Lecture Notes in Computer Science 8766

Commenced Publication in 1973
Founding and Former Series Editors:
Gerhard Goos, Juris Hartmanis, and Jan van Leeuwen

T0212651

Luiz DeRose   Bronis R. de Supinski
Stephen L. Olivier   Barbara M. Chapman
Matthias S. Müller (Eds.)

Using and Improving OpenMP for Devices, Tasks, and More

10th International Workshop on OpenMP, IWOMP 2014
Salvador, Brazil, September 28-30, 2014
Proceedings

 Springer

Volume Editors

Luiz DeRose
Cray Inc., St. Paul, MN, USA
E-mail: ldr@cray.com

Bronis R. de Supinski
Lawrence Livermore National Laboratory, Livermore, CA, USA
E-mail: bronis@llnl.gov

Stephen L. Olivier
Sandia National Laboratories, Albuquerque, NM, USA
E-mail: slolivi@sandia.gov

Barbara M. Chapman
University of Houston, Houston, TX, USA
E-mail: chapman@cs.uh.edu

Matthias S. Müller
RWTH Aachen, Aachen, Germany
E-mail: mueller@itc.rwth-aachen.de

ISSN 0302-9743   e-ISSN 1611-3349
ISBN 978-3-319-11453-8   e-ISBN 978-3-319-11454-5
DOI 10.1007/978-3-319-11454-5
Springer Cham Heidelberg New York Dordrecht London

Library of Congress Control Number: 2014948474

LNCS Sublibrary: SL 2 – Programming and Software Engineering

Typesetting: Camera-ready by author, data conversion by Scientific Publishing Services, Chennai, India

Printed on acid-free paper

Springer is part of Springer Science+Business Media (www.springer.com)

Preface

OpenMP is a widely accepted, standard application programming interface (API) for high-level shared-memory parallel programming in Fortran, C, and C++. Since its introduction in 1997, OpenMP has gained support from most high-performance compiler and hardware vendors. Under the direction of the OpenMP Architecture Review Board (ARB), the OpenMP specification has evolved up to the recent release of version 4.0. This version includes several new features like accelerator support for heterogeneous hardware environments, an enhanced tasking model, user defined reductions, and thread affinity to support binding for performance improvements on non-uniform memory architectures.

The evolution of the standard would be impossible without active research in OpenMP compilers, runtime systems, tools, and environments. OpenMP is both an important programming model for single multicore processors and as part of a hybrid programming model for massively parallel, distributed memory systems built from multicore or manycore processors. In fact, most of the growth in parallelism of the upcoming Exascale systems is expected to be coming from an increased parallelism within a node. OpenMP offers important features that can improve the scalability of applications on such systems.

The community of OpenMP researchers and developers in academia and industry is united under cOMPunity (www.compunity.org). This organization has held workshops on OpenMP around the world since 1999: the European Workshop on OpenMP (EWOMP), the North American Workshop on OpenMP Applications and Tools (WOMPAT), and the Asian Workshop on OpenMP Experiences and Implementation (WOMPEI) attracted annual audiences from academia and industry. The International Workshop on OpenMP (IWOMP) consolidated these three workshop series into a single annual international event that rotates across Asia, Europe, and the Americas. The first IWOMP workshop was organized under the auspices of cOMPunity. Since that workshop, the IWOMP Steering Committee has organized these events and guided development of the series. The first IWOMP meeting was held in 2005, in Eugene, Oregon, USA. Since then, meetings have been held each year, in Reims, France, Beijing, China, West Lafayette, USA, Dresden, Germany, Tsukuba, Japan, Chicago, USA, Rome, Italy, and Canberra, Australia. Each workshop has drawn participants from research and industry throughout the world. IWOMP 2014 continues the series with technical papers, tutorials, and OpenMP status reports. The IWOMP meetings have been successful in large part due to the generous support from numerous sponsors.

The cOMPunity website (www.compunity.org) provides access to the talks given at the meetings and to photos of the activities. The IWOMP website (www.iwomp.org) provides information on the latest event. This book contains proceedings of IWOMP 2014. The workshop program included 16 technical papers, two keynote talks, a tutorial on OpenMP, an invited talk, and a sponsor talk. The paper by Artur Podobas, Mats Brorsson and Vladimir Vlassov was selected for the Best Paper Award. All technical papers were peer reviewed by at least three different members of the Program Committee.

In a special way, the OpenMP community remembers Ricky Kendall, former member of the IWOMP Steering Committee. He passed away March 18, 2014 and is greatly missed.

September 2014   Luiz DeRose
                                                        Bronis R. de Supinski
                                                          Stephen L. Olivier

Organization

Organizing Co-chairs

Luiz DeRose   Cray Inc., USA
Adhvan Novais Furtado   SENAI Unidade CIMATEC, Brazil

Program Co-chairs

Luiz DeRose   Cray Inc., USA
Bronis R. de Supinski   LLNL, USA

Sponsors Chair

Barbara Chapman   University of Houston, USA

Tutorials Chair

Christian Terboven   RWTH Aachen University, Germany

Publication Chair

Stephen L. Olivier   Sandia National Laboratories, USA

Local Coordination Chair

Adhvan Novais Furtado   SENAI Unidade CIMATEC, Brazil

Program Committee

Eduard Ayguadé   BSC and Universitat Politecnica de Catalunya, Spain
Mark Bull   EPCC, University of Edinburgh, UK
Jacqueline Chame   ISI, USC, USA
Barbara Chapman   University of Houston, USA
Nawal Copty   Oracle Corporation, USA
Alejandro Duran   Intel, Spain
Nasser Giacaman   University of Auckland, New Zealand
Chunhua Liao   LLNL, USA

IWOMP Steering Committee

Steering Committee Chair

Steering Committee

Table of Contents

Tasking Models and Their Optimization

Understanding and Verifying Correctness of OpenMP Programs

OpenMP Memory Extensions

Extensions for Tools and Locks

Experiences with OpenMP Device Constructs

Task-Parallel Reductions in OpenMP and OmpSs

Jan Ciesko[1], Sergi Mateo[1], Xavier Teruel[1], Vicenç Beltran[1],
Xavier Martorell[1,2], Rosa M. Badia[1,3],
Eduard Ayguadé[1,2], and Jesús Labarta[1,2]

[1] Barcelona Supercomputing Center
[2] Universitat Politècnica de Catalunya
[3] Artificial Intelligence Research Institute (IIIA)
- Spanish National Research Council (CSIC)
{jan.ciesko,sergi.mateo,xavier.teruel,vicenc.beltran,
xavier.martorell,rosa.m.badia,eduard.ayguade,
jesus.labarta}@bsc.es

Abstract. The wide adoption of parallel processing hardware in mainstream computing as well as the raising interest for efficient parallel programming in the developer community increase the demand for parallel
programming model support for common algorithmic patterns. In this
work we present an extension to the OpenMP task construct to add
support for reductions in while-loops and general-recursive algorithms.
Further we discuss implications on the OpenMP standard and present a
prototype implementation in OmpSs. Benchmark results confirm applicability of this approach and scalability on current SMP systems.

Keywords: OpenMP, Task, Reduction, Recursion, OmpSs.

1 Introduction

Reductions are a reoccurring algorithmic pattern in many scientific, technical
and mainstream applications. Their characteristic non-atomic update operation
over arbitrary data types makes their execution computationally expensive and
parallelization challenging.

In programming, a reduction occurs when a variable, *var*, is updated itera-
tively as

$$iter : \; var = op(var, expression),$$

where *op* is a commutative and associative operator performing an update on
var and where *var* does not occur in *expression*. In case of parallel execution,
mutual exclusive access is required to ensure data consistency.

Taking a broader look at usage patterns across applications reveals three common types of reductions: *for-loop* (bounded loop), *while-loop* (unbounded loop)
and *recursive*. For-loop reductions enclose a reduction in a for-loop body. They
are often used in scientific applications to update large arrays of simulation data
in each simulation step (such as updating particle positions by a displacement

L. DeRose (Eds.): IWOMP 2014, LNCS 8766, pp. 1–15, 2014.

corresponding to a time slice) or in numerical solvers where values are accumulated over a scalar to indicate convergence behavior and break conditions [7].
They are often referred to as array or scalar reductions.

For-loops represent the class of primitive-recursive algorithms where the iteration space is computable and where control structures of no greater generality are
allowed. The iterative formulation of primitive-recursive functions is currently
supported in OpenMP [9].

While-loop reductions represent another usage pattern and define the class of
general-recursive functions. They appear in algorithms where the iteration space
is unknown such as in graph search algorithms.

The last occurrence represents recursions. Recursive reductions can be found
in backtracking algorithms used in combinatorial optimization. Even though
one could argue that for each recursion an iterative formulation exists (either
as a for-loop or a while-loop), recursions often allow very compact and readable
formulations. Examples of a recursive and while-loop reduction are shown in
Figure 1.

```
1 int nqueens (...) {                    1 ...
2   if (cond1 (...)) return 1;           2 int red = 0;
3   int count = 0;                       3 int foo (node_t node ,...) {
4   for (int row = 0; row < n; row++){   4   while (node->next) {
5     if (cond2 (...)))                   5     red+=bar (node->value);
6       count += nqueens (...);          6     node=node->next;
7   }                                     7   }
8   return count;                        8 }
9 }                                       9 ...
```

(a)   (b)

Fig. 1. The recursive, schematic implementation of n-Queens (a) and a graph algorithm
(b) show the different occurrences of reductions in applications

In this work we propose an extension to the OpenMP standard by adding
support for while-loop and recursive reductions through the *task reduction* directive. Formally, this extends the existing support for primitive-recursive, iterative algorithms by the class of general-recursive algorithms for both, iterative
and recursive formulations. In terms of parallel programming, the proposed task
reduction allows the expression of so called task-parallel reductions. Further we
propose a compliant integration into OpenMP and present a prototype implementation based on OmpSs [1].

The rest of the paper is structured as follows. Chapter 2 introduces the language construct. In Chapter 3 we introduce OmpSs, discuss compiler transformations and runtime implementation. Benchmark results are shown in Chapter 4.
Finally we discuss related work in Chapter 5 and conclude this work in Chapter 6
with a summary and outlook on future work.

2   Task-Parallel Reductions with OpenMP

The idea to support task-parallel reductions builds on top of the conceptual framework introduced with explicit tasking in OpenMP. Since tasking allows to express concurrent while-loops and recursions, it represents a convenient mechanism to support task-parallel reductions as well. For its definition we use the current standard specification [9] as a baseline and add a set of rules describing data consistency and nesting. While this work is written with a certain formalism in mind, it does not represent a language specification.

2.1   Definition

The task reduction directive[1] is defined as:

```
1 #pragma omp task [clauses] reduction (identifier : list)
2 structured-block
```

The *reduction* clause in the task construct declares an asynchronous reduction task over a list of items. Each item is considered as if declared *shared* and for each item a private copy is assigned for each implicit task participating in the reduction. At implicit or explicit barriers or task synchronization, the original list item is updated with the values of the private copies by applying the combiner associated with the *reduction-identifier*. Consequently, the scope of a reduction over a list item begins at the first encounter of a reduction task and ends at an implicit or explicit barrier or task synchronization point. We call this region a *reduction domain*. Implications on synchronization in case of domain nesting is conforming to the OpenMP specification.

We would like to point out that the provided definition is generic and does not restrict the usage of task-parallel reductions to any particular enclosing construct. However, as in this case the scope of a task-parallel reduction is defined by both task synchronization as well as by barriers, its support would require to modify their current implementations. In particular they would need to check for outstanding private copies and reduce them. A solution to minimize the impact on unrelated programming constructs is to restrict the use of task-parallel reductions to the context of a *taskgroup*.

In the rest of this Chapter we discuss implications of this proposal on *taskwait* and taskgroup directives, reductions on data dependencies and nesting.

2.2   Reductions on Taskwait

The *taskwait* construct specifies a wait on the completion of child tasks in the context of the current task and combines all privately allocated list items of all child tasks associated with the current reduction domain. A taskwait therefore represents the end of a domain scope. The previous example shown in Figure 1b can be easily parallelized as shown in Figure 2.

---

[1] Shown in C and C++ syntax.

```
 1 ...
 2 int red=0;
 3 while(node->next)    {
 4     #pragma omp task reduction (+:red)
 5     {
 6         red+=bar(node->value);
 7     }
 8     node=node->next;
 9 }
10 #pragma omp taskwait
11 return red;
```

Fig. 2. A concurrent reduction using a *taskwait* to ensure data consistency so a function would return a correct value of *red*

2.3   Support in Taskgroups

The *taskgroup* construct specifies a deep wait on all child tasks and their descendent tasks. After the end of the taskgroup construct, all enclosed reduction domains are ended and original list items are updated with the values of the private copies. Similarly to a taskwait construct, task-parallel reductions require to extend their role of task synchronization to actively perform a memory operation to restore consistency. Figure 3 shows an example where a reduction domain is ended implicitly at the end of a taskgroup construct.

```
 1 ...
 2 int red=0;
 3 #pragma omp taskgroup
 4 {
 5     while(condition(){
 6         #pragma omp task reduction (+:red)
 7         red += foo ();
 8     }
 9 }
10 return red;
```

Fig. 3. A concurrent reduction within the *taskgroup* performs a wait on all children and their descendant tasks (this is often referred to as deep wait)

2.4   Reductions on Data Dependencies

Data-flow based task execution allows a streamline work scheduling that in certain cases results in higher hardware utilization with relatively small development effort. Task-parallel reductions can be easily integrated into this execution model but require the following assumption. A list item declared in the task reduction directive is considered as if declared *inout* by the *depend* clause. As this would effectively serialize the execution of reduction tasks due to the "inout" operation over the same variable, dependencies between reduction tasks of the same domain need to be overridden.

An example, where a reduction domain begins with the first occurrence of a participating task and is ended implicitly by a dependency introduced by a successor task, is shown is Figure 4. In this example the actual reduction of private copies can by overlapped by the asynchronous execution of *bar* which again might improve hardware utilization.

```
 1 ...
 2 int red=0;
 3 for(int i=0; i<SIZE; i+=BLOCK){
 4     #pragma omp task shared(array) reduction (+:red)
 5     for(int j=i; j< i+BLOCK; ++j){
 6         red += array[j];
 7     }
 8 }
 9 #pragma omp task
10 bar();
11 #pragma omp task shared(red) depend(in:red)
12 printf("%i\n",red);
13 ...
```

Fig. 4. The reduction domain over the variable *red* is ended by a task dependency

2.5 Nesting Support

Nested task constructs typically occur in two cases. In the first, each task at each nesting level declares a reduction over the same variable. This is called multi-level reduction. In this case, a taskwait at each nesting level is not mandatory as long as a deep wait ensures proper synchronization later on. It is important to point out that only task synchronization that occurs at the same nesting level at which a reduction scope was created (that is the nesting level that first encounter a reduction task for a list item), ends the scope and reduces private copies. Within the reduction domain, the value of the reduction variable is unspecified. An example for a multi-level domain reduction is shown in Figure 5.

```
 1 ...
 2 int red = 0;
 3 for(int i=0; i<SIZE; i+=BLOCK){
 4     #pragma omp task shared(array) reduction (+:red)
 5     for(int j=i; j< i+BLOCK; ++j){
 6         #pragma omp task shared(array) reduction (+:red)
 7         red += array[j] + bar(/*long_computation*/);
 8     }
 9     #pragma omp taskwait
10     printf("Unspecified value of red:%i\n",red);
11 }
12 #pragma omp taskwait
13 ...
```

Fig. 5. A multi-level domain reduction is computed over the same variable by tasks participating at different nesting levels

In the second occurrence each nesting level reduces over a different reduction variable. This happens for example if a nested task performs a reduction on task-local data. In this case a taskwait at the end of each nesting level is required. We call this occurrence a nested-domain reduction. Figure 6 shows an example of an element-wise matrix summation, where inner tasks iterate over rows and compute partial results that are then reduced by outer tasks to compute the final value. Since in this example the nested domain is ended by the inner taskwait, accessing *red_ local* returns a correct value.

```
1 ...
2 int red = 0;
3 for(int i = 0; i < SIZE_Y; i++){
4     #pragma omp task shared(array) reduction(+:red)
5     {
6         int red_local = 0;
7         for(int j = 0; j < SIZE_X; j+=BLOCK_X) {
8             #pragma omp task reduction(+:red_local)
9             for (int k = j; k < j + BLOCK_X; ++k){
10                red_local += array[i][k];
11            }
12        }
13        #pragma omp taskwait
14        printf("Correct value of red_local:%i\n",red_local);
15        red += red_local;
16    }
17 }
18 #pragma omp taskwait
19 ...
```

Fig. 6. Element-wise matrix sum implemented as a nested-domain reduction, where each dimension is processed in a different nesting level over a different variable

General Nesting Support. The general support for nesting requires to inspect scenarios where a task-parallel reduction is nested within the *parallel* and *worksharing* constructs.

An example for such a scenario where a reduction is computed over a shared variable in a *parallel for* construct on one level and reduction tasks on the second level is shown in Figure 7. This example represents a multi-domain reduction because even though both directives declare a reduction over the same variable (similarly to Figure 5), the inner reduction is performed on private copies that were created for each implicit task of the parallel region. In this case the outer reduction domain starts at the encounter of the first reduction task (implicit in this case) and ends at the implicit barrier at the end of the parallel region. The inner reduction domain starts on each thread with the encounter of the first explicit task and ends at the taskwait.

In case the reduction variable in the work-sharing construct would be declared *shared* instead, each implicit task would perform a reduction on the shared variable by its nested reduction tasks. Here the scopes of the inner reductions would end at implicit synchronization points within the implicit tasks and the runtime would need to make sure to update the shared variable atomically.

```
 1 ...
 2 int red = 0;
 3 #pragma omp parallel for shared(array) reduction (+:red)
 4 for(int i=0; i<SIZE; i+=BLOCK){
 5     for(int j=i; j< i+BLOCK; ++j){
 6         #pragma omp task shared(array) reduction (+:red)
 7         red += array[j] + bar(/*long_computation*/);
 8     }
 9     #pragma omp taskwait
10 }
11 ...
```

Fig. 7. Nested task-parallel reduction in a worksharing construct performs a reduction over the shared variable *red*

Currently OpenMP does not support nesting data-parallel and task-parallel reductions because of the following restriction.

– A list item that appears in a reduction clause of the innermost enclosing worksharing or parallel construct may not be accessed in an explicit task.

Adjusting this restriction as shown below, would add support for the general nesting support while maintaining the afford of discouraging programming errors.

– A list item that appears in a reduction clause of the innermost enclosing worksharing or parallel construct may not be accessed in an explicit task unless it appears in its reduction clause.
– Nested reductions over the same list item must perform the same reduction operation.

If a general support of task-parallel reductions as discussed in this sections is desirable depends on its necessity. Currently task-parallel reductions enclosed in the taskgroup construct represent a satisfactory approach that reduces the impact of tasking on barriers.

Figure 8 shows two implementations of the n-Queens application from Chapter 1, that compute a reduction over a global (a) and local (b) variable.

3 Implementation in OmpSs

To evaluate requirements for compilers as well as for runtime support we implemented the presented proposal in the OmpSs programming model. OmpSs is a high-level, task-based, parallel programming model supporting SMPs, heterogeneous systems (like GPGPU systems) and clusters.

OmpSs consists of a language specification, a source-to-source compiler for C, C++ and Fortran [2] and a runtime [3]. The language defines a set of directives that allow a descriptive expression of tasks. With this information the runtime is capable of dependency-aware task scheduling. While this is similar to OpenMP,

```
1 int count = 0;
2 int nqueens(...){
3   if (cond1(...))
4     return 1;
5   for(int row=0;row<n;row++){
6     if (cond2(...)))
7       #pragma omp task\
8       reduction(+:count)
9       count += nqueens(...);
10  }
11  #pragma omp taskwait
12  return 0; //neutral element
13 }
```

```
1 int nqueens(...){
2   if (cond1(...))
3     return 1;
4   int count = 0;
5   for (int row=0;row<n;row++){
6     if (cond2(...)))
7       #pragma omp task\
8       reduction(+:count)
9       count += nqueens(...);
10  }
11  #pragma omp taskwait
12  return count;
13 }
```

(a)   (b)

Fig. 8. A concurrent implementation of N-Queens as a multi-level (a) and nested-level domain (b) reduction over the variable *count*

the OmpSs runtime implements a different execution model. In OmpSs, an application is launched as a single implicit task in an implicit parallel region over all available threads. Therefore nor the parallel construct nor barriers are needed and memory consistency is ensured through data dependencies and task synchronization directives. Even though these differences exist, OmpSs is suited to serve as a reference implementation for the specific use-cases presented in Chapter 2.

3.1 Runtime Support

The runtime implementation is based on the idea of privatization. In order to avoid the need for mutual exclusive access to the reduction variable, a thread-private copy (TPRS) is created and used as a temporal reduction target. Since its creation, initialization and processing later on are expensive operations, it is important to maximize the life span and reuse of a TPRS.

Therefore we introduce a thread-team private reduction manager object that tracks privatized memories and assigns them to requesting tasks. Consequently all tasks that are executed on the same thread and belong to the same reduction domain always receive the same allocated thread-private memory. Once the domain ends, one of the participating threads reduces all corresponding TPRSs serially.

Allocation Strategies and Storage Handling. To evaluate memory allocation we implemented two strategies called static and dynamic allocation.

Static allocation preallocates and initializes an array of thread-private reduction storages for all threads of a team (as defined by *omp_ get_ num_ threads()*) at the moment when the first reduction task is created. This marks the beginning of a reduction domain. During execution, the runtime provides previously allocated TPRS objects according to a domain and thread identifier to requesting child tasks.

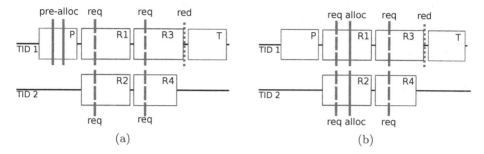

Fig. 9. Static (a) and dynamic (b) allocation differs in when and where thread-private memory is requested (req), allocated (alloc) and reduced (red)

With dynamic allocation, memory is allocated and initialized on demand at task execution. Once a task requests a thread-private storage, the runtime performs an allocation, registers the storage in the reduction manager and returns a TPRS. An allocation is performed for each first execution of a reduction task of a domain on a participating thread. In this case a reduction domain begins at the execution of the first reduction task. This allocation strategy does not create any work for the encountering thread as the allocation is called at execution time of child tasks in parallel.

An execution diagram of an application where a parent task P creates four reduction tasks $R1$-4 running on two threads (TID 1, 2) is shown in Figure 11. In this scenario a following task T has an input dependency on the reduction variable and expects a correct value in memory at the moment of its execution. In OmpSs, finding the right point in time to reduce TPRSs is implemented via data dependencies. TPRSs are reduced in the moment when data dependencies are satisfied, or in other words, when the last task of a dependency domain has finished execution. In this example, reduction task $R3$ is the task that satisfies the dependency requirements for task T and once completed it instructs the current thread TID 1 to reduce all private storages of the reduction domain.

The advantage of static allocation is that it allows to allocate memory in a single call (to malloc for example) and its implementation is lock free once all TPRSs have been allocated. On the other hand, allocation is in the critical path and potentially can result in allocating unused storage in case not all threads participate in the computation. Further this approach does not adapt to changing numbers of participating threads.

Dynamic allocation allocates and initializes memory in parallel and avoids unnecessary allocation for busy threads that will not participate in the reduction computation. Since the number of registered TPRS storages changes over time, this implementation requires a lock in the global manager which can potentially introduce lock contention for fine grained tasks. This approach corresponds to the idea of dynamic parallelism where problem size nor thread counts are known.

Nesting Support. In case of nesting, synchronization constructs might occur at any nesting level. In this case the runtime must be able identify storage locations that correspond to an ending domain.

For this purpose the reduction manager object implements a list of TPRSs and two maps that point to individual items in that list. One map uses task identifiers while the other one uses target addresses (pointers to the original reduction variable) as primary keys.

At the first execution of a task of new reduction domain, a new TPRS is allocated and initialized for the current thread and the parent work descriptor identifier as well as the address of the reduction variable are stored in the corresponding maps. Each successive task running on that thread and reducing over same variable will receive the same TPRS because of matching addresses. Once tasks finish, and the recursion starts to collapse, only those tasks that have a matching task identifier stored in the map are allowed to reduce TPRS storages. This corresponds exactly to those tasks that created a new reduction domain.

3.2   Compiler Support

The goal of the Mercurium compiler is to generate code transformations according to OmpSs annotations provided by the programmer. In case of encountering a task reduction, the compiler replaces all occurrences of the original reduction variable within the task by a reference to a previously requested thread-private reduction store, called TPRS. This transformation includes the following steps.

- Generate call to the runtime to obtain a TPRS. The runtime serves a TPRS corresponding to the current thread that is executing the task
- Replace all references to the original reduction variable within the task by a reference to the TPRS
- Apply the above transformation on the final task code block (code that is executed in the final task region).

The final task code block represents the original user written code without runtime calls and is invoked when the task's final clause evaluates to true. The final clause in the task construct is typically used to set a cut-off value for task generation in order to control task granularity. In this way recursive functions can be stopped from task generation in order to avoid large runtime overheads.

In case of task reductions, multiple tasks can invoke the final code block that is performing a reduction over a global reduction variable in parallel. Consequently in order to avoid race conditions, accesses to the reduction variable within the final code block need to be redirected to the thread-private storage as well. Since requesting a TPRS is typically implemented as a runtime call, careful implementation is needed to minimize its impact on performance. Alternatively an additional final code block can be generated and invoked that accepts a TPRS pointer as an additional parameter. This would make the runtime call to request a TPRS obsolete.

Compiler transformations applied to Figure 5 are shown in Figure 10.

```
1 void outline_task1(struct ArgsTask1 args);
2 void outline_task2(struct ArgsTask2 args);
3 int foo() {
4    ...
5    for(int i=0; i<SIZE; i+=BLOCK)
6        rt_create_task({array, i, &red}, &outline_task1);
7    rt_taskwait();
8    return red;
9 }
10 void outline_task1(struct ArgsTask1 args) {
11    int *tp_red = rt_get_thread_storage(args.red);
12    for(int j=i; j< args.i + BLOCK; ++j)
13        rt_create_task({array, j, tp_red}, &outline_task2);
14    rt_taskwait();
15 }
16 void outline_task2(struct ArgsTask2 args) {
17    int *tp_tp_red = rt_get_thread_storage(args.tp_red);
18    (*tp_tp_red) += args.array[args.j] + bar(/*long_computation*/);
19 }
```

Fig. 10. Transformations applied by the compiler redirecting accesses to a thread-private reduction store

4   Evaluation

The evaluation of the presented runtime support is based on four application kernels that include while-loop and recursive reductions. The first two applications, n-Queens and Knight's tour, represents the satisfiability problem in numerical combinatorics. They compute in one case the maximum number of different configurations of n queens, in the other, the number of knight's paths covering all fields on a chess board of size n. These applications are implemented as recursive backtracking algorithms in two versions. In one version the reduction is performed over a task-local variable (nested-domain reduction) and in the other over a global variable (multi-level domain reduction). The schematic concurrent code for n-Queens is shown in Figure 8. Execution traces obtained from the n-Queens application running on 16 threads are shown in Figure 11 and illustrate task execution and lifetimes of TPRSs for both implementations. In these executions, task granularity was set to an optimum by using the *final* clause in the task construct. As visible in the execution trace, a multi-level domain reduction allows high reuse rates of thread-private memory across nesting levels.

Max-height, another application, computes the longest path over a directed, unbalanced and acyclic graph. This application represent a while-loop reduction. Due to its frequent, irregular memory accesses, its scalability is limited by memory bandwidth when running on 16 processor cores. The Powerset benchmark computes the number of all possible sets over a given number of elements. This application is implemented recursively where unlike the n-Queens application, each recursive branch is of the same length.

Figure 12 shows application scalability for the aforementioned applications implemented as nested-domain (a) and multi-level domain (b) reduction as well as their implementations with tasking and atomic updates (using built-in atomics

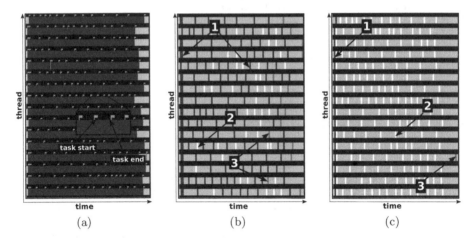

Fig. 11. An execution trace for the n-Queens application (n=15 and creating tasks in two nesting levels) shows tasks (a) and allocation (1), reuse (2) and reduction (3) of thread-private reduction storages over a task-local(b) and global variable(c) as shown in Figure 8

where possible). For each benchmark we have selected the best task granularity and the following problem sizes: n-Queens with n=15, Knight's tour with board size 5x5; Max-height with a graph height 15, 7 edges per node and Powerset over 32 items. Results show that all benchmarks benefit from reduction support, especially in cases where lock contention and atomic updates degrade performance.

While all applications were executed with both allocation strategies, they did not exhibit significant performance differences. Allocation and initialization strategies are relevant especially in case of user-defined reductions over larger data types and array reductions where the cost of memory allocation and initialization becomes expensive. As a more detailed analysis exceeds the scope of this paper, we defer it to future work.

Inspecting overheads of the current implementation for both allocation strategies revealed that the additional time introduced by runtime calls specific to reduction support did not exceed 1% of total time spent in the runtime irregardless of granularity or problem size. We expect that this behavior will change in case of user-defined and array-type reductions.

4.1   Environment

All benchmark results presented in this work were obtained from the MareNostrum 3 supercomputer located at the Barcelona Supercomputing Center. Each system node contains two 8-core Intel Xeon E5-2670 CPUs running at 2.6 GHz with 20MB L3 cache and 32GB of main memory. Applications were compiled

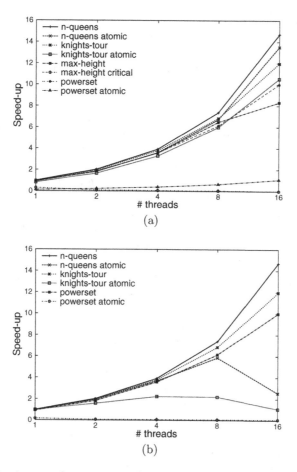

Fig. 12. Application speed-up over serial execution implemented with nested (a) and multi-level domain (b) reductions as well as with regular tasking using atomics

using Mercurium compiler v1.99.1 and GCC v4.8.2 back-end/native compiler with -O3. The runtime is based on the Nanos++ RTL v0.7a.

5 Related Work

OpenMP has allowed concurrent reductions in work-sharing constructs since its first specification (OpenMP 1.0) in 1997. The supported clauses allow the use of a reduction operator and a list of scalar, shared locations. During parallel execution, the runtime creates private copies for each list item and thread in the team. The result variable is initialized with the identity value according to the operator that is declared in the clause. In successive versions of the OpenMP specification, additional features have been added to the standard. These include min- and max-operators for C/C++ in version OpenMP 3.1, extended reduction support to Fortran Allocatable Arrays (OpenMP 3.0) and User Defined Reduction (OpenMP 4.0). Aside from small incremental updates, the OpenMP specification has never allowed OpenMP tasking in reductions. In fact it explicitly forbids the use of reduction symbols in combination with tasks: "A list item that appears in a reduction clause of the innermost enclosing work-sharing or parallel construct may not be accessed in an explicit task." [9] This restriction reduces flexibilities achieved by dynamic parallelism in many algorithms.

Other programming models, such as the Cilk++ [8], introduce different types of linguistic mechanisms, so called hyperobjects [6], that are coordinating local views of the same variable. Based on a `cilk_spawn` mechanism that starts parallel execution, the parent creates a private copy of the original view initialized with the identity value, while the child receives the original view of the symbol. These two views join just before synchronization occurs (`cilk_sync`). In the first step, the child view is updated with the value of the parent view according to a reducer function. Then the parent view is discarded, and replaced by the view of the child. Unlike lazy-reduction implemented in OmpSs that is able to reuse storage across nesting levels, in this case an allocation, reduction and deallocation always occur.

X10 [4], another popular programming model, introduces a phaser-accumulator [10,11] construct for dynamic parallelism. A X10-phaser is a coordination construct allowing to unify point-to-point synchronization among different X10-tasks (activities). The phaser-accumulators support two logical operations. It sends a value for accumulation that has been produced in the current phase or it receives the accumulated value from the previous phase. This implementation entirely eliminates race conditions through the accumulator object that handles read and write accesses. This encapsulation of functionality allows to define implementation strategies that differ as to when the reduction itself is performed. That is either when data is supplied or when a synchronization point is reached. In this respect this implementation is comparable to OmpSs.

6   Conclusions and Future Work

In this paper we presented an extension to OpenMP tasking to support reductions in while-loops and general-recursive functions. In turned out that the OpenMP taskgroup is suited to support task-parallel reductions as it minimizes implications on unrelated constructs. A general support in OpenMP is possible but requires further analysis of deep task synchronization and of implementation and performance implications on barriers. This effort should be made in the future if applications exist that render the taskgroup construct insufficient. The presented runtime implementation offers two different allocation strategies and maximizes storage reuse. Dynamic allocation follows the idea of dynamic parallelism where neither the amount of work nor the number of participating threads are known beforehand. Results show that task granularity is important and in case of recursive algorithms can be efficiently controlled by the final clause. In the case of while-loops, task granularity needs to be taken into account by the programmer through appropriate application design. Performance results obtained on a MareNostrum 3 system node show a near-linear speed-up for test cases with optimal granularity. Future work includes runtime support for efficient array reductions through software caching [5], user-defined reductions and execution on accelerators.

Acknowledgments. This work has been developed with the support of the grant SEV-2011-00067 of Severo Ochoa Program, awarded by the Spanish Government and by the Spanish Ministry of Science and Innovation (contracts TIN2012-34557, and CAC2007-00052) by the Generalitat de Catalunya (contract 2009-SGR-980) and the Intel-BSC Exascale Lab collaboration project.

Also the authors would like to thank the OpenMP community for their substantial contribution to this work.

References

1. Barcelona Supercomputing Center: OmpSs Specification (April 25, 2014), http://pm.bsc.es/ompss-docs/specs
2. BSC - Parallel Programming Models group: Mercurium C/C++ source-to-source compiler (May 2014), http://pm.bsc.es/projects/mcxx
3. BSC - Parallel Programming Models group: Nanos++ runtime library (May 2014), http://pm.bsc.es/projects/nanox
4. Charles, P., Grothoff, C., Saraswat, V., Donawa, C., Kielstra, A., Ebcioglu, K., von Praun, C., Sarkar, V.: X10: An Object-oriented Approach to Non-uniform Cluster Computing. SIGPLAN Not. 40(10), 519–538 (2005)
5. Ciesko, J., Bueno-Hedo, J., Puzovic, N., Ramirez, A., Badia, R.M., Labarta, J.: Programmable and scalable reductions on clusters, pp. 560–568. IEEE, Boston (2013)
6. Frigo, M., Halpern, P., Leiserson, C.E., Lewin-Berlin, S.: Reducers and Other Cilk++ Hyperobjects. In: Proceedings of the Twenty-first Annual Symposium on Parallelism in Algorithms and Architectures, SPAA 2009, pp. 79–90. ACM, New York (2009)
7. Komatitsch, D., Tromp, J.: Introduction to the spectral-element method for 3-D seismic wave propagation 139(3), 806–822 (1999)
8. Leiserson, C.E.: The Cilk++ Concurrency Platform. In: Proceedings of the 46th Annual Design Automation Conference, DAC 2009, pp. 522–527. ACM, New York (2009)
9. OpenMP Architecture Review Board: OpenMP application program interface version 4.0 (July 2013)
10. Shirako, J., Peixotto, D.M., Sarkar, V., Scherer, W.N.: Phasers: A Unified Deadlock-Free Construct for Collective and Point-to-point Synchronization. In: ICS 2008: Proceedings of the 22nd Annual International Conference on Supercomputing, pp. 277–288. ACM, New York (2008)
11. Shirako, J., Peixotto, D.M., Sarkar, V., Scherer, W.N.: Phaser accumulators: A new reduction construct for dynamic parallelism. In: IEEE International Symposium on Parallel and Distributed Processing, IPDPS 2009, pp. 1–12. IEEE, Rome (2009)

Evaluation of OpenMP Dependent Tasks with the KASTORS Benchmark Suite

Philippe Virouleau[1], Pierrick Brunet[1], François Broquedis[4], Nathalie Furmento[2], Samuel Thibault [3], Olivier Aumage[1], and Thierry Gautier[1]

[1] INRIA,
[2] CNRS,
[3] University of Bordeaux,
[4] Grenoble Institute of Technology
MOAIS and RUNTIME Teams, Computer Science Laboratories of Grenoble and Bordeaux,
France
firstname.lastname@inria.fr,
thierry.gautier@inrialpes.fr

Abstract. The recent introduction of task dependencies in the OpenMP specification provides new ways of synchronizing tasks. Application programmers can now describe the data a task will read as input and write as output, letting the runtime system resolve fine-grain dependencies between tasks to decide which task should execute next. Such an approach should scale better than the excessive global synchronization found in most OpenMP 3.0 applications. As promising as it looks however, any new feature needs proper evaluation to encourage application programmers to embrace it. This paper introduces the KASTORS benchmark suite designed to evaluate OpenMP tasks dependencies. We modified state-of-the-art OpenMP 3.0 benchmarks and data-flow parallel linear algebra kernels to make use of tasks dependencies. Learning from this experience, we propose extensions to the current OpenMP specification to improve the expressiveness of dependencies. We eventually evaluate both the GCC/libGOMP and the CLANG/libIOMP implementations of OpenMP 4.0 on our KASTORS suite, demonstrating the interest of task dependencies compared to taskwait-based approaches.

Keywords: OpenMP, task dependencies, benchmarks, runtime systems, KASTORS.

1   Introduction

HPC architectures evolved so rapidly that it is now common to build shared-memory configurations with several dozens of cores. The recent appearance of technologies such as the Intel Xeon Phi co-processor makes affordable configurations with thousands of cores a not-so-far reality. Efficiently programming such large-scale platforms requires to express more and more fine-grain parallelism.

Standard parallel programming environments such as OpenMP have evolved to address this requirement, introducing new ways of designing highly parallel programs. Extending OpenMP to support task parallelism stands as a first step to improve the scalability of OpenMP applications on large-scale platforms. Indeed, task parallelism

L. DeRose (Eds.): IWOMP 2014, LNCS 8766, pp. 16–29, 2014.

usually comes with lower runtime-related overhead than thread-based approaches, allowing OpenMP programmers to create a large amount of tasks at low cost. Task parallelism also promotes the runtime system to a central role, as having more units of work to execute requires smarter scheduling decisions and load balancing capabilities.

OpenMP was recently extended to support task dependencies. Instead of explicitly synchronizing all the tasks of a parallel region at once, the application programmer can now specify a list of variables a task will read as input or write as output instead. This information is transmitted to the task scheduling runtime system. The runtime then marks a task as ready for execution only once all its dependencies have been resolved. Dependencies therefore provide a way to define finer synchronizations between tasks, able to scale better than global synchronizations on large-scale platforms. Dependencies also give the runtime system more options to efficiently schedule tasks, as these become ready for execution as soon as the data they access has been updated.

As promising as it looks however, any new feature needs proper evaluation to encourage application programmers to embrace it. While several compilers and runtime systems are now beginning to support OpenMP 4.0 task dependencies, no benchmark suite currently exists to evaluate their respective benefits and compare them to traditional task parallelism.

This paper highlights two major contributions. We first introduce a new benchmark suite to experiment with OpenMP 4.0 task dependencies. We present performance results for both the GCC/libGOMP and the CLANG[1]/libIOMP compilers and their runtime systems, comparing kernels involving either dependent or independent tasks. Secondly, we comment on the issues we met while implementing these benchmarks along the lines of current 4.0 revision of the OpenMP specification. Building on this experience, we contribute some extension proposals to the existing OpenMP specification, to improve the expressiveness of the task dependency support.

The remainder of this paper is organized as follows. Section 2 describes the task dependency programming model in OpenMP 4.0. It then analyzes the strategies adopted by GCC/libGOMP and CLANG/libIOMP to implement this model. Section 3 introduces the KASTORS benchmark suite we have designed to evaluate OpenMP 4.0's task model implementations. Section 4 presents the performance results of KASTORS using two different hardware configurations. We identify and discuss practical issues with the current OpenMP specification, and we propose extensions in section 5 to address these issues. We finally present some related works in section 6 before concluding.

2 The Way OpenMP Specifies Dependencies between Tasks

The OpenMP Architecture Review Board recently introduced a new way of expressing task parallelism using OpenMP, through the task dependencies extension that comes with revision 4.0 of the specification. This section gives some insight into how programmers can use task dependencies to advantageously replace the often excessive global task synchronizations found in many OpenMP 3.0 applications. We also study the way the development teams of GCC/libGOMP and CLANG/libIOMP choose to implement this new OpenMP task model within their compilers and associated runtime systems.

---

[1] Intel branch with support for OpenMP: http://clang-omp.github.io/

2.1 Task Dependencies by the Example

OpenMP 4.0 introduces the `depend` keyword to specify the access mode of each shared variable a task will access during its execution. Access modes can be set to either `in`, `out` or `inout` whether the corresponding variable is respectively read as input, written as output or both read and written by the considered task. This information is then processed by the underlying runtime system to decide whether a task is ready for execution or should first wait for the completion of other ones.

Listing 1.1 shows the implementation of a LU factorization. It is inspired by the SparseLU kernel from the BOTS [5] benchmark suite, which generates OpenMP independent tasks. The matrix being factorized is divided into a set of smaller sub-matrices on which are applied three computation kernels, called `fwd`, `bdiv` and `bmod`. At iteration k, the update of sub-matrix (i,j) by the `bmod` function requires an update of both sub-matrices (k,j) and (i,k) from the `fwd` and `bdiv` functions respectively. For each iteration, we make sure no `bmod` task starts executing before tasks `fwd` and `bdiv` have completed using the broad range, explicit `taskwait` synchronization keyword on line 11. This keyword indiscriminately waits for the completion of every task created by the parallel section so far.

While respecting the algorithm semantics, this solution limits the potential parallelism that can be generated out of such an application. Listing 1.2 shows the same algorithm implemented with OpenMP task dependencies. Instead of waiting for the termination of *all* previous tasks before executing `bmod` tasks, we specify dependencies to make sure `bmod` tasks can execute as soon as the data they access has been updated by the corresponding `fwd` and `bdiv` tasks. Running this `depend` version of the program leads to the creation of a dependency graph. When an OpenMP thread turns idle,

Listing 1.1. LU with independent tasks

```
1  for (k=0; k<NB; k++) {
2    lu0(M[k*NB+k]);
3    for (j=k+1; j<NB; j++)
4  #pragma omp task untied shared(M)
5      fwd(M[k*NB+k], M[k*NB+j]);
6
7    for (i=k+1; i<NB; i++)
8  #pragma omp task untied shared(M)
9      bdiv(M[k*NB+k], M[i*NB+k]);
10
11 #pragma omp taskwait
12
13   for (i=k+1; i<NB; i++)
14     for (j=k+1; j<NB; j++)
15 #pragma omp task untied shared(M)
16       bmod(M[i*NB+k],
17             M[k*NB+j],
18             M[i*NB+j]);
19 #pragma omp taskwait
20 }
```

Listing 1.2. LU with task dependencies

```
1  for (k=0; k<NB; k++) {
2  #pragma omp task untied shared(M) \
3      depend(inout: M[k*NB+k:BS*BS])
4    lu0(M[k*NB+k]);
5    for (j=k+1; j<NB; j++)
6  #pragma omp task untied shared(M) \
7      depend(in: M[k*NB+k:BS*BS]) \
8      depend(inout: M[k*NB+j:BS*BS])
9      fwd(M[k*NB+k], M[k*NB+j]);
10
11   for (i=k+1; i<NB; i++)
12 #pragma omp task untied shared(M) \
13     depend(in: M[k*NB+k:BS*BS]) \
14     depend(inout: M[i*NB+k:BS*BS])
15     bdiv(M[k*NB+k], M[i*NB+k]);
16
17   for (i=k+1; i<NB; i++)
18     for (j=k+1; j<NB; j++)
19 #pragma omp task untied shared(M) \
20     depend(in: M[i*NB+k:BS*BS]) \
21     depend(in: M[k*NB+j:BS*BS]) \
22     depend(inout: M[i*NB+j:BS*BS])
23     bmod(M[i*NB+k],M[k*NB+j],M[i*NB+j
24 ]);
   }
```

the runtime system browses this graph to decide which task should be executed next, according to tasks' current state and resolved dependencies.

Task dependency support comes with several benefits. First, task dependencies involve decentralized, selective synchronization operations that should scale better than the broad-range taskwait-based approaches. In some situations, this way of programming unlocks more valid execution scenarios than explicitly synchronized tasks, which provides the runtime system with many more valid task schedules to choose from. For example, many instances of the **fwd**, **bdiv** and **bmod** computations can legally run concurrently with the version of the LU factorization expressing task dependencies. On the contrary, this level of concurrence is not possible with the `taskwait` version because the lack of accurate dependency information leads to an over-conservative synchronization scheme. As an added benefit, information about task dependencies also enables the runtime system to optimize further, such as improving task and data placement on NUMA systems.

In expressing dependencies, the programmer needs to strike the right balance however. Indeed, dependencies expressed too coarsely might limit the amount of available parallelism. On the other hand, defining fine-grain dependencies may increase runtime-related overheads, depending on the way the underlying runtime system keeps track of the variables set inside a `depend` clause and the method it uses to enforce dependencies.

2.2 Maturity of Compiler Support

Both the GCC (4.9) and CLANG[2] compilers now support most of the functionalities of OpenMP 4.0. The GNU libGOMP runtime system is responsible for executing OpenMP applications compiled with GCC, while the CLANG compiler generates calls to the Intel libIOMP library. Please note that support for OpenMP 4.0 dependent tasks is still very recent in these compilers at the time of this writing. GCC 4.9 was released on April 22, 2014. The CLANG branch with Intel OpenMP support is under active development. However, even though both compilers are still maturing their support for OpenMP dependent tasks, the tests that we conducted and that we present in Section 4 show that the OpenMP dependent task support in these compilers already favorably compares to the legacy independent task support.

Compiler Support for the "`depend`" Clause. The GCC 4.9 compiler stores the entire list of dependencies into a **void*** * array. This array is passed as argument to the `GOMP_task` function call generated out of a `#pragma omp task` directive. It contains the addresses of all the variables referenced in the `depend` clause.

The Clang 3.4 compiler also generates a list out of the `depend` clause, and passes it to the `__kmpc_omp_task_with_deps` runtime function. This structure stores the addresses of all the variables described inside the `depend` clause, as well the length and flags of associated dependencies.

---

[2] In this article, we designate as "CLANG" the branch developed and maintained by Intel to integrate OpenMP support into the CLANG compiler. This branch is available there: http://clang-omp.github.io/

Runtime Support for Task Dependencies. The libGOMP library that comes with GCC 4.9 uses two data structures to manage task dependencies. The first data structure is the `depend` variable list generated by the compiler for the newly created task, as mentioned above. The second data structure is a hashtable located in the parent of the created task, which keeps track of all the pending dependencies between all the already created child tasks of the parent task. Upon creating the new child task, the runtime walks the list of `depend` variables and looks every variable up in the pending dependency table. If any unresolved dependency is found, the task creation enter the *deferred path*. Otherwise, the task is fully instantiated immediately.

The libIOMP used with Clang 3.4 has a very similar approach. Each parent task maintains a hashtable containing the pending dependencies for its children tasks. If a newly created task is found clear of any pending dependency, the `__kmpc_omp_task_with_deps` runtime function immediately instantiates it by calling the `__kmpc_omp_task` function. Otherwise, the new task is added as a successor to all tasks from which it expects some data, and the `__kmpc_omp_task_with_deps` function returns a code indicating that the new task has not yet been queued. The waiting new task will subsequently be woken up upon completion of its last predecessor.

3   The KASTORS Suite Overview

We designed the KASTORS benchmark suite to evaluate implementations of the OpenMP dependent task paradigm, introduced as part of the OpenMP 4.0 specification [11]. This section introduces the different benchmarks and describes how we extended them to express task dependencies.

Cholesky and QR Decompositions from PLASMA. The PLASMA [9] library developed at ICL/UTK provides a large number of key linear algebra algorithms optimized for multi-core architectures. Several implementations of each algorithm are available, using either static or dynamic scheduling. Dynamic scheduled algorithms are built on top of the QUARK [12] runtime system, which uses a data-flow dependency model to

Listing 1.3. Dynamic algorithm pattern

```
1  wrapper_algorithm_dynamic_call(...)
      {
2      // sequential work
3      for (...)
4        QUARK_Insert_Task(
             wrapper_blas_function,
             packed_parameters);
5      // sequential work
6      for (...)
7        QUARK_Insert_Task(
8           wrapper_another_blas_function
             ,
9           packed_parameters);
10     // sequential work
11 }
```

Listing 1.4. OpenMP algorithm pattern

```
1  algorithm_call(...) {
2      // sequential work
3      for (...)
4  #pragma omp task depend(inout:
          array[...])
5          blas_function(...);
6      // sequential work
7      for (...)
8  #pragma omp task depend(inout:
          array[...])
9          another_blas_function(...)
             ;
10     // sequential work
11 }
```

schedule tasks. The two algorithms we selected are a Cholesky decomposition and a QR decomposition, respectively known as DPOTRF and DGEQRF in PLASMA, which all operate on double precision floating point matrices (**double** type).

The initial implementation uses multiple levels of wrappers, packing and unpacking parameters at each level, which affects the readability of algorithms and can be error prone. Listings 1.3 and 1.4 show the initial dynamic version and the transformations we made for the OpenMP 4.0 port respectively. On the original version the `wrapper_blas_function` performs parameters unpacking before calling the actual BLAS/LAPACK routines it is built on. The OpenMP 4.0 modification led to the removal of multiple wrapper levels, thus improving code readability and maintainability, and removing the need for such parameter management.

Poisson2D. This algorithm solves the Poisson equation on the unit square [0,1]x[0,1], which is divided into a grid of NxN evenly-spaced points. This benchmark relies on a 5-point 2D stencil computational kernel that is repeatedly applied until convergence is detected. We implemented two main blocked versions of this kernel, using either independent tasks and tasks with dependencies.

SparseLU. This benchmark computes the LU decomposition of a sparse matrix. We modified the original BOTS implementation to express task dependencies like described on listings 1.1 and 1.2, except only non-NULL blocks are updated to adapt the traditional LU decomposition to sparse matrices.

Strassen. The Strassen algorithm uses matrix decompositions to compute the multiplication of large dense matrices. Similarly to SparseLU, we modified the BOTS implementation to add parallelism to the addition part of the algorithm and express task dependencies instead of using taskwait-based synchronizations.

4   Performance Evaluation

All experiments were performed with the libGOMP library distributed with GCC 4.9 (git-mirror commit 6ed3847ffd0), and the libIOMP library distributed with clang-omp 3.4 (llvm commit 233b1e3f034, clang-omp commit 7580e521e51f).We conducted our experiments on two different NUMA configurations.

The first one holds 8 AMD Magny Cours processors for a total of 48 cores. Each core has access to 64 KB of L1 cache, 512 KB of L2 cache. Both L1 and L2 caches are private, while L3 cache is shared between the 6 cores of a processor. This configuration provides a total of 256 GB (32 GB per NUMA node) of main memory. We will refer to this configuration as **AMD48**.

The second one holds 4 Intel Xeon E5-4620 processors for a total of 32 cores. Each core has access to 64 KB of L1 cache, 256 KB of L2 cache. Both L1 and L2 caches are private, while L3 cache is shared between the 8 cores of a processor. This configuration provides a total of 380 GB (95 GB per NUMA node) of main memory. We will refer to this configuration as **INTEL32**.

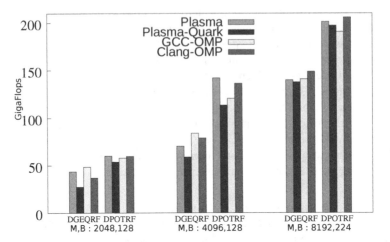

Fig. 1. Plasma on AMD48

Plasma. The DPOTRF and DGEQRF algorithms from Plasma rely on the BLAS library. We used different versions of optimized BLAS depending on the machine: ATLAS 3.10.1 was used on INTEL32, and ATLAS 3.8.4 was used on AMD48. Measurements were conducted using the maximum number of CPUs for each machine. The performance results are expressed in gigaflops (the higher the better), from an average of 10 runs, with an average standard deviation of 2 Gflops.

We compared four versions of these algorithms: The original PLASMA implementation with static scheduling (Plasma), the dynamic scheduling implementation on top of Quark runtime (Plasma-Quark) and two KASTORS OpenMP versions compiled with GCC/libGOMP (GCC-OMP) and CLANG/libIOMP (Clang-OMP), respectively. Each version was run on the following matrix size (M) / block size (B) couples: (2048 / 128), (4096 / 128), (8192 / 224).

For both algorithms the results are positive: On both machines the OpenMP versions compete with the original versions. In several cases, the Clang-OMP version even leads by a slight margin. The overall good results of the original static version can be explained by the fact that it does not have to pay the overhead of task creation. One can also notice that QUARK-based versions always are slightly slower than both CLANG and GCC implementations for small matrix sizes, which leads to the conclusion that the libGOMP and libIOMP runtimes induce less overhead and provide a better handling of fine-grain tasks than QUARK. The conclusion is encouraging, as we were able to get similar or better performance results using a portable OpenMP-based approach than with a specifically designed runtime.

Poisson2D. The results are shown in figure 3 and the corresponding sequential times are reported in table 1. The speedup of both independent tasks and dependent tasks versions are low: Less than 14 on AMD48 and 6 on INTEL32. The application is memory bound with about the same number of arithmetic operations per load and store. The Poisson2D code is an iterative computation in which tasks are created at each time-step to update

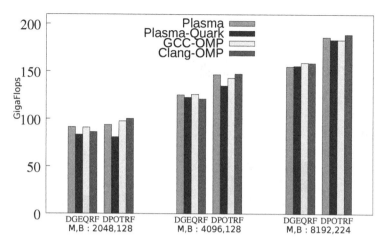

Fig. 2. Plasma on INTEL32

Table 1. Sequential Poisson2D, Strassen and SparseLU execution time (s)

Platform	Compiler	Poisson2D		SparseLU		Strassen	
		8192	16384	128x64	64x128	4096	8192
AMD48	GCC	5.28	21.34	97.74	94.36	38.35	269.93
AMD48	CLANG	5.42	21.66	99.34	95.08	32.92	234.16
INTEL32	GCC	1.64	6.53	77.88	71.97	25.32	180.11
INTEL32	CLANG	1.77	6.79	76.74	71.58	20.12	142.54

the sub domain of the initial grid. One of the important problem is that tasks are not bound to resources in order to take data locality into account. Typical scenario is that tasks between successive iterations may be performed by different threads of the same parallel region. Neither the CLANG or the GCC runtime tries to schedule tasks in order to maximize data reuse. Moreover, tasks that access to same data (due to sharing of frontiers between two sub-domains) may be better scheduled if they are mapped to cores on the same NUMA node. It is challenging for OpenMP runtime developers to take data dependencies into account in order to better schedule tasks to improve data locality.

SparseLU. For this benchmark we used two matrices and sub-matrices sizes : 128x64 and 64x128. Speed up were measured from an average of 10 runs, with an average standard deviation of 0.5. Results are shown on Figure 4 and reference sequential times are listed in Table 1.

For every tested configuration, the dependent task version outperforms the independent task version for both compilers. The best speed up is achieved using the 64x128 configuration. The OpenMP 4.0 version using dependencies performs slightly better in most cases because it is able to exploit inter-iteration parallelism. The version using independent tasks cannot exploit it, because of the global synchronization steps (see

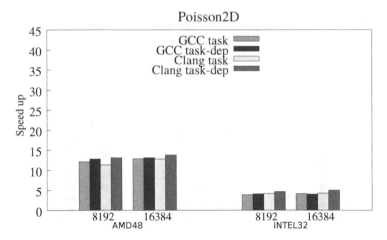

Fig. 3. Poisson 2D

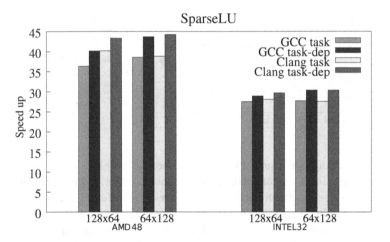

Fig. 4. SparseLU

listings 1.1 and 1.2). It is therefore unable to provide enough parallelism to fully benefit from the available number of cores. This confirms that using data-flow dependencies can lead to a better use of CPUs.

Strassen. The Strassen matrix multiplication is typically performed in 3 steps: a matrix add, a matrix multiply and a matrix add again. The most expensive part is the multiply, but the first adds are not negligible. Thus we define dependences between these two parts. We apply a recurse cutoff of 5, and for matrix smaller than 128x128, multiplies are computed with the usual algorithm instead of Strassen. Experiments were made using two matrix/blocksize combinations: 8192/128, 16384/128. Speed up were measured

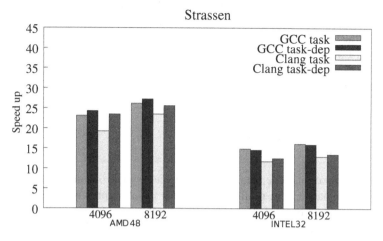

Fig. 5. Strassen

from an average of 10 runs. Results are shown on Figure 5 and reference sequential times are listed on Table 1. The dependent task version very slightly outperforms the independent task version for both compilers on most test cases. We can also notice that these fine-grain dependency expressions are at the bleeding-edge of the OpenMP 4.0 implementation for both GCC and Clang, as some finer dependencies are not yet supported by these compilers.

The general conclusion of these experiments with early implementations of the new OpenMP 4.0's data-flow paradigm is that there is little reason not to make use of it for the benchmarked codes. Under the large majority of the cases tested, the new paradigm incurs no performance regression. Moreover, the finer-grain synchronization scheme it provides is able to deliver more parallelism to feed large multicore configurations, usually leading to better performance results.

5   Extending OpenMP Dependency Expressiveness

5.1   Enabling Reductions for OpenMP Tasking: The Cumulative-Write Mode

OpenMP supports reduction for several directives such as `section`, `parallel` and `for`. Since the introduction of task-based programming within OpenMP 3.0, programs increasingly use loops to generate tasks, instead of performing computations directly within an `omp for` loop. OpenMP 4.0's task dependencies should strengthen this tendency even further, to enable more load-balancing flexibility. Unfortunately, the `reduction` clause is not available for the `omp task` directive, nor any alternative mechanism, leaving programmers to build it by themselves.

The approach we propose is to extend the set of **in,out** and **inout** data access modes with a new *cumulative-write* mode **cw**. This new mode indicates that several tasks may contribute to a piece of data in any order (but not simultaneously). It is inspired by the reduction support implemented in runtime system Kaapi [7]. One might suggest to use the existing `inout` mode instead. However, the `inout` mode imposes a strong ordering between tasks, that proves to be unnecessary in that case. The following example illustrates this idea with a modified version of the LU decomposition code from Fig. 1.2. Using a *cumulative write* mode `cw` for the `bmod` computation (line 23) breaks the strong inter-iteration dependency that was caused by the `inout` mode, thus enabling more parallelism.

```
1    #pragma omp task untied shared(M) \
2        depend(in: M[i*NB+k:BS*BS]) \
3        depend(in: M[k*MSIZE+j:BS*BS]) \
4        depend(cw: M[i*NB+j:BS*BS])
5    bmod(M[i*NB+k], M[k*NB+j], M[i*NB+j]);
```

On the next input or inout dependency, or at the next synchronization point (taskwait, explicit or implicit barrier), the runtime ensures that variables previously accessed using the `cw` mode may then be read. The reduction operator can be a pre-defined operators or a user defined reduction operator such as introduced with OpenMP-4.0. We plan to extend reduction operators to enable non-commutative operators as well (such as appends on a string or matrix multiplication) such as in [7] or [1].

5.2 Expressing Dependencies on Non-contiguous Memory Areas

OpenMP 4.0 makes it possible to express task dependencies on the slice of an array, by specifying the offset and the length of the dependent slice. These slices specifications can be chained to express dependencies on 2D-subarrays.

```
1    #pragma omp task depend(inout:array[offset1:length1][offset2:length2])
2        blas_function(...);
```

Chained array slices are available only for constant arrays and variable length arrays, however. The lack of leading dimension information makes them impractical for pointers, which strongly limits their interest. Temporarily copying data to constant arrays is tedious and time consuming. Variable length arrays on the other hand, are passed by value (copy) from a function to another, and only integrated the C language standard since C99. However, VLA is an optional feature in C11. A possible workaround could be to cast the pointer to a variable length array or constant array, such as this:

```
1    double *f_ = malloc(NX * NY * sizeof(double));
2    double (*f)[NX][NY] = (double (*)[NX][NY])f_;
3    #pragma omp task depend(inout:f[offset1:length1][offset2:length2])
4        blas_function(...);
5    free(f_);
```

This solution is not very much elegant, however. Our proposal is thus to extend the slice syntax to enable the specification of the missing leading dimension information. Following this extension, 2D sub-arrays may be specified such as this:

```
1    double *f = malloc(NX * NY * sizeof(double));
2    #pragma omp task depend(inout:f[offset1:length1:NX][offset2:length2])
3        blas_function(...);
4    free(f);
```

6   Related Work

OpenMP Benchmarks. To the best of our knowledge, KASTORS is the only benchmark suite focusing on OpenMP task dependencies. This section describes existing benchmarks evaluating other aspects of the OpenMP specification.

The Barcelona OpenMP Tasks Suite [5] evaluates the addition of tasking to the OpenMP 3.0 specification, comparing several ways of generating tasks out of small computing kernels. We adapted two of these kernels, *SparseLU* and *Strassen*, to express task dependencies, and we added the modified versions to our KASTORS suite.

Older OpenMP benchmark suites such as PARSEC [3], SPECOMP [10] and Rodinia [4] could be extended to benefit from task parallelism, as well as the NAS Parallel Benchmark suite [2] (NPB). NPB was originally introduced to evaluate the performance of parallel supercomputers. It was later extended to provide OpenMP 2.5 compatible versions of most kernels. We consider modifying some of them to exploit task parallelism, especially the "multi-zone" ones [8] involving nested parallelism.

Compilers and Runtime Systems Supporting Task Dependencies. KAAPI [7][3], StarPU [1][4], Quark [12] and OMPSs [6] are libraries that support task dependencies in a different context than OpenMP. We present them here focusing on the different access modes they propose, and the way application programmers can provide task dependencies using these libraries.

The KAAPI and StarPU runtime systems were designed to improve the performance of task-based parallel applications on large-scale heterogeneous platforms. Unlike the current OpenMP specification, KAAPI and StarPU support the expression of dependencies on multi-dimensional arrays. StarPU provides ways of splitting a data with user-defined filters that can help to express dependencies on sub-matrices, for example.

The Quark runtime system that comes with the PLASMA library is responsible for executing tasks created out of BLAS operators in a dynamic way. Unlike KAAPI and StarPU, Quark only considers unidimensional arrays, but comes with an original scratch access mode to reuse thread-specific temporary data.

OMPSs [6] is a programming model inspired by OpenMP with specific directives to support task dependencies and heterogeneity. The OMPSs programming model includes the concurrent clause to express that tasks will perform reductions on the listed variables. Similar access-modes also exist in KAAPI and StarPU.

7   Conclusion

The introduction of task dependencies in the revision 4.0 of the OpenMP specification provides application programmers with a new, powerful way of describing synchronizations in task-based parallel applications. OpenMP compilers and runtime systems will play a key role in the adoption of such a new feature by the community, as they are responsible for tracking and resolving variable dependencies before executing tasks.

---

[3] http://kaapi.gforge.inria.fr
[4] http://starpu.gforge.inria.fr

The performance of OpenMP applications expressing task dependencies will be closely related to how efficiently compilers and runtime systems implement this new feature.

We introduced a new benchmark suite, called KASTORS, composed with small kernels ported on the OpenMP dependent task model. We then compared their performance with taskwait-based versions of the same kernels for both the GCC/libGOMP and the CLANG/libIOMP compilers and runtime systems. While the support for task dependencies in these compilers is still very recent, experiments run on two different hardware configurations show that the versions with task dependencies offer performances comparable and sometimes better to taskwait-based versions on most kernels. The results obtained by rewriting some PLASMA kernels to use OpenMP task dependencies also demonstrated that this model even outperforms dedicated data-flow solutions in some situations, while improving portability.

In the near future, we plan to extend the KASTORS suite with new benchmarks coming from either modified versions of existing benchmarks or small kernels inspired from real-life scientific applications. Based on CLANG, we are also developing a source-to-source compiler that generates direct calls to the KAAPI or StarPU runtime systems out of C/C++ OpenMP programs. We are currently working on releasing this compiler with a full support of the extensions proposed in section 5.

Acknowledgments. This work has been partially supported by the INRIA ADT K'STAR Project, the ANR-11-BS02-013 HPAC Project and the IRSES2011-295217 HPC-GA Project.

References

1. Augonnet, C., Thibault, S., Namyst, R., Wacrenier, P.-A.: STARPU: A Unified Platform for Task Scheduling on Heterogeneous Multicore Architectures. In: Sips, H., Epema, D., Lin, H.-X. (eds.) Euro-Par 2009. LNCS, vol. 5704, pp. 863–874. Springer, Heidelberg (2009)
2. Bailey, D., Barszcz, E., Barton, J., Browning, D., Carter, R., Dagum, L., Fatoohi, R., Fineberg, S., Frederickson, P., Lasinski, T., Schreiber, R., Simon, H., Venkatakrishnan, V., Weeratunga, S.: The NAS Parallel Benchmarks. Report RNR-94-007, Department of Mathematics and Computer Science, Emory University (March 1994)
3. Bienia, C.: Benchmarking Modern Multiprocessors. PhD thesis, Princeton University (January 2011)
4. Che, S., Sheaffer, J., Boyer, M., Szafaryn, L., Wang, L., Skadron, K.: A characterization of the rodinia benchmark suite with comparison to contemporary cmp workloads. In: 2010 IEEE International Symposium on Workload Characterization (IISWC), pp. 1–11 (December 2010)
5. Duran, A., Teruel, X., Ferrer, R., Martorell, X., Ayguade, E.: Barcelona openmp tasks suite: A set of benchmarks targeting the exploitation of task parallelism in openmp. In: International Conference on Parallel Processing, ICPP 2009, pp. 124–131. IEEE (2009)
6. Duran, A., Ayguadé, E., Badia, R.M., Labarta, J., Martinell, L., Martorell, X., Planas, J.: Ompss: a proposal for programming heterogeneous multi-core architectures. Parallel Processing Letters 21(02), 173–193 (2011)
7. Gautier, T., Besseron, X., Pigeon, L.: Kaapi: A thread scheduling runtime system for data flow computations on cluster of multi-processors. In: PASCO 2007 (2007)

8. Jin, H., der Wijngaart, R.F.V.: Performance characteristics of the multi-zone nas parallel benchmarks. In: IPDPS. IEEE Computer Society (2004)
9. Kurzak, J., Luszczek, P., YarKhan, A., Faverge, M., Langou, J., Bouwmeester, H., Dongarra, J.: Multithreading in the PLASMA Library, pp. 119–141. Chapman and Hall/CRC (2013)
10. Müller, M.S., et al.: Spec omp2012 – an application benchmark suite for parallel systems using openmp. In: Chapman, B.M., Massaioli, F., Müller, M.S., Rorro, M. (eds.) IWOMP 2012. LNCS, vol. 7312, pp. 223–236. Springer, Heidelberg (2012)
11. OpenMP Architecture Review Board. OpenMP application program interface version 4.0 (July 2013)
12. YarKhan, A., Kurzak, J., Dongarra, J.: Quark users' guide: Queueing and runtime for kernels. Technical report, Innovative Computing Laboratory, University of Tennessee (2011)

METAFORK: A Framework for Concurrency Platforms Targeting Multicores

Xiaohui Chen[1], Marc Moreno Maza[1], Sushek Shekar[1], and Priya Unnikrishnan[2]

[1] Department of Computer Science, University of Western Ontario
[2] Compiler Development Team, IBM Toronto Lab

Abstract. We present METAFORK, a metalanguage for multithreaded algorithms based on the fork-join concurrency model and targeting multicore architectures. METAFORK is implemented as a source-to-source compilation framework allowing automatic translation of programs from one concurrency platform to another. The current version of this framework supports CILKPLUS and OPENMP. We evaluate the benefits of the METAFORK framework through a series of experiments, such as narrowing performance bottlenecks in multithreaded programs. Our experiments show also that, if a native program, written either in CILKPLUS or OPENMP, has little parallelism overhead, then the same property holds for its OPENMP or CILKPLUS counterpart translated by METAFORK.

1 Introduction

In the past decade the pervasive ubiquity of multicore processors has stimulated a constantly increasing effort in the development of concurrency platforms, such as CILKPLUS, OPENMP and TBB. While those programming languages are all based on the fork-join concurrency model, they largely differ in their way of expressing parallel algorithms and scheduling the corresponding tasks. Therefore, developing software code combining libraries written with several of those languages is a challenge.

Nevertheless there is a real need for facilitating interoperability between concurrency platforms. Consider for instance the field of symbolic computation. The DMPMC library[1] provides sparse polynomial arithmetic and is entirely written in OPENMP, meanwhile the BPAS library[2] provides dense polynomial arithmetic and is entirely written in CILKPLUS. Polynomial system solvers require both sparse and dense polynomial arithmetic and thus could take advantage of a combination of the DMPMC and BPAS libraries. However, CILKPLUS and OPENMP have different run-time systems. In order to achieve interoperability between them, we propose an automatic source-to-source translation mechanism.

Another motivation for such a software tool is *comparative implementation* with the objective of narrowing performance bottlenecks. The underlying observation is that the same multithreaded algorithm, based on the fork-join

---

[1] From the TRIP project www.imcce.fr/trip developed at the *Observatoire de Paris*.
[2] From the *Basic Polynomial Algebra Subprograms* www.bpaslib.org developed at the University of Western Ontario.

L. DeRose (Eds.): IWOMP 2014, LNCS 8766, pp. 30–44, 2014.
© Springer International Publishing Switzerland 2014

parallelism model, implemented with two different concurrency platforms, say CILKPLUS and OPENMP, could result in very different performance, often very hard to analyze and compare. If one code scales well while the other does not, one may suspect an inefficient implementation of the latter as well as other possible causes such as higher parallelism overheads. Translating the inefficient code to the other language can help narrowing the problem. Indeed, if the translated code still does not scale, one can suspect an implementation issue (say the programmer missed to parallelize one portion of the algorithm) whereas if the translated code does scale, then one can suspect a parallelism overhead issue in the original code (say the grain-size of a parallel for-loop is too small).

In this paper, we propose METAFORK, a metalanguage for multithreaded algorithms based on the fork-join parallelism model [5] and targeting multicore architectures. By its parallel programming constructs, the METAFORK language is currently a super-set of CILKPLUS [4, 13, 11] and offers counterparts for the following widely used parallel constructs of OPENMP [16, 1]: #pragma omp parallel, #pragma omp task, #pragma omp sections, #pragma omp section, #pragma omp for, #pragma omp taskwait, #pragma omp barrier, #pragma omp single and #pragma omp master. However, METAFORK does not make any assumptions about the run-time system, in particular about scheduling strategies (work sharing, work stealing [6]). In fact, METAFORK is not designed to be a target language, but rather as the internal intermediate representation (IR) of a source-to-source compiler framework for multithreaded languages.

The syntax and the semantics of METAFORK's parallel constructs are specified in Sections 2, 3 and 4. Since METAFORK is a faithful extension of the C/C++ language, this is actually sufficient to completely define METAFORK.

Recall that a driving motivation of the METAFORK project is to facilitate automatic translation of programs between concurrency platforms. To date, our experimental framework includes translators between CILKPLUS and METAFORK (both ways) and, between OPENMP and METAFORK (both ways). Hence, through METAFORK, we perform program translations between CILKPLUS and OPENMP (both ways). Integrating TBB in this framework is work in progress.

Despite of the fact that it does not support all features of OPENMP, the METAFORK language is rich enough to capture the semantics of large bodies of OPENMP code, such as the *Barcelona* OPENMP *Tasks Suite* (BOTS) [10] and translate faithfully to CILKPLUS each of the BOTS test cases. In the other direction, we could translate the BPAS library to OPENMP.

In Section 5, we briefly explain how the translators of the METAFORK compilation framework are implemented. In particular, we specify which OPENMP data-sharing clauses are captured by the METAFORK translators. Simple examples of code translation are provided.

In Section 6, we evaluate the benefits of the METAFORK framework through a series of experiments. First, we show that METAFORK can help narrow down performance bottlenecks in multithreaded programs by means of comparative implementation, as discussed above. Secondly, we observe that, if a native CILKPLUS (resp. OPENMP) program has little parallelism overhead, then the same holds for its OPENMP (resp. CILKPLUS) counterpart translated by METAFORK. We tested more than 20 examples in total for which experimental results can be found in the technical report [8] and for which code can be found on the web site of the METAFORK project. Moreover, the source code of the METAFORK translators can be downloaded from the same web site at http://www.metafork.org.

Related work. While the well-developed source-to-source compiler framework ROSE[3] has been used to support many programming languages, including OPENMP and UPC, we are not aware of a ROSE-based platform similar to METAFORK, that is, providing source-to-source translation between multithreaded languages. On the other hand, several projects offer automatic one-way translation from a concurrency platform running on one hardware architecture to another concurrency platform running on another hardware architecture, e.g. OPENMP shared-memory code to MPI distributed-memory code as in the papers [2] [9] (HOMPI Project) or [15] (OPENMP Accelerator Model). Other projects offer extension of a concurrency platform from one hardware architecture to another hardware architecture, like HOMP [15] or OPENMPC [12] which allow extended OPENMP code to run on NVIDIA GPUs. In contrast to these two types of projects, METAFORK is currently dedicated to a single type of hardware architecture, namely multicore processors. However, METAFORK offers automatic *two-way* translations. Moreover, the generated code is human-readable, as illustrated by the examples available on the METAFORK web site.

2   Parallel Constructs and Execution Model of METAFORK

METAFORK extends both the C and C++ languages into a multithreaded language based on the fork-join concurrency model. Thus, concurrent execution is obtained by a parent thread creating and launching one or more child threads so that the parent and its children execute a so-called *parallel region*. An important example of parallel regions are for-loop bodies. METAFORK has the following natural requirement regarding parallel regions: control flow cannot branch into or out of a *parallel region*.

METAFORK has four parallel constructs: function call spawn, block spawn, parallel for-loop and synchronization barrier. The first two use the keyword meta_fork while the other two use respectively the keywords meta_for and meta_join. The parallel constructs of METAFORK grant permission for concurrent execution but do not command it. Hence, a METAFORK program can execute on a single core machine. We emphasize the fact that meta_fork allows the programmer to spawn a function call (like in CILKPLUS) as well as a block (like in OPENMP). Examples of METAFORK code with CILKPLUS and OPENMP can be found through Figures 5, 6, 7, 8, 9, 10, 11, 12 and 13.

As mentioned, the keyword meta_fork is used to express the fact that a function call or a block is executed by a child thread, concurrently to the execution

---

[3] http://en.wikibooks.org/wiki/ROSE_Compiler_Framework

of the parent thread. If the program is run by a single processor, the parent thread is suspended during the execution of the child thread; when this latter terminates, the parent thread resumes its execution after the function call (or block) spawn.

If the program is run by multiple processors, the parent thread may continue its execution[4] after the function call (or block) spawn, without being suspended, meanwhile the child thread executes the function call (or block) spawn. In this latter scenario, the parent thread waits for the completion of the execution of the child thread, as soon as the parent thread reaches a synchronization point.

Spawning a function call with `meta_fork`. Spawning a call to the function `f`, with the argument sequence `args`, is done by `meta_fork f(args)`. The semantics is similar to that of the CILKPLUS counterpart `cilk_spawn f(args)`. In particular, all the arguments in the sequence `args` are evaluated before spawning the function call `f(args)`. However, the execution of `meta_fork f(args)` differs from that of `cilk_spawn f(args)` on one feature. While there is an implicit `cilk_sync` at the end of the Cilk block [11] surrounding this latter `cilk_spawn`, no such implicit barriers are assumed with `meta_fork`. This feature is motivated by the fact that, in addition to the fork-join parallelism, we plan to extend the METAFORK language to other forms of parallelism such as *parallel futures* [17, 3].

Spawning a block with `meta_fork`. The other usage of the `meta_fork` construct is for spawning a basic block B, which is done as follows: `meta_fork { B }`. If B consists of a single instruction, then the surrounding curly braces can be omitted. We also refer to this construction as a *parallel region*. There is no equivalent in CILKPLUS while it is offered by OPENMP. Similarly to a function call spawn, this parallel region is executed by a child thread (once the parent thread reaches the `meta_fork` construct) meanwhile the parent thread continues its execution after the parallel region. Similarly also to a function call spawn, no implicit barrier is assumed at the end of the surrounding region. Hence synchronization points have to be added explicitly, using `meta_join`. A variable v which is not local to B may be shared by both the parent and child threads; alternatively, the child thread may be granted a private copy of v. Precise rules about data attributes, for both parallel regions and parallel for-loops, are stated in Section 3.

Parallel for-loops with `meta_for`. Parallel for-loops in METAFORK have the following format `meta_for (I, C, S) { B }` where I is the *initialization expression* of the loop, C is the *condition expression* of the loop, S is the *stride* of the loop and B is the loop body. The specifications of C, S, B are standard and similar to the initialization expression, condition expression and stride of a CILKPLUS for-loop. We refer to the METAFORK specifications document [7] for details. The parent thread will share the work of executing the iterations of the loop with

---

[4] In fact, the parent thread does not participate to the execution of a function call (or block) spawn, but will participate to the execution of the iterations of a parallel for-loop.

the child threads. An implicit synchronization point is assumed after the loop body. That is, the execution of the parent thread is suspended when it reaches `meta_for` and resumes when all children threads (executing the loop body iterations) have completed their execution. As one can expect, the iterations of the parallel loop `meta_for (I, C, S) { B }` must execute independently of each other in order to guarantee that this parallel loop is semantically equivalent to its serial version `for (I, C, S) { B }`.

Synchronization point with `meta_join`. The construct `meta_join` indicates a *synchronization point* (or *barrier*) for a parent thread and its children tasks. More precisely, a parent thread reaching this point must wait for the completion of its children tasks but not for those of the subsequent descendant tasks.

3   Variable Attribute Rules

Variables that are *non-local* to the block of a parallel region may be either *shared* by or *private* to the threads executing the code paths where those variables are defined. After a terminology review, we specify the rules that METAFORK uses in order to decide whether such a non-local variable is shared or private.

Shared and private variables. Consider a parallel region with block Y (or a parallel for-loop with loop body Y). X denotes the immediate outer scope of Y. We say that X is the *parent region* of Y and that Y is a *child region* of X. A variable v which is defined in Y is said to be *local* to Y; otherwise we call v a *non-local* variable for Y. Let v be a non-local variable for Y. Assume v gives access to a block of storage before reaching Y. (Thus, v cannot be a non-initialized pointer.) We say that v is *shared* by X and Y if its name gives access to the same block of storage in both X and Y; otherwise we say that v is *private* to Y. In particular, if Y is a parallel for-loop we say that a local variable w is *shared* by Y whenever the name of w gives access to the same block of storage in any loop iteration of Y, which means that all the threads that execute this parallel for-loop share the same variable w; otherwise we say that w is *private* to Y.

Value-type and reference-type variables. In the C programming language, a *value-type variable* contains its data directly as opposed to a *reference-type variable*, which contains a reference to its data. Value-type variables are either of primitive types (`char`, `float`, `int`, `double`, `void`) or user-defined types (`enum`, `struct`, `union`). Reference-type variables are pointers, arrays and functions.

`static` *and* `const` *type variables.* In the C programming language, a *static* variable is a variable that has been allocated statically and whose lifetime extends across the entire run of the program. This is in contrast to *automatic* variables (*local* variables are generally *automatic*) whose storage is allocated and deallocated on the call stack and, other variables (such as objects) whose storage is dynamically allocated in heap memory. When a variable is declared with the qualifier *const*, the value of that variable cannot typically be altered by the program during its execution.

```
/* This file starts here ... */          /* ... and  continues here ... */
#include<stdio.h>                         void subcall(int *a,int *b){
#include<time.h>                                for(int i=0;i<10;i++)
#include<stdlib.h>                                    printf("%d %d\n",a[i],b[i]);
int a;                                    }
long par_region(long n){                  int main(int argc,char **argv){
      int b;                                    long n=10;
      int *c = (int *)malloc(sizeof(int)*10);   par_region(n);
      int d[10];                                return 0;
      const int f=0;                      }
      static int g=0;                     /* ... and finishes here. */
      meta_fork{
          int e = b;
          subcall(c,d);
      }
}
```

Fig. 1. Various variable attributes in a parallel region

Variable attribute rules of meta_fork. A non-local variable v which gives access to a block of storage before reaching Y is shared between the parent X and the child Y whenever v is: (1) a global variable, (2) a file scope variable, (3) a reference-type variable, (4) declared static or const, or (5) qualified shared. In all other cases, the variable v is private to the child. In particular, value-type variables (that are not declared static or const, or qualified shared ,and that are not global or file scope variables) are private to the child. In Figure 1, the variables a, c, d, f and g are shared, meanwhile the b and e are private.

```
/* To illustrate variable attributes, three    /* This file is b.cpp*/
    files (a headerfile "a.h" and two source    #include<stdio.h>
    files "a.cpp" and "b.cpp") are used.        #include<stdlib.h>
This file is a.cpp  */                          #include<time.h>
#include<stdio.h>                               #include"a.h"
extern int var;                                 int var = 100;
void test(int *array)                           int main(int argc,char **argv)
{                                               {
  int basecase = 100;                               int *a=(int*)malloc(sizeof(int)*10);
  meta_for(int j = 0; j < 10; j++)                  srand((unsigned)time(NULL));
  {                                                 for(int i=0;i<10;i++)
          static int var1=0;                          a[i]=rand();
          int i = array[j];                         test(a);
          if( i < basecase )                        return 0;
              array[j]+=var;                    }
  }                                             /* This file is a.h*/
}                                               void test(int *a);
```

Fig. 2. Example of shared and private variables with meta_for

Variable attribute rules of meta_for. A non-local variable which gives access to a block of storage before reaching Y is *shared between parent and child*. A variable local to Y is *shared by* Y whenever it is declared static, otherwise it is private to Y. In particular, loop control variables are private to Y. In the example of Figure 2, the variables array, basecase, var and var1, are shared by all threads while the variables i and j are private. In the example of Figure 9, the variable

```
long fib_parallel(long n)
{
        long x, y;
        if (n < 2)
            return n;
        else{
            x = meta_fork fib_parallel(n-1);
            y = fib_parallel(n-2);
            meta_join;
            return (x+y);}
}
```

```
long fib_parallel(long n)
{
        long x, y;
        if (n < 2)
            return n;
        else{
            meta_fork shared(x)
            {
                x = fib_parallel(n-1);
            }
            y = fib_parallel(n-2);
            meta_join;
            return (x+y);}
}
```

Fig. 3. Parallel fib code using a function spawn

Fig. 4. Parallel fib code using a block spawn

b is private, thus the OPENMP, METAFORK, CILKPLUS codes of Figures 8, 9 and 10 are semantically equivalent.

The shared *keyword.* Programmers can explicitly qualify a given variable as shared by using the shared keyword. In the example of Figure 3, the variable n is private to fib_parallel(n-1). In Figure 4, we specify the variable x as shared and the variable n is still private. Notice that the programs in Figures 3 and 4 are semantically equivalent. In the parallel regions of the example of Figure 12, the variables sum_a and sum_b are qualified shared. Hence the OPENMP, METAFORK and CILKPLUS programs of Figure 11, 12 and 13 are semantically equivalent.

4   Semantics of the Parallel Constructs in METAFORK

In order to formally define the semantics of each of the parallel constructs in METAFORK, we introduce the *serial C-elision* of a METAFORK program $\mathcal{M}$: this is a program $\mathcal{C}$ expressed in the C-language and with the same semantics as $\mathcal{M}$. In [7], we obtain such a serial C-elision $\mathcal{C}$ from the program $\mathcal{M}$ by means of a series of rewriting rules. Due to space consideration, we cannot include this algorithmic definition here. However, we believe that sketching its principle is sufficient for understanding the rest of this paper.

As mentioned before, spawning a function call in METAFORK has the same semantics as spawning a function call in CILKPLUS. More precisely: meta_fork f(args)   and   cilk_spawn f(args) are semantically equivalent.

A meta_for loop allows iterations of the loop body to be executed in parallel. By default, each iteration of the loop body is executed by a separate thread. However, using the grainsize compilation directive, one can specify the number of loop iterations executed per thread[5]: #pragma meta grainsize = expression.   Nevertheless, in order to obtain the *serial C-elision* of a METAFORK for-loop, we require that the meta_for construct could be replaced

---

[5] The loop iterations of a thread are then executed one after another by that thread.

by the C-language `for` - whatever is the grainsize of this METAFORK for loop - without changing the initialization expression, condition expression and stride. (Of course, the loop-body must be replaced with its serial C-elision.)

Specifying the semantics of the spawning of a block in METAFORK is the difficult part. We do it in [7] in an algorithmic fashion, using rewriting rules, that are similar to a LEX-YACC program. The main idea is to use *outlining*, a widely used technique in the OPENMP community, see [14]. To have a taste of that transformation, one should observe how the METAFORK code of Figure 12 is transformed into the CILKPLUS code of Figure 13. Obtaining the serial elision of that latter code is easy and one can finally derive a serial C-elision for our input METAFORK code.

5   Translation

In this section, we briefly explain how the translators of the METAFORK compilation framework are implemented. Obviously, for each translator, the semantics of each input program are preserved into the output program. However, scheduling strategies (like an OPENMP clause `schedule(static, chuksize)`) are ignored by our translators. Retaining them (at least as structured comments) will be explored in a future release of METAFORK.

From CILKPLUS code to METAFORK code. Translating code from CILKPLUS to METAFORK is easy in principle since, up to the vectorization constructs of CILKPLUS, the METAFORK language is a superset of CILKPLUS. However, implicit CILKPLUS barriers need to be explicitly inserted in the target METAFORK code. This implies that, during translation, it is necessary to trace the instruction stream DAG of the CILKPLUS program in order to properly insert barriers in the generated METAFORK code.

From METAFORK code to CILKPLUS code. Since CILKPLUS has no constructs for spawning a block of code, we naturally use the *outlining technique* to: (1) wrap the parallel region as a function, and then (2) call that function concurrently. In fact, the problem of translating code from METAFORK to CILKPLUS is equivalent to that of defining the serial elision of a METAFORK program.

From OPENMP code to METAFORK code. We first consider the translation of an OPENMP task directive: if it is a function call spawn, as in Figure 7, we use the METAFORK construct for spawning a function call. Otherwise, we use the METAFORK construct for spawning a block. Currently, we translate faithfully the following OPENMP optional clause directives: `shared`, `private` and `firstprivate`. For the translation of OPENMP sections to the METAFORK parallel regions we only support the default variable attribute and note that this case leads us to insert extra synchronization points. Finally, for the translation of an OPENMP parallel for-loop to METAFORK, we note that: (1) the `private` and `firstprivate` optional clause directives are faithfully translated,

(2) every variable specified `private` is re-declared in the parallel for-loop of the METAFORK translation, (3) the loop control variables are initialized inside the loop, and (4) scheduling strategies of OPENMP parallel for loops are ignored,

From METAFORK *code to* OPENMP *code.* This is easy in principle, since the METAFORK language can be regarded as a subset of the OPENMP language. We note that function calls spawned with the `meta_fork` construct are translated using the task constructs of OPENMP.

```
long fib(long n)
{
  long x, y;
  if (n<2) return n;
  else if (n<BASE)
    return fib_serial(n);
  else
  {
    x = cilk_spawn fib(n-1);
    y = fib(n-2);
    cilk_sync;
    return (x+y);
  }
}
```

```
long fib(long n)
{
  long x, y;
  if (n<2) return n;
  else if (n<BASE)
    return fib_serial(n);
  else
  {
    x = meta_fork fib(n-1);
    y = fib(n-2);
    meta_join;
    return (x+y);
  }
}
```

```
long fib(long n)
{
  long x, y;
  if (n<2) return n;
  else if (n<BASE)
    return fib_serial(n);
  else
  {
    #pragma omp task shared(x)
    x = fib(n-1);
    y = fib(n-2);
    #pragma omp taskwait
    return (x+y);
  }
}
```

Fig. 5. CILKPLUS code   **Fig. 6.** METAFORK code   **Fig. 7.** OPENMP code

```
int main()
{
  int a[N];
  int b = 0;
  #pragma omp parallel
  #pragma omp for private(b)
  for(int i=0; i<N; i++)
  {
    b = i ;
    a[i] = b;
  }
}
```

```
int main()
{
  int a[N];
  int b = 0;

  meta_for(int i=0; i<N; i++)
  {
    int b;
    b = i ;
    a[i] = b;
  }
}
```

```
int main()
{
  int a[N];
  int b = 0;

  cilk_for(int i=0; i<N; i++)
  {
    int b;
    b = i ;
    a[i] = b;
  }
}
```

Fig. 8. OPENMP code   **Fig. 9.** METAFORK code   **Fig. 10.** CILKPLUS code

6   Experimentation

In this section, we evaluate the performance and the usefulness of the four METAFORK translators (METAFORK to CILKPLUS, CILKPLUS to METAFORK, METAFORK to OPENMP, OPENMP to METAFORK). To this end, we run these translators on various input programs written either in CILKPLUS or OPENMP, or both.

We emphasize the fact that our purpose is not to compare the performance of the CILKPLUS or OPENMP run-time systems. The reader should notice that the codes used in this study were written by different persons with different levels

```
int main(){
  int sum_a=0, sum_b=0;
  int a[5] = {0,1,2,3,4};
  int b[5] = {0,1,2,3,4};
  #pragma omp parallel
  {
    #pragma omp sections
    {
      #pragma omp section
      {
        for(int i=0; i<5; i++)
          sum_a += a[i];
      }
      #pragma omp section
      {
        for(int i=0; i<5; i++)
          sum_b += b[i];
      } } }
}
```

```
int main()
{
  int sum_a=0, sum_b=0;
  int a[5] = {0,1,2,3,4};
  int b[5] = {0,1,2,3,4};

  meta_fork shared(sum_a){
            for(int i=0; i<5; i++)
              sum_a += a[i];
  }

  meta_fork shared(sum_b){
            for(int i=0; i<5; i++)
              sum_b += b[i];
  }

  meta_join;
}
```

```
void fork_func0(int* sum_a,int* a)
{
    for(int i=0; i<5; i++)
      (*sum_a) += a[i];
}
void fork_func1(int* sum_b,int* b)
{
    for(int i=0; i<5; i++)
      (*sum_b) += b[i];
}
int main()
{
  int sum_a=0, sum_b=0;
  int a[5] = {0,1,2,3,4};
  int b[5] = {0,1,2,3,4};
  cilk_spawn fork_func0(&sum_a,a);
  cilk_spawn fork_func1(&sum_b,b);
  cilk_sync;
}
```

Fig. 11. OPENMP
code

Fig. 12. METAFORK
code

Fig. 13. CILKPLUS code

of expertise. In addition, the reported experimentation is essentially limited to one architecture (AMD Opteron) and one compiler (GCC). Therefore, it would be delicate to draw any clear conclusions comparing CILKPLUS and OPENMP. We conducted three sets of experiments:

- In the first one, we compared the performance of hand-written codes. The motivation, specified in the introduction, is *comparative implementation.*
- In the second one, we translated large portions of the BPAS library from CILKPLUS to OPENMP, motivated by the *interoperability* question raised in the introduction.
- In the last experiment, we compared the *parallelism overheads* measured the original codes (either CILKPLUS or OPENMP) and their translated counterparts.

Before reporting on these three sets of experiments:

- we describe the *setup* (hardware, software) in which they were conducted and,
- we explain how we verified the *correctness* of the multithreaded code generated by our translators.

Experimentation setup. For all experiments, apart from student's code, we use codes from the following sources:

- The BPAS library http://www.bpaslib.org,
- John Burkardt's Home Page
  http://people.sc.fsu.edu/~%20jburkardt/c_src/openmp/openmp.html,
- the BOTS [10] and
- the CILK distribution examples http://sourceforge.net/projects/cilk/.

The source code of those test cases was compiled as follows:

- CILKPLUS code with GCC 4.8 using -O2 -g -lcilkrts -fcilkplus
- OPENMP code with GCC 4.8 using -O2 -g -fopenmp

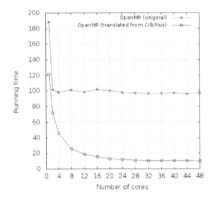
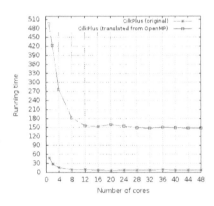

Fig. 14. Parallel mergesort in size 5×10^8

Fig. 15. Matrix inversion of order 4096

We run all our programs on AMD Opteron 6168 48-core nodes (with 256GB RAM and 12MB L3) and Intel Xeon 2.66GHz/6.4GT with 12-cores nodes.

Correctness. Validating the correctness of our translators was a major requirement of our work. Depending on the test-case, we could use one of the following strategies.

- Assume that the original program, say $\mathcal{P}$, contains both a parallel code and its serial elision (manually written). When program $\mathcal{P}$ is executed, both codes run and compare their results. Let us call $\mathcal{Q}$ the translated version of $\mathcal{P}$. Since serial elisions are unchanged by our translation procedures, then $\mathcal{Q}$ can be verified by the same process used for program $\mathcal{P}$. This first strategy applies to the `Cilk++` distribution examples and the BOTS (Barcelona OpenMP Tasks Suite) examples.
- If the original program $\mathcal{P}$ does not include a serial elision of the parallel code, then the translated program $\mathcal{Q}$ is verified by comparing the output of $\mathcal{P}$ and $\mathcal{Q}$. This second strategy had to be applied to the FSU (Florida State University) examples.

Comparative implementation. For this first purpose, we use a series of test-cases, each of them consisting of a pair of hand-written programs: one written in OPENMP and the other in CILKPLUS. Within each pair, a program S, written by a student, has a performance bottleneck; meanwhile its counterpart E, written by an expert does not. For each pair, we translate one program (either S or E) to the other language. For these two programs (expressed in the same concurrency platform) we measure the running time on p processors, for $1 \leq p \leq 48$, and compare the resulting data so as to narrow down the performance bottleneck in the inefficient program. Figures 14 and 15 illustrate two test-cases: *Parallel mergesort, Matrix inversion.* More test-cases can be found in this technical report [8].

Table 1. BPAS timings with 1 and 16 workers: original CilkPlus code and translated OpenMP code

Test	Input size	CilkPlus		OpenMP	
		T_1	T_{16}	T_1	T_{16}
8-way	2048	0.423	0.231	0.421	0.213
Toom-Cook	4096	1.849	0.76	1.831	0.644
	8192	9.646	2.742	9.241	2.774
	16384	39.597	9.477	39.051	8.805
	32768	174.365	34.863	172.562	33.032
DnC	2048	0.874	0.259	0.867	0.299
Plain	4096	3.95	1.264	3.925	1.123
Polynomial	8192	18.196	3.335	18.154	4.428
Multiplication	16384	77.867	12.778	75.885	12.674
	32768	331.351	55.841	332.126	55.925

Table 2. Timings on AMD 48-core: underlined timings refer to original code and non-underlined timings to translated code

Test	Input size	CilkPlus		OpenMP	
		Serial	T_1	Serial	T_1
Protein alignment (for)	100	568.07	566.10	_568.79_	_568.16_
quicksort	$5 \cdot 10^8$	_94.42_	_96.23_	94.15	97.20
prefixsum	$1 \cdot 10^9$	_27.06_	_28.48_	27.14	28.42
Fibonacci	$1 \cdot 10^9$	_96.24_	_96.26_	97.56	97.69
DnC_MM	$1 \cdot 10^9$	_752.04_	_752.74_	751.79	750.34
Mandelbrot	500×500	0.64	0.64	_0.64_	_0.65_

– For *Parallel mergesort*, the original OpenMP code (written by a student) misses to parallelize the merge phase (and simply spawns the two recursive calls using OpenMP sections) while the original CilkPlus code (written by an expert) does parallelize the merge phase. On Figure 14, the running time curve of the translated OpenMP code is as theoretically expected while the curve of the original OpenMP code shows a limited scalability. This suggests that the original hand-written OpenMP code should expose more parallelism.

– For *Matrix inversion*, the two original parallel programs are based on different serial algorithms for inverting a dense matrix. The original OpenMP code uses Gauss-Jordan elimination while the original CilkPlus code uses a divide-and-conquer approach based on Schur's complement. Figure 15 shows that the code translated from CilkPlus to OpenMP is more appropriate for fork-join multithreaded languages targeting multicores. In other words the Schur's complement approach should be prefered in this context.

Interoperability. Our second experiment is dedicated to automatic translation of highly optimized libraries. The motivation, presented in the introduction, is to facilitate interoperability between libraries developed for different concurrency platforms, namely CILKPLUS and OPENMP. For this question, we want to determine whether or not the translated programs have similar serial and parallel running times as their hand-written-and-optimized counterparts. For this experiment, we have used the BPAS library which counts more than 150,000 lines of CILKPLUS code. Half of those lines are dedicated to polynomial multiplication and we translated those to OPENMP. In Table 1, we report on timings of two of the main algorithms for polynomial multiplication, namely 8-way Toom-Cook and divide-and-conquer plain multiplication. One can see that the original and translated codes have similar running times on 1 and 16 cores, for all input data sizes that we tested. Therefore, the OPENMP version of the BPAS library retains the good performance of the original version written in CILKPLUS.

Parallelism overheads. Our third experiment is devoted to the following question: do the METAFORK translators add extra parallelism overheads to the generated code w.r.t. the original code? We focus here on *work overhead*. By work overhead, we mean the time ratio between a multithreaded program run on one core and its serial elision. For this experiment, we have considered original programs using different parallelism patterns (divide-and-conquer, parallel for-loops) and written in both OPENMP and CILKPLUS. Our results are collected in Table 2. For all the examples that we tested, we could observe that, if the original program has little work overhead, then the same holds for the translated program.

7   Concluding Remarks

METAFORK allows for rapidly mapping algorithms written for one concurrency platform to another. As we have seen in Section 6, METAFORK can be applied for (1) comparing algorithms written with different concurrency platforms and (2) porting more programs to systems that may have a highly optimized run-time for one paradigm (say divide-and-conquer algorithms, or producer-consumer).

The METAFORK translation framework may also avoid the negative interferences of having multiple interfaces between the different components of a large solver written with various concurrency platforms. Along the same idea, the METAFORK translators can be used to transform legacy code into a more adequate concurrency platform.

Last but not least, we think that a great benefit of METAFORK is the abstraction that it provides. It can be useful for parallel language design (for example in designing parallel extensions to C/C++) as well as a good tool to teach parallel programming.

In the future work, as discussed in the METAFORK specifications document [7], we will consider parallel reduction as an important extension and include other parallel computing models like pipelining.

Acknowledgments. This work was supported in part by NSERC of Canada and in part by an IBM CAS Fellowship in 2013 and 2014. We are also grateful to Abdoul-Kader Keita (IBM Toronto Lab) for his advice and technical support.

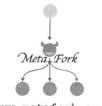

www.metafork.org

References

[1] Ayguadé, E., Copty, N., Duran, A., Hoeflinger, J., Lin, Y., Massaioli, F., Teruel, X., Unnikrishnan, P., Zhang, G.: The design of OpenMP Tasks. IEEE Trans. Parallel Distrib. Syst. 20(3), 404–418 (2009)

[2] Basumallik, A., Eigenmann, R.: Towards automatic translation of OpenMP to MPI. In: Proceedings of the 19th Annual International Conference on Supercomputing, ICS 2005, pp. 189–198. ACM, New York (2005)

[3] Blelloch, G.E., Reid-Miller, M.: Pipelining with futures. Theory Comput. Syst. 32(3), 213–239 (1999)

[4] Blumofe, R.D., Joerg, C.F., Kuszmaul, B.C., Leiserson, C.E., Randall, K.H., Zhou, Y.: Cilk: An efficient multithreaded runtime system. In: Proceedings of the Fifth ACM SIGPLAN Symposium on Principles and Practice of Parallel Programming, PPOPP 1995, pp. 207–216. ACM, New York (1995)

[5] Blumofe, R.D., Leiserson, C.E.: Space-efficient scheduling of multithreaded computations. SIAM J. Comput. 27(1), 202–229 (1998)

[6] Blumofe, R.D., Leiserson, C.E.: Scheduling multithreaded computations by work stealing. J. ACM 46(5), 720–748 (1999)

[7] Chen, X., Moreno Maza, M.: MetaFork: A metalanguage for concurrency platforms targeting multicores. Technical report, U. of Western Ontario (2013)

[8] Chen, X., Moreno Maza, M., Shekar, S.: Experimenting with the MetaFork framework targeting multicores. Technical report, U. of Western Ontario (2013)

[9] Dimakopoulos, V.V., Hadjidoukas, P.E.: HOMPI: A hybrid programming framework for expressing and deploying task-based parallelism. In: Jeannot, E., Namyst, R., Roman, J. (eds.) Euro-Par 2011, Part II. LNCS, vol. 6853, pp. 14–26. Springer, Heidelberg (2011)

[10] Duran, A., Teruel, X., Ferrer, R., Martorell, X., Ayguade, E.: Barcelona OpenMP Tasks Suite: A set of benchmarks targeting the exploitation of task parallelism in OpenMP. In: Proc. of the 2009 International Conference on Parallel Processing, ICPP 2009, pp. 124–131. IEEE Computer Society, Washington, DC (2009)

[11] Intel Corporation. Intel CilkPlus language specification, version 0.9 (2013)

[12] Lee, S., Eigenmann, R.: OpenMPC: Extended OpenMP programming and tuning for GPUs. In: Proceedings of the 2010 ACM/IEEE International Conference for High Performance Computing, Networking, Storage and Analysis, SC 2010, pp. 1–11. IEEE Computer Society (2010)

[13] Leiserson, C.E.: The Cilk++ concurrency platform. The Journal of Supercomputing 51(3), 244–257 (2010)

[14] Liao, C., Hernandez, O., Chapman, B., Chen, W., Zheng, W.: OpenUH: An optimizing, portable OpenMP compiler: Research articles. Concurr. Comput.: Pract. Exper. 19(18), 2317–2332 (2007)

[15] Liao, C., Yan, Y., de Supinski, B.R., Quinlan, D.J., Chapman, B.: Early experiences with the OpenMP accelerator model. In: Rendell, A.P., Chapman, B.M., Müller, M.S. (eds.) IWOMP 2013. LNCS, vol. 8122, pp. 84–98. Springer, Heidelberg (2013)

[16] OpenMP Architecture Review Board. OpenMP application program interface, version 4.0 (2013)

[17] Spoonhower, D., Blelloch, G.E., Gibbons, P.B., Harper, R.: Beyond nested parallelism: Tight bounds on work-stealing overheads for parallel futures. In: Meyer auf der Heide, F., Bender, M.A., (ed.) SPAA, pp. 91–100. ACM (2009)

TurboBŁYSK: Scheduling for Improved Data-Driven Task Performance with Fast Dependency Resolution

Artur Podobas, Mats Brorsson, and Vladimir Vlassov

KTH, Royal Institute of Technology
Stockholm, Sweden
{podobas,matsbror,vladv}@kth.se

Abstract. Data-driven task-parallelism is attracting growing interest and has now been added to OpenMP (4.0). This paradigm simplifies the writing of parallel applications, extracting parallelism, and facilitates the use of distributed memory architectures. While the programming model itself is becoming mature, a problem with current run-time scheduler implementations is that they require a very large task granularity in order to scale. This limitation goes at odds with the idea of task-parallel programing where programmers should be able to concentrate on exposing parallelism with little regard to the task granularity. To mitigate this limitation, we have designed and implemented TurboBŁYSK, a highly efficient run-time scheduler of tasks with explicit data-dependence annotations. We propose a novel mechanism based on pattern-saving that allows the scheduler to re-use previously resolved dependency patterns, based on programmer annotations, enabling programs to use even the smallest of tasks and scale well. We experimentally show that our techniques in TurboBŁYSK enable achieving nearly twice the peak performance compared with other run-time schedulers. Our techniques are not OpenMP specific and can be implemented in other task-parallel frameworks.

1 Introduction

The idea behind data-driven task-parallelism is to automatically derive inter-task dependencies based on the use of data-regions by tasks. Data-driven task-parallelism extends the fork-join model (for example Cilk [7]) by allowing out-of-order execution of tasks, conceptually similar to instruction-level parallelism in out-of-order processors. There is, however, one significant problem with current state-of-the-art data-driven solutions: the granularity of tasks must be large in order to amortize the cost of automatically solving inter-task dependencies. Workloads where parallelism is composed of fine-grained tasks thus becomes harder to manage, and can sometimes lead to sub-serial performance. Some run-time systems reduce the overhead cost by forcing the programmer to specify dependencies manually (see for instance OpenSTREAM [14] and OpenUH [9]) but at the same time reducing user-friendliness.

L. DeRose (Eds.): IWOMP 2014, LNCS 8766, pp. 45–57, 2014.

Some major benefits of task-based parallel programming is the promise of *composability*, i.e. a task-parallel program component can be arbitrarily composed with other task-parallel program components, and *decoupling the expression of concurrency from the mapping onto available cores* (threads). The latter is important as it enables the possibility to write programs that automatically can benefit from new hardware generations with more cores. Both of these encourage programmers to create tasks without considering the available resources or scheduling overhead, something current task schedulers cannot handle well.

We present novel techniques that improve the possibility to use fine-grained tasks. While we show results from an OpenMP run-time system, the techniques are general and can be used in any task-based framework supporting data-dependences among tasks. We had a hypothesis that many task-parallel programs exhibit *static* data dependency patterns that reoccur frequently and which could be exploited in the task scheduler. Our *novel* techniques allow the programmer to specify which tasks are known to have static iterative dependencies. The tasks still undergo the automatic dynamic dependency resolver for the first invocation and maintain all benefits of dynamic data-driven parallelism, but when the dependencies have been resolved once, they are optimized and re-applied at a smaller cost for subsequent invocations.

Our contributions are as follows.

- TurboBŁYSK: a compiler and highly efficient run-time task scheduler capable of handling OpenMP 4.0 tasks;
- an evaluation of TurboBŁYSK against state-of-the-art frameworks supporting data-driven task parallelism;
- a proposed extension of OpenMP 4.0 tasks to support dep_patterns that enable the run-time system to conserve task dependencies between iterations;
- a detailed overview of the design decisions in *TurboBŁYSK* that explains why *TurboBŁYSK* performs better than similar state-of-the-art implementations for fine-grained parallelism.

On the same hardware platform we nearly double the performance for fine-grained task-parallel programs compared to current state-of-the-art alternative implementations. We will now further motivate the need for this work before describing the implementation in more detail.

2   Motivation

It is computationally expensive to resolve data dependencies dynamically at run-time. In order to quantify this overhead we modified gcc's OpenMP 4.0 run-time system (libgomp in gcc 4.9 snapshot 20131103) to measure the time spent handling dependencies and compared it with the time consumed in other parts of the execution. We have created a benchmark that performs Gauss-Seidel computations over a 2048x2048 matrix and executed it with two block-sizes: 128x128 block size for coarse-grained tasks with 6k dependencies to solve, and 24x24 for fine-grained task execution with 180k dependencies to solve.

The performance results were striking; the time consumed managing dependencies in the coarse-grained case was only 1.2% of the total execution time while the time consumed for dependency resolution in the fine-grained case exceeded 40%. The execution time of the fine-grained execution was even slower than the serial version.

Practically this means that there is no benefit of using multiple cores for executing a Gauss-Seidel on a 256x256 matrix. Other applications behaved in a similar fashion. Our opinion is that programmers should not need to concern themselves with decomposition granularities of tasks. The task scheduler should work with as fine granularities as possible. Some applications really *require* tasks to be fine-grained in order to exploit parallelism. While we realize that it is unrealistic to completely ignore task granularity, we strive to do as best as possible to relieve the programmers from task granularities constraints.

In the next section we explain what we do to significantly improve on current state-of-the-art.

3   TurboBŁYSK: A Framework for Fast-Dependency Resolution

This section describes the *TurboBŁYSK* framework which implements OpenMP 4.0 and consists of a transcompiler (BłyskCC) and a run-time system (TurboBŁYSK). Our framework includes support for the **depend**-clause that allows for data-driven task execution of disjoint data-regions. *BłyskCC* is a source-to-source compiler which transforms the OpenMP code to run-time system API calls; a hand-written recursive-descend parser converts the source code into an Abstract-Syntax-Tree (AST) where the OpenMP pragmas are transformed and tasks outlined (similar to Mercurium [2]).

3.1   Automatic Dependency Resolution

Task dependencies are extracted by keeping track of each task that will work on a specific data-region(s). A data-region is defined by its virtual address coming from the application such as an address of a variable or parts of an array, and the size of that region. Each known data-region is inserted into a *dependency-structure* that keeps track of all tasks that use this particular data-region. There are private dependency-structures for each parent task, allowing hierarchical decomposition of dependent tasks. When a new task is submitted from the application to the run-time system, each data-region to be used is looked up given its virtual address, obtaining the dependency-structure for that data-region. If the obtained dependency-structure is empty, then the task claims that data-region.

If the new task and existing tasks using that data-region only read from it, then the dependency is marked as resolved (Read-After-Read). Only Flow- (Read-After-Write), Anti- (Write-After-Read) and Output- (Write-After-Write) dependencies are considered. Note that even if a Read-after-Read dependency is

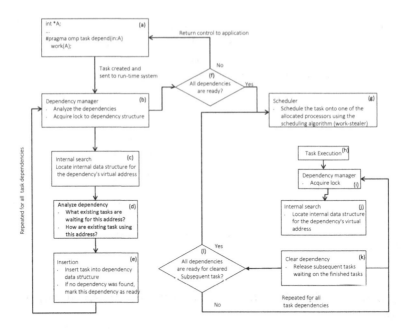

Fig. 1. Flow-chart representing the steps required to solve a task's dependencies including the steps performed when a task finishes executing

encountered, the task will still need to be entered into the dependency-structure for subsequent tasks.

Fig. 1 shows actions performed by our run-time system when a task is created and we will refer to this figure in the following text.

Task Creation. When the application creates a task (Fig. 1:a) a run-time system call is performed to submit the task. At this point, if the run-time system finds that the task does not use the **depend** clause it will immediately schedule the task for execution (Fig. 1:g); otherwise, it will proceed to analyze the dependencies (Fig. 1:b).

The run-time system needs to locate the *dependency-structure* that is associated with the task's data-regions. This search (Fig. 1:c) is the most computationally intensive part in resolving dependencies. Multiple threads can be using the dependency-structures, hence they need to be protected by a lock. In many run-time systems (for example GCC's libgomp) this lock is global, preventing concurrent access to the dependency-structure. In TurboBŁYSK, we allow partial concurrent access. We keep each dependency-structure sorted in a *bitwise trie* – a binary tree where searching for a dependency-structure is done by traversing all bits in the data-region's virtual address. To allow concurrent access, the root-node for our trie contains 64 independent entries; each of the 64 entries is protected by a lock. The lock is internally represented as a 64-bit variable where each bit represents a lock for one of the 64 entries. Mapping from a data-region to the required lock is done by examining the six least-significant bits of the data-region's *word address*; we found that when task-granularities are fine, tasks tend to work on data-regions whose virtual addresses are close to each other and will therefore use different locks (different value in the least-significant six bits). When a lock has been calculated for each data-region a task will use, the locks are acquired and the search in the trie begins. The search is an $O(log(n))$ operation that results in either a found data-region's dependency-structure or the creation of a new dependency-structure. The lock and the found dependency-structure are saved in the task-structure for later use.

Inside the Dependency-Structure. When the dependency structure (Fig. 1:d,e) has been found for a particular data-region, the run-time system will insert the task into the end of a list. The list contains all previous tasks waiting for/or currently using the data-region. The dependency structure contains a variable we call the dependency $q\_position$(queuing_position). The $q\_position$ is increased when we detect a Flow-, Anti- or Output- dependence. The type of dependency is determined by comparing the current task with the previously inserted tasks (for that data-region). We also maintain a state variable called $a\_position$ (active position) which corresponds to the position that is currently executing. When all tasks for a given $a\_position$ finish executing, the run-time system releases subsequently dependent tasks. If a new task enters a dependency region, and the $a\_position$ is the same as the $q\_position$ (active_position==queue_position) and both the tail-task and the new task will *Read* from the data region, then there are no dependencies on other previous tasks using the data-region.

When the Dependencies-Analysis Is Complete. When a task's data-regions have had their dependencies detected, the run-time system checks if any dependencies were found (Fig. 1:f). If none were found then the task is scheduled for execution (Fig. 1:g), otherwise the run-time system returns control to the application.

When Task Finishes Executing. When a processor finishes executing a task (Fig. 1:h), the previously saved lock will be re-acquired in order to lock-on to the dependency-structures associated with the finished task (Fig. 1:i,j). The run-time system goes through each of the recently completed task's dependency structures and reduce the number of tasks in the $a\_position$ (Fig. 1:k). If the tasks in the $a\_position$ reaches zero, the processor increments the $a\_position$ and remove the dependency of subsequent tasks in the list until it detects anything other than a Read-After-Read dependency. If, when clearing dependencies of tasks, a task has no other dependencies in other data-regions then it is scheduled for execution (Fig. 1:l).

3.2   Dependency Pattern

Data-driven parallelism allows the programmer to be oblivious towards dependencies between tasks as they are transparently derived by the run-time system.

We can relax this model by allowing the programmer to specify whether a task's sub-graph is static or not. Should a task's sub-graph be static, the run-time system can dynamically extract task dependencies from the first run of the task and re-use them in later invocations. Note that the programmer still does not need to know the dependencies between tasks – she only specifies whether the tasks will have static dependencies.

We propose a new OpenMP keyword called dep_pattern, which together with a unique tag enables the run-time system to extract task-graph dependencies for that tag and re-apply them on the next invocation of the tagged task. Consider the following code:

```
void matmul(float *A,float *B, float *C,int DIM) {
    for (int i=0;i<DIM;i+=4)
        for (int j=0;j<DIM;j+=4)
            for (int k=0;k<DIM;k+=4)
#pragma omp task depend(in:A[k+(j*DIM)],B[k+(j*DIM)]) \
            depend(inout: C[i+(j*DIM)]
                matmul_block( &A[k+(j*DIM],...);
}

...

#pragma omp task dep_pattern("matmul_16x16") depend(in:A,B) depend
    (inout:C)
    matmul(A,B,C,16);
```

The above example code is a standard blocked matrix multiplication. We create a top-level task to perform the matrix multiplication and specify the data-regions that will be used; in addition, we tell the compiler that this task will contain tasks whose dependencies are static regardless of which virtual addresses they use. When the run-time system encounters a dep_pattern clause it will first try to determine if the dependencies are known for the tag from previous invocations. If the run-time system fails to locate the tag ("matmul_16x16" in the example above), it will use the automatic dependency manager to derive the (static) dependencies and sample them. It is up to the programmer to chose the tag's name and use it consistently with the dep_pattern-clause – a tag for a wavefront pattern will not work on a e.g. matrix-multiplication and will yield data-races.

Sampling is performed by renaming dependency structures which we refer to as *reservation stations* to further the analogy with out-of-order execution of instructions. Recall that *TurboBLYSK* uses a *bitwise trie* to keep track of all dependency structures. The difference when sampling is that each of the dependency structures is given a unique integer ID and that the run-time system saves what dependency IDs each data-region in each sequentially spawned task used. This information is saved in a stream where each task is represented as: [int]#ID [int]#deps [int]dep1 [int]modifier1. The modifier specifies how the task will access the reservation station (Read,Write or both). When the task has finished, the raw stream will be processed (optimized). Information in the stream will be losslessly encoded and each integer can potentially be reduced to a nibble in size. Similarly, the modifiers for the reservation stations are encoded in the least significant bits of the static *reservation station* used with the dependency. To further increase the compression and improve performance, the run-time system will perform the following when compressing the stream.

- It will simulate all tasks' dependencies. If a reservation station (data-region) will only be *read* from, it will be completely removed. As an example, a matrix multiplication will always read from two matrices and produce results into a third. The dependencies on the two first matrices will thus be removed when analyzing the stream which results in a 66% reduction in amount of dependencies and reservation stations. It can be argued that those two dependencies can be removed from the source code; doing so would however remove information required to use distributed memory architectures or to improve scheduling [11].
- For each task, and its reservation station usage, a lock will be mapped. We look at the histogram of reservation stations that are used the most, and construct the locks such that the most intensively used reservation stations can be worked on concurrently. This results in a better lock mapping compared with the heuristic used in the automatic dependency phase.

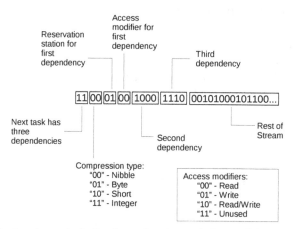

Fig. 2. Example showing a task, its dependencies and the modifiers encoded in the bit stream

An example encoding can be seen in Fig. 2. Here, since the reservation stations used by each dependency fits into a nibble (4-bit), the stream will start with b1100 indicating three dependencies to follow (b11=3) and that the dependencies will be represented in a nibble form specified by the b00 prefix- other prefixes indicate other compressions schemes. What follows are 12 bits (3 x 4-bit) that represent each dependency of the task; the least-significant two bits express the type of dependency (read/write/read-write) and the two most-significant bits represents the *reservation station* to be used.

Using the Stream. The stream is now encoded and ready to be used. On the next invocation of a task with a "matmul_16x16" tag, the encoded stream will be used to apply the dependencies. The run-time system, knowing that a tag-stream pair exists, will proceed to create a set of reservation stations rather than a trie. When tasks start spawning, the stream is parsed and the dependency-structure is quickly ($O(1)$ instead $O(logN)$) found in a reservation station – unlike the automatic dependency resolver, the locks and addresses need not be analyzed and the cost of searching for a dependency structure in the bitwise trie is completely removed.

Note that using the dep_pattern keyword does not remove the ability to know the different data-regions (address ranges) a task uses, nor does it remove the ability to offload tasks onto distributed devices (such as GPUs). It only indicates that the dependencies are static. Our approach also allows for other static analyzing techniques to be used on task-graphs, helping the scheduler's decision making. We allow mixing tasks marked with dep_pattern (i.e., tasks with static dependencies) with tasks whose dependencies are dynamic in a hierarchical manner. Finally, the streams could also be saved to persistent storage for use in future executions.

4   Evaluation Methodology

System Architecture. We used a shared memory NUMA multiprocessor with four AMD Opteron 6172 processors totalling 48 cores and 64 GB DRAM. All 48 cores were used in our evaluations. The Operating System used is Red Hat version 6.5 (kernel version 2.6.32).

Comparison. We compared our implementation against OmpSs [6] using Mercurium 1.3.5.8 (OmpSs's compiler) and Nanos++ (OmpSs's run-time system) version 0.7a. We also compared against gcc's OpenMP implementation libgomp, taken from the gcc 4.9 snapshot archive version 3.455. OmpSs is a well-known task-library that, arguably, is one of the pioneers of data-driven computing in the task-based paradigm, which is why we chose to compare against it.

Benchmarks. We used five different benchmarks in our performance evaluation. We executed each benchmark/input pair ten times, using the median to eliminate extreme corner cases. Resilience to fine-grained parallelism was evaluated by varying the amount of concurrency exposed, typically by altering the block-size each task works on. The benchmarks are:

- **Matrix Multiplication** Parallel blocked Matrix Multiplication where each task handles a blocked region. We used the ATLAS BLAS [4] library for the multiplication.
- **SparseLU** Parallel LU matrix factorization. Original code from BOTS [5] which we converted to OpenMP v4 and OmpSs.

- **Gauss-Seidel** Parallel, blocked and iterative Gauss-Seidel calculation derived from previous studies [14,13].
- **Cholesky** factorization based on the ATLAS BLAS library [4].
- **N-Body** a parallel version of this classical problem.

Schedulers. To ensure fairness, both TurboBŁYSK and OmpSs used the same work-stealing baseline scheduler. Each processor has its own queue into which tasks are spawned. Processors unable to find work in their own queue will attempt to steal work from other processors. Victim selection is pseudo-random. The libgomp scheduler uses a global task queue.

Speedup Calculations. We calculated the speedup when running our evaluated run-time systems by normalizing it against the *fastest* serial version we found: $Speedup = {}^{t_{ser}}/{}_{t_{par}}$ where t_{ser} is the time taken for the serial version, and t_{par} is the parallel makespan (time taken for the parallel region). Initialization phases (e.g. memory allocation or dep_pattern[1] stream encoding) were not included in the evaluation.

5   Results

5.1   Resilience to Fine-Grained Parallelism

We constructed a micro-benchmark where we simulate a wave-front pattern of dependencies. Each task has a read dependency on the north and west elements in a matrix. The benchmark iterates five times over the matrix. We first evaluated the task-overheads (Fig. 3:a). This was done by creating empty tasks and thus isolating the run-time system's management of the tasks and their dependencies. As we gradually increased the wave-front matrix (increasing the number of dependencies), we found that TurboBŁYSK has a $1.88\mu s$ task-overhead compared to gcc's $7.38\mu s$ and OmpSs's $19.26\mu s$. The dep_pattern clause had an even smaller average overhead of $1.21\mu s$, where $0.42\mu s$ task-overheads could also be observed. Also note that the overhead in TurboBŁYSK remains fairly constant independent ($1.88\pm0.21\mu s$) of how many dependencies the application has.

We also simulated an artificial work-load in each task to make it possible to vary task granularity while keeping the same number of tasks. The purpose is to see at what granularity each framework starts to scale efficiently. We fixed the micro-benchmark to have 245,760 dependencies to solve. We found (Fig. 3:b) that TurboBŁYSK started to scale already with 6μ long tasks. Both the automatic-dependency solver and the dep_pattern-clause outperformed all other implementations, reaching peak-performance much earlier than the other implementations. Gnu C's libgomp starts scaling when the task granularities reach $35\mu s$, but the performance is not very stable until granularities of $42\mu s$ or longer. OmpSs requires granularities that are larger than $300\mu s$ to scale well.

---

[1] Which is fair, since the stream is encoded once and can be used forever.

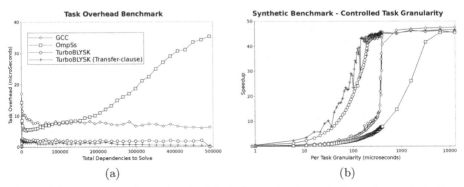

Fig. 3. (a): Average task-overhead with different implementations. Lower is better. (b): Speedup with different controlled granularities on tasks. Higher is better.

5.2 Experimental Results

Fig. 4 shows speedup profiles for all the evaluated benchmarks. Overall, our run-time system performs consistently better than both OmpSs and gcc's libgomp. TurboBŁYSK starts to scale at much lower granularities and to a higher number of cores in most cases; the reason for this increase in scalability is that there simply is not enough parallelism exposed at the granularities required by the other run-time systems.

For example, SparseLU (Fig. 4:c) using the `dep_pattern` clause allows scaling already with a block-size of 18x18 while gcc's libgomp and OmpSs require a block-size of 30x30 and 25x25 respectively – a similar behaviour is seen for all the benchmarks. The results for Cholesky (Fig. 4:d) show that the peak-performance of our run-time system is nearly twice as high as for the other run-time systems, and four times as high using the `dep_pattern`-clause.

Many of the evaluations showed a trend where the automatic dependency-manager (TurboBŁYSK) and the `dep_pattern`-clause (TurboBŁYSK (Dep_Pattern)) had equal performance, diverging only when the granularity of tasks was so small that even our fast automatic dependency-manager failed to handle them. Using the `dep_pattern` clause, performance could be maintained or even increased at these fine granularities (Fig. 4:a,b,c,e).

6 Related Work

Vandierendonck et. al [16] compared different methods of dependency-analysis. Our implementation of the dependency-management is very similar to their Hypergraph scheme, with minor implementation differences. The evaluation took place in SWAN and their prototype run-time system based on data-driven parallelism but which does not focus on automatic dependency management on virtual addresses (which we do). Our `dep_pattern` clause receive the same level of algorithm complexity as their algorithm, while still conveying information to the run-time system regarding virtual addresses.

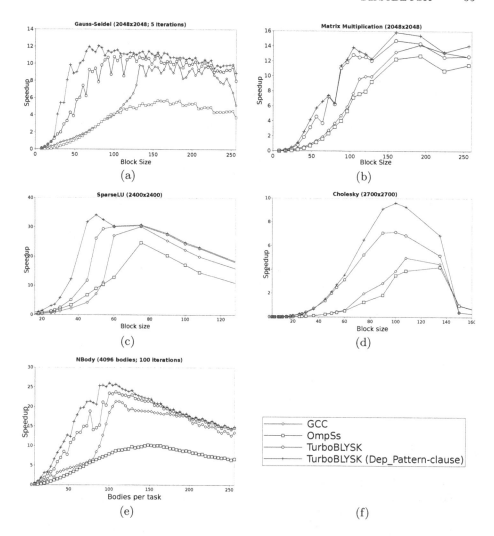

Fig. 4. Experimental evaluation of TurboBŁYSK, gcc's OpenMP 4.0 implementation and OmpSs. We increase the task granularity (reducing parallelism) moving from left to right on the x-axis. Speedup–how much faster parallel execution is over the serial– is seen on the y-axis.

The OSCAR compiler [12] supports a similar concept to our, but in the fork-join paradigm. *During compilation*, static tasks are identified and statically scheduled to optimize cache behavior. However, our work has two differences: we use dynamic dependencies to figure out static properties of a Direct-Acyclic-Graph and our method uses a different paradigm (data-driven) where compiler detected strategies are significantly harder (if possible).

OmpSs [6] is an OpenMP based run-time system and compiler framework targeting data-driven parallelism. OmpSs is a merge between a data-driven model, StarSs [10], and OpenMP. OmpSs supports both region based [13] and address-based (as in the present study) data-driven parallelism, and also has GPU-support.

OpenUH [9] supports task dependencies using IDs/TAGs [9] that are used to specify dependencies between tasks and removes the overhead of dynamically finding the dependencies, but expects more from the programmer. Conceptually our dep_pattern clause converts a dynamic data-driven task graph to a graph such as OpenUHs.

X-Kaapi [8] is a OpenMP-like parallel model supporting multiple paradigms, amongst others data driven parallelism. Similar to OmpSs and the OpenMPv4 specification, the user conveys information regarding the use of memory regions to the run-time system, which inserts dependencies between different tasks. X-Kaapi also supports the removal of WAR-dependencies by renaming regions. X-Kaapi is used in the libKOMP [3] run-time system, featuring OpenMP like execution.

OpenSTREAM [14] is a run-time system featuring *streams* in which data flows between different tasks. It uses the streams to detect producer-consumer patterns between tasks (dependencies). OpenSTREAM was evaluated against StarSs, showing what a large impact the dependency management had on the execution time of fine-grained parallel application.

StarPU [1] is a framework for both accelerators and homogeneous general-purpose systems. It supports the notion of data-regions which the run-time system exploits to provide efficient multi-GPU performance. It uses a variant of the HEFT [15] to schedule workloads on resources using a model based on the size of the input regions.

7   Conclusions

We presented TurboBŁYSK: an OpenMP4.0 tasking framework for data-driven parallelism, which we used to show that even the finest of granularities can scale well. We experimentally showed that our techniques in TurboBŁYSK enable achieving nearly twice the peak performance compared with other run-time schedulers. The techniques are not OpenMP specific and can be implemented in other task-parallel frameworks. We also introduced the dep_pattern-clause; a novel and intuitive method of re-using dependency patterns commonly found in task-based application. Using the dep_pattern-clause programmers can further leverage the performance. Our experimental evaluation verified all our methods, which we compared to existing state-of-the-art models.

Acknowledgements. This work was funded by the Artemis PaPP Project nr. 295440, and SRA Serc OpCoReS project. The authors are members of Scalable Computing Systems, SCALE. We thank the researchers Alejandro Rico and Alex Ramirez from Barcelona Supercomputer Center for sample OmpSs applications used in this study. Further thanks goes to Xavier Teruel for answering questions related to Nanos++/OmpSs regarding dependencies. Thank you!

References

1. Augonnet, C., Thibault, S., Namyst, R., Wacrenier, P.-A.: StarPU: A unified platform for task scheduling on heterogeneous multicore architectures. Concurrency and Computation: Practice and Experience 23(2), 187–198 (2011)
2. Balart, J., Duran, A., Gonzàlez, M., Martorell, X., Ayguadé, E., Labarta, J.: Nanos Mercurium: A research compiler for OpenMP. In: Proceedings of the European Workshop on OpenMP, vol. 8 (2004)
3. Broquedis, F., Gautier, T., Danjean, V.: LIBKOMP, an efficient openMP runtime system for both fork-join and data flow paradigms. In: Chapman, B.M., Massaioli, F., Müller, M.S., Rorro, M. (eds.) IWOMP 2012. LNCS, vol. 7312, pp. 102–115. Springer, Heidelberg (2012)
4. Clint Whaley, R., Petitet, A., Dongarra, J.J.: Automated empirical optimizations of software and the ATLAS project. Parallel Computing 27(1), 3–35 (2001)
5. Duran, A., Teruel, X., Ferrer, R., Martorell, X., Ayguade, E.: Barcelona openmp tasks suite: A set of benchmarks targeting the exploitation of task parallelism in openmp. In: International Conference on Parallel Processing, ICPP 2009, pp. 124–131. IEEE (2009)
6. Duran, A., Ayguadé, E., Badia, R.M., Labarta, J., Martinell, L., Martorell, X., Planas, J.: OmpSs: A proposal for programming heterogeneous multi-core architectures. Parallel Processing Letters 21(02), 173–193 (2011)
7. Frigo, M., Leiserson, C.E., Randall, K.H.: The implementation of the Cilk-5 multithreaded language. ACM Sigplan Notices 33(5), 212–223 (1998)
8. Gautier, T., Lementec, F., Faucher, V., Raffin, B.: X-Kaapi: A Multi Paradigm Runtime for Multicore Architectures. Rapport de recherche RR-8058, INRIA (February 2012)
9. Ghosh, P., Yan, Y., Chapman, B.: Support for dependency driven executions among OpenMP tasks. In: Data-Flow Execution Models for Extreme Scale Computing, DFM 2012, pp. 48–54 (2012)
10. Labarta, J.: StarSS: A programming model for the multicore era. In: PRACE Workshop New Languages & Future Technology Prototypes at the Leibniz Supercomputing Centre in Garching, Germany (2010)
11. Muddukrishna, A., Jonsson, P.A., Vlassov, V., Brorsson, M.: Locality-Aware Task Scheduling and Data Distribution on NUMA Systems. In: Rendell, A.P., Chapman, B.M., Müller, M.S. (eds.) IWOMP 2013. LNCS, vol. 8122, pp. 156–170. Springer, Heidelberg (2013)
12. Nakano, H., Ishizaka, K., Obata, M., Kimura, K., Kasahara, H.: Static coarse grain task scheduling with cache optimization using OpenMP. In: Zima, H.P., Joe, K., Sato, M., Seo, Y., Shimasaki, M. (eds.) ISHPC 2002. LNCS, vol. 2327, pp. 479–489. Springer, Heidelberg (2002)
13. Planas, J., Badia, R.M., Ayguadé, E., Labarta, J.: Hierarchical task-based programming with StarSs. International Journal of High Performance Computing Applications 23(3), 284–299 (2009)
14. Pop, A., Cohen, A.: OpenStream: Expressiveness and data-flow compilation of OpenMP streaming programs. ACM Transactions on Architecture and Code Optimization (TACO) 9(4), 53 (2013)
15. Topcuoglu, H., Hariri, S., Wu, M.-Y.: Performance-effective and low-complexity task scheduling for heterogeneous computing. IEEE Transactions on Parallel and Distributed Systems 13(3), 260–274 (2002)
16. Vandierendonck, H., Tzenakis, G., Nikolopoulos, D.S.: Analysis of dependence tracking algorithms for task dataflow execution. ACM Transactions on Architecture and Code Optimization (TACO) 10(4), 61 (2013)

Classification of Common Errors in OpenMP Applications

Jan Felix Münchhalfen[1,3,4], Tobias Hilbrich[2], Joachim Protze[1,3,4],
Christian Terboven[1,3,4], and Matthias S. Müller[1,3,4]

[1] IT Center, RWTH Aachen University, D - 52074 Aachen
[2] ZIH, Technische Universität Dresden, D - 01062 Dresden
[3] Chair for High Performance Computing, RWTH Aachen University, D - 52074 Aachen
[4] JARA – High-Performance Computing, Schinkelstraße 2, D – 52062 Aachen
{muenchhalfen,protze,terboven,mueller}@itc.rwth-aachen.de,
tobias.hilbrich@tu-dresden.de

Abstract. With the increased core count in current HPC systems, node level parallelization has become more important even on distributed memory systems. The evolution of HPC therefore requires programming models to be capable of not only reacting to errors, but also resolving them. We derive a classification of common OpenMP usage errors and evaluate them in terms of automatic detection by correctness-checking tools, the OpenMP runtime and debuggers. After a short overview of the new features that were introduced in the OpenMP 4.0 standard, we discuss in more detail individual error cases that emerged due to the `task` construct of OpenMP 3.0 and the `target` construct of OpenMP 4.0. We further propose a default behavior to resolve the situation if the runtime is capable of handling the usage error. Besides the specific cases of error we discuss in this work, others can be distinctly integrated into our classification.

1 Introduction

With the advent of multi- and manycore architectures, node-level parallelization has become increasingly important in the field of high performance computing (HPC). In fact, OpenMP has emerged as the most widely used standard for shared memory parallel programming in HPC. Although the nature of OpenMP programming greatly enhances the development of parallel applications, parallel programming with OpenMP is still error prone to generic mistakes in parallel programming and those specific to OpenMP. In addition, resilience capabilities will become of greater importance with the availability of exascale supercomputers. Parallel programs must be able to detect and respond to certain events that may lead to program termination or incorrect results, e.g., runtime failures. In this context, the development of an error model is a high priority in the OpenMP language committee.

In this work, we propose a classification for OpenMP usage errors (*defects*) to summarize known types of syntactic and semantic mistakes. We further distinguish these from performance issues. Particularly, this includes defect classes that involve the OpenMP 3.0 task and OpenMP 4.0 target constructs. This classification may serve tool developers and the OpenMP community as a framework and overview of the common defects introduced when parallelizing with OpenMP.

L. DeRose (Eds.): IWOMP 2014, LNCS 8766, pp. 58–72, 2014.

Additionally, our examples provide input for test suites that evaluate the correct operation of OpenMP compilers and runtimes. We also investigate the failures that these defects may induce on an application, the possibilities towards automatic detection, and the correctness-checking tools that are capable of detecting them. This classification extends and incorporates existing studies [8,10] and our long term experience in application developer support.

Our investigation first discusses related work (Section 2) and an overview of the latest standard specification released by the OpenMP language committee — OpenMP 4.0 [4] (Section 3).

In Section 4 we discuss our classification of defects, with respect to syntax, semantics and performance. Sections 4.1, 4.2 and 4.3 discuss the individual defect classes in detail and the possibilities for tool developers to detect them automatically. Finally we draw our conclusions in sec. 6.

2   Related Work

Suess et al. discussed common mistakes in OpenMP [10]. They conducted a study over two years and observed which mistakes their students made when parallelizing with OpenMP. A classification and coarse relationship between correctness and performance achievement is made in the paper, and best practices into avoiding common mistakes are presented. Additionally, different compilers and tools are evaluated for their ability to detect certain defects. At the time of this study, OpenMP 2.5 was the most recent standard specification. Thus, it does not include the defect classes that we introduce for the task and target constructs of later OpenMP versions.

Our classification subsumes the defect classes of this study and extends them by syntactic as well as semantic defects the students did not encounter, besides covering newer OpenMP constructs.

P. Petersen and S. Shah also published a classification of threading errors [8] (Section 4, Figure 1). In contrast to our classification, they further distinguish the class of semantic defects, especially the logical defects, into *stalls* and *live-locks*. As we do not see an increased potential of detection out of this differentiation, we summarize these defects in a class of *Conceptual defects*. Apart from that, we subsumed this classification and extend it by classes for syntactic defects and performance issues.

A. Duran et al. proposed an error handling clause [7]. Their proposal draws a callback based mechanism that defines a set of different failure severities and predefines actions to handle specific failures. In case of a failure, the predefined action, or a specified callback is executed and may decide how to handle the failure. This callback can receive additional information about the region- or source code location where the failure occurred. The proposal was evaluated using a modified NANOS [2] OpenMP runtime library. Two benchmark suites, the EPCC micro-benchmarks [6] and the NAS parallel benchmarks [3] (v3.0) are further evaluated to determine which overhead the error handling functionality adds to the OpenMP runtime.

Another work from Wong et al. [11] evaluates three different possibilities to make the OpenMP standard capable of handling erroneous situations. The proposal motivates extended error handling capabilities by demonstrating how C++ exception based error handling can be used to catch unexpected failures within the OpenMP runtime. Wong et al. then discuss requirements that proposed error handling addition to the standard should conform to. They introduce three different approaches for error handling in OpenMP: a done construct, which was included (see *cancellation points*) in the latest OpenMP standard: an error-code dependent approach that would be compatible with languages that are exception unaware; and a callback based approach which slightly extends the one proposed by Duran et al. [7]. For the failure class "*SIMD aligned with unaligned data*" we present in the following, the error handling approaches with error-codes and the done construct would be insufficient, the latter at least in exception unaware languages.

Motivated by these works [7][11] there are efforts in the OpenMP language committee to establish error handling capabilities in the OpenMP standard. To support the work of the OpenMP language committee we provide a classification of defects and evaluate possibilities for their automatic detection as shown in several examples. When appropriate, we also include a recommendation on how the failure should be handled by the OpenMP runtime.

3   Overview of OpenMP 4.0

The OpenMP standard is a directive based approach to express parallelism. It uses a strict fork-join model in which multiple threads process *tasks*, which can be either implicit or explicit. The terms implicit and explicit are used to distinguish between a task originating from programmer effort by using the task directive, and a task created implicitly when a parallel region is encountered.

Every OpenMP program can be compiled either as a parallel program by interpreting the OpenMP directives and clauses, or as purely sequential by ignoring all OpenMP directives.

The standard does not impose requirements on the behavior of an OpenMP application if it is compiled as a sequential program. The execution results of such a binary can deviate from the parallel results. In other respects there are several requirements to applications that are parallelized with OpenMP, e.g., OpenMP strictly holds on to the Single Entry, Single Exit principle, which means no branch or jump statements from the base language may be used to enter or leave OpenMP regions. Programs which do not adhere to the OpenMP standard's requirements are called *nonconforming*. An OpenMP program starts with one thread that executes the main program on the *host* and subsequently is able to spawn other threads using the corresponding OpenMP directives. Several worksharing constructs then distribute workload among multiple threads, e.g., the *do*, and *for*-loop, and sections constructs assign workloads. Whenever a thread is not idle, it can process a task.

In version 4.0, the OpenMP standard distinguishes between *host* and *target* devices. The two terms correspond to host computer and accelerators respectively. Code that is enclosed in a target region, is compiled to be executed on accelerators. This extension enables OpenMP to reach out to heterogeneous architectures that previously required different programming models like CUDA, OpenCL, or OpenACC. The new simd construct controls execution in the vector units. Other additions to the standard include user defined reductions, task dependency and thread affinity control.

Currently the Intel compiler, the Cray compiler, and the GNU Compiler Collection (GCC) support OpenMP 4.0, although GCC has no functionality implemented yet for the `target` directive and always executes this code on the host.

4 Error Classification

We collected common defects in OpenMP applications from our own experiences, long lasting support activities from various HPC users and our projects, and summarized them in a classification. Figure 1 presents this classification in which we distinguish between syntactic and semantic defects, as well as performance issues. The latter covers performance flaws that do not actually lead to wrong results or nonconforming applications, but affect the efficiency of the application. We will discuss the defects and failure handling, as well as tools that are able to detect them below.

We carefully assembled this classification based on our experiences and available studies [8,10], in order to incorporate all types of defects that we are aware of, as well as novel defects that extensions of OpenMP 3.0 and OpenMP 4.0 introduced. This classification provides a framework for common OpenMP programming defects and forms a basis for future extension.

The naming *error* is ambiguous; therefore we use the notion from [12]:

- *defect* to address programming errors, i.e., incorrect source code, and
- *failure* to address error manifestation, e.g., execution abortion or deadlocks.

To remove a failure from a program a trace-back is needed to the defect in the source code. But there is no distinct correlation between classes of failures and defects, and an error could be assigned to both a failure and a defect class. Compilers and static analysis tools typically detect defects. Runtime analysis tools typically spot failures, but may also spot defects. The same holds for debuggers. When we expect an error to be spotted as a defect we assign it to a defect class. We assign an error to a failure class if we think that this error is only detectable as a failure.

4.1 Syntactic Defects

A syntactic defect in general is code that is not compliant by the grammar of a programming language. With respect to OpenMP parallelization we limit syntactic defects to OpenMP compiler directives. We distinguish between mistyped and correct OpenMP prefixes (e.g. `#pragma omp` in C++); mistyped prefixes are not recognized as OpenMP compiler directives, the compiler will ignore them by default. We do not classify syntactic errors caught by compilers, and refrain from examining them further here. For misspellings, the compiler could recommend similar keywords from the OpenMP grammar.

4.2 Semantic Defects

We recognize programming mistakes that are semantic defects. These are compiled into executable code, but otherwise cause failures within the OpenMP runtime, which may

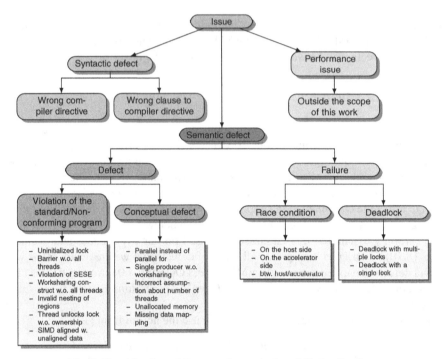

Fig. 1. Classification of Common Issues in OpenMP Applications

manifest themselves as execution aborts, deadlocks, or incorrect results. Most importantly, the exact behavior of a semantic defect depends on the runtime at hand. Thus these defects may introduce portability problems that only become visible with specific runtimes. Semantic defects form the biggest class of possible mistakes — not only when parallelizing with OpenMP — but with programming in general. In the following, we will discuss the four sub-classes of semantic defects in Figure 1. Some of these sub-classes involve additional child classes.

Violations of the Standard/Nonconforming Program: In this class we integrate defects that are a clear violation to one or more of the definitions of the OpenMP standard. The standard strictly prohibits developers from using certain combinations of OpenMP compiler directives or the usage of runtime functions in specific contexts. We do not claim completeness at this point. The amount of possible standard violations simply exceeds the scope of this work, thus we focus on a smaller, respresentative portion of defects.

Uninitialized locks: OpenMP offers different mechanisms to synchronize threads. The most commonly used are *barriers* and *critical sections*. It is more difficult to induce a defect using the latter two high level approaches than doing so with *locks*. Locks are a low level mechanism for synchronization and enable the programmer to coordinate threads with finer and increased control, but also with increased potential to create defects. OpenMP features two types of locks: regular and nested locks. The difference between the two types is that nested locks may be locked repeatedly by the same thread without blocking, while regular locks would block if the thread that currently owns them tries to acquire the lock again. In both cases a lock needs to be released the same number of times it was locked. Additionally, locks, need to be initialized before they are used. The standard does not specify how programs will behave if programmers make use of an uninitialized lock. Detection of this is either possible in the OpenMP runtime, or by keeping track of initialized locks, e.g., in a correctness tool. The OpenMP runtime could issue a mild severity level, i.e., a warning and handle the failure appropriately by e.g. just initializing the lock to resolve the situation without terminating the application. We do not propose to terminate the application in this case, despite this being a violation to the standard, because the defect is a minor violation and can be resolved quite easily. In our experiments the defect could be found by using Valgrind (memcheck), the Intel Inspector XE or a debugger.

Barriers not reached by all threads of a team: As mentioned previously, barriers are less error prone than locks. Nevertheless they still offer potential for defects as barriers must always be encountered by all threads of a team. Some OpenMP regions have implicit barriers at their end unless a `nowait` clause is present. Thus, this defect may or may not be a special case of *Violation of the Single Entry, Single Exit principle (SESE).* It is possible to induce this situation by using barriers inside conditional statements which depend on a condition that is special to a thread, or by implementing irregular execution patterns using statements such as `goto`. An example of this situation for a barrier inside a conditional statement, is given in code Example 1.

If the code is of low complexity and only includes a few conditional statements that determine if a thread reaches a barrier or not, the defects of this class may be detectable by static code analysis. In more complex codes, e.g., where the barrier is hidden in a third party library, the detection proves far more difficult. A runtime analyzer may identify this situation if the waiting states of all threads are clearly known, e.g. if all threads wait at different barriers. More exhaustive approaches could utilize model checking techniques to detect defects of this class. If this situation can be detected, a runtime may decide to terminate the application, since the program exhibits a serious nonconformance to the standard.

Violation of the Single Entry, Single Exit principle (SESE): The OpenMP execution model requires each thread encountering an OpenMP region to also exit the region in a regular fashion (without skipping the end of the region). A team of threads that is spawned at the start of a `parallel` region must correctly exit the parallel region. Parallel execution in OpenMP strictly follows a fork-join-model and consequently the generated team threads must join at the end of a parallel region. Any deviation from this principle violates the OpenMP standard and will cause undefined behavior ranging from program termination to deadlock, as well as partially executed worksharing directives. Detection is possible through static code analysis or by keeping track of individual threads and their paths of execution during runtime. The default behavior of the runtime should be immediate termination of the application or cancellation of all `parallel` regions because the program behavior is undefined from this point on.

Worksharing constructs not reached by all threads of a team: Special constructs like worksharing constructs must be encountered by all threads of a team or none at all. As described in *Violation of the Single Entry, Single Exit principle (SESE)*, these situations are created by using the `goto` keyword or by placing worksharing constructs inside conditional code paths. An example is given in code Example 1. The most promising approach to detect this kind of defect is static code analysis. If the runtime is able to detect this automatically, it should terminate the innermost `parallel` region with an appropriate error level because the successful parallel execution of this region is then rendered impossible. This would enable developers to implement different strategies and, if necessary, rely on (possibly serial) fallback algorithms to deliver correct results.

```
1    #pragma omp parallel
2        if( omp_get_thread_num() % 2 ){
3            #pragma omp for
4            for( int i=0; i < N; ++i )
5                ...
6            #pragma omp barrier
7        }else{
8            #pragma omp barrier
9        }
```

Example 1. Worksharing construct/barrier is not reached by all threads of a team

```
1    double a[N], b[N], c[N];
2    ...
3    #pragma omp parallel
4        for(int i=0; i < N; i++)
5            a[i] = b[i] * c[i];
```

Example 2. Parallel for should be used

Invalid nesting of regions: The current OpenMP standard [4] covers the nesting of regions and places a set of restrictions on which regions may not be directly nested. For example it is strictly forbidden to directly nest worksharing constructs, because each worksharing construct requires the context of a single `parallel` region. Any violation to this restriction fits into this defect class. The compiler is in many cases able to identify this kind of defect. An exception to this is when OpenMP regions are *orphaned* and hidden inside third-party libraries or subroutines in other source files. This effectively prevents some compilers from identifying a relationship between the OpenMP region and its parent region. In this case, identifying the violation to the standard is far more difficult and requires more sophisticated approaches such as modifications to the OpenMP runtime to keep track of which regions are reached by individual threads. Termination of the innermost parallel region may in some cases suffice to handle the failure, but that depends on the combination of regions which violate the standard and it may as well be required to terminate the application if e.g. `critical` regions of the same name are nested (see *Deadlocks*). While this would render further execution impossible, termination of the innermost parallel region on the other hand may enable developers to implement recovery mechanisms, e.g., a fallback approach. Compilers with interprocedural analysis capabilities will most probably be able to even detect invalid nesting of *orphaned* constructs properly.

Unlocking locks that are not owned by the current task: The OpenMP standard states that calls to `omp_unset_lock` and `omp_unset_nest_lock` with a lock as argument that is neither locked nor owned by the current *task* is nonconforming. It is easy to avoid this kind of situation when using OpenMP locks: Using higher level approaches, e.g., C++ classes that lock in the constructor and unlock in the destructor, or always placing the lock and unlock in pairs, and near to each other in the source code. When tasks are tied to threads in OpenMP (default behaviour), the constraint that the lock needs to be owned by the current task is equivalent to the constraint of lower-level mechanisms like pthreads, that the current threads need to own the lock. So far, none of the major compilers mentioned in Section. 3 have implemented this clause, but this possibly might create problems when locks are used inside untied tasks. Unlocking attempts by threads/tasks which don't own the lock can easily be detected by keeping track of the locking and unlocking operations in the runtime. As the program state is undefined after this operation, the runtime should either terminate the program if this failure occurs or exit all parallel regions with a descriptive error code.

SIMD aligned with unaligned data: OpenMP 4.0 includes a `SIMD` directive that enables programmers to manually instruct the compiler to translate a loop into vectorized code. An `aligned` clause can be used to specify the alignment of loop data in bytes. This may be beneficial because some instruction sets, e.g., the x64 instruction set, include SIMD instructions for aligned and unaligned data, of which the former generally needs less loads to complete. The developer can align data either by using special `malloc`-variants like `posix_memalign` or by manually allocating $(N + alignment)$ bytes and then adjusting the pointer appropriately.

The task of detecting the incorrect use of the `aligned` clause can be very difficult at compile time as it is not known then how the data will be aligned when the program is run. A debugger will certainly detect this (after execution) as the CPU will raise an interrupt when this defect occurs. Because the runtime will most probably not be able to detect this kind of defect before an interrupt occurs, we do not propose a default behavior here.

Conceptual Defect: A *conceptual defect* occurs when code does not explicitly violate the OpenMP standard and may as such be called a conforming OpenMP program, but nevertheless results in unwanted or unintended program behavior. Cases of this class represent correct applications in terms of the restrictions of the OpenMP standard, but fail to meet intended specifications, due to another software defect or due to an incorrect specification. As an example, an application meant to calculate π could be correctly parallelized, but simply have a defect in its formulas or logic. It may be either caused by a program condition that only occurs under specific circumstances that were not considered by the developer or simply by lack of knowledge on the developer. We explicitly exclude race conditions (see *Race Conditions*) and deadlocks (see *Deadlocks*) from this class.

Parallel instead of parallel for: The mistake of using a `parallel` directive when a `parallel for` directive was intended is quite common and can lead to different failures, depending on the pre-parallized code. This defect may not have any impact on compilation at all and thus go unnoticed. This is the case, e.g., when all threads execute the same code in parallel, without any worksharing or data races. The result will be correct, but there will be no benefit in runtime because each thread does the same work as the serial program. See Example 2 for this case. Because there are situations where it actually may make sense to use `parallel` over `parallel for`, this defect is hard to detect. If data races occur during execution of this defect, the defect is detectable by applying detection methods for race conditions (see *Race Conditions*). If no race conditions occur during execution of this defect we do not think a tool would be able to detect it.

Single producer without worksharing: An often used concept in parallel programming is the *single producer*. In the single producer pattern one thread creates one or multiple tasks inside a `single` construct. Subsequently those tasks are processed by the threads of the underlying parallel region. Because the absence of the single construct does not violate the standard or renders the code syntactically incorrect, it is easily overlooked. Another well known design pattern is the *parallel producer*. As the name suggest, here tasks are created in parallel and possibly without a `single` construct. Hence it is not easy to determine the correctness of applications which utilize these parallel programming patterns. They might however trigger other defects which are covered in this work, e.g. *Race Conditions*. We do not consider this sort of mistake to be detectable by correctness checking tools because the intention of the application remains ambiguous without deeper insight.

Locks as barriers: An OpenMP lock that was locked by one thread will block all other threads that call `omp_set_lock` until the thread which owns the lock executes a call to `omp_unset_lock`. Therefore, a programmer with a lack of understanding of OpenMP constructs might try to use locks as a concept for barriers, unaware of the `barrier` directive and assuming that a single call to `omp_unset_lock` enables the continuation of all threads. We do not expect that the intention to create a barrier is detectable by a tool when this situation is encountered. Potentially, a deadlock or a possible deadlock can be detected and does not differ from the situation in the subsequent deadlock defect class.

Incorrect assumptions about the number of threads: The `OMP_DYNAMIC` environment variable may raise unexpected situations in OpenMP programs if set to true and the developer relies on the number of threads being set by other methods, such as a previous argument to `omp_set_num_threads` or the value of the environment variable `OMP_NUM_THREADS`. While this situation does not interfere with dynamic loop scheduling, it is probably best to allow the runtime to choose the number of threads arbitrarily to optimize the utilization of system resources. Therefore the programmer may not rely on the number of threads being equal to what was requested. Even if a certain number of threads was requested and the value of `OMP_DYNAMIC` equals to false, a different number of threads may be provided by the runtime, e.g., if less threads are available than what was requested. This kind of defect is logical nature and thus very difficult to spot automatically because an analyzing application needs to know what is to be accomplished in the first place. The runtime therefore cannot detect it.

Unallocated memory (host/accelerator): If an OpenMP application fails to allocate memory and thus uses a NULL-pointer in a subsequent OpenMP clause, the behavior of the runtime library is undefined. This sort of defect could be handled by a mechanism like the one proposed in [7,11]. The runtime should take care of the error handling in this case. To resolve the failure, the region should either be completely skipped with an adequate error code given back to the application developer — or transfer execution to a callback function that could be specified by the developer. While NULL-pointers are quite easy to detect, a pointer to a memory region that is not allocated or only partially allocated may prove more difficult to spot. To achieve this, the runtime would need to track the application heap, or all calls to malloc. This erroneous situation is also detectable using a debugger: An application raises a SEGFAULT-interrupt when it accesses unallocated memory in any way. The proposed way to handle this failure is either program termination or termination of the innermost parallel region with a suitable error code.

Missing data mapping to accelerator: In OpenMP 4.0 the target and target data directives were introduced to that enable the programmer to offload computations to accelerator devices. The directives support a map clause that is responsible for the mapping (or migration) of data from the host to the accelerator and vice versa. The developer has to name each variable that was declared outside the scope of the target region in a corresponding map clause. Depending on the type of accelerator, host and device may either share their memory, portions of their memory or have separate memories. Therefore it is important to specify the type of mapping in the map clause which may either be alloc, to, from or tofrom. Global variables inside a target region must be declared with the declare target directive. If the accelerator and host do not share a common memory, on the device side the data will be allocated, received from the host and copied back, corresponding to their mapping. If a data mapping for the target region is missing, the compiler will raise an error and most likely interrupt the compilation process.

Race Conditions: A race condition is defined as a situation during program runtime in which two or more executing units, usually threads, access a shared resource simultaneously in such a way that at least one unit is modifying the resource. This may lead to failures, if the resource does not provide sufficient internal synchronization to allow for multiple executing units/threads accessing it at the same time, e.g. a memory location. This usually requires the programmer to employ suitable synchronization. To this class we assign all defects which can lead to race conditions. Detecting this class of defects usually induces a significant overhead on application runs. We therefore do not consider this class recommendable to be handled by the OpenMP runtime automatically.

Race conditions on the host side: Race conditions are a problem not only specific to OpenMP but to parallel programming in general. OpenMP parallelized applications which do not make use of the `target` directive to offload data for computation to an accelerator, may execute with false assumptions about the default data sharing behavior of OpenMP or forgotten data sharing clauses when entering a parallel region. There are several works in progress on the detection of data races on the host side, e.g. the thread sanitizer that is part of the latest version of GCC [9] and commercial tools like the Intel Inspector XE [1] and Oracle Solaris Studio Thread Analyzer [5]. Most of them are able to properly detect those types of data races.

Race conditions on the accelerator side: If an application with target directives is compiled to offload code to an accelerator, OpenMP directives and runtime functions may be utilized on the device as well as on the host with few limitations [4]. The developer may spawn a team of threads on the accelerator using the `parallel` directive — same as on the host side — and forget to specify adequate data sharing clauses for the variables used inside the parallel region. In principal the problem is very similar to the one described in *Race conditions on the host side*, but its detection can be much more complicated because not all accelerator systems offer the same repertoire of debugging/tracing capabilities as most host processors. Additionally, detecting race conditions usually requires a lot of device memory because each memory access needs to be traced for later analysis. On accelerator devices this may prove challenging, as memory is generally very limited. An approach for GPGPU accelerators [13] provides insight into such data race detection capabilities, but has not yet been applied to OpenMP applications.

Race conditions between host/accelerator: With the introduction of the `target` directive it is possible to offload computations to an accelerator device. As explained in *Missing data mapping to accelerator* it is further possible that the host and the accelerator truly share memory. In this case, race conditions will occur if both the host and the accelerator device operate on the same data without synchronization. As a consequence, data is copied from and to the accelerator as `target` or `target data` regions are encountered. While the OpenMP runtime should take care that no data is overwritten when data is copied to the accelerator, it is very well possible that the host changed the data that was transferred to the accelerator in the meantime. A copy-back operation from the accelerator may overwrite this data and lead to a data race if the user has not synchronized the access. If host and accelerator share a common memory, the detection of this requires tracing both host and device memory accesses because both can modify the same memory transparently. If host and accelerator have seperate memories, it is sufficient to trace only host memory accesses because one thread will always block until the target region is completed and only then, copy back data (see *Race conditions on the host side*).

Deadlocks: A deadlock is a situation in which a program is in a waiting state for an indefinite amount of time. In this class we categorize defects which can lead to deadlocks. If the OpenMP runtime is able to identify a deadlock situation, it should handle the failure by either terminating the application or, more preferably, by terminating all parallel regions with an error code. Unfortunately, not all deadlock situations will be detectable by the runtime. OpenMP 4.0 introduced the feature of task dependencies which we evaluated with regard to their potential of introducing deadlocks. Task dependencies by design prevent programmers from creating circular dependencies and therefore it is effectively impossible to run into a deadlock by only using task dependencies.

Deadlock with multiple locks: The explicit use of the locking API is in general error-prone and susceptible to deadlocks. Especially when more than one lock is involved, deadlocks can occur if locking operations overlap. In a real world application this may be difficult to detect at compile time if calls to omp_set_lock and omp_unset_lock are concealed in subroutines (*orphaned*). If all threads are blocked due to a call to omp_set_lock, the deadlock situation is clear and can be identified by the OpenMP runtime or correctness-checking tools.

Deadlock with a single lock: This type of defect describes a situation where a deadlock occurs due to the order in which locks are accessed. The deadlock situation might not always occur but only under specific circumstances, e.g., specific scheduling of threads/tasks. In Example 3 it very much depends on the scheduling of tasks if the application will deadlock or not. If two or more tasks operate on locks concurrently and there is a task scheduling point after a call to omp_set_lock without a preceding omp_unset_lock, a deadlock might occur. This situation is also called a *potential* deadlock. A tool could spot this situation via a model checking approach or at runtime by keeping track of locks and their owners and taskwait constructs. We are not aware of any tools which are currently able to spot such failures.

```
1   omp_lock_t lock; omp_init_lock( &lock );
2   #pragma omp parallel
3       #pragma omp master
4           #pragma omp task
5           {
6               #pragma omp task
7               {
8                   omp_set_lock( &lock );
9                   omp_unset_lock( &lock );
10              }
11              omp_set_lock( &lock );
12              #pragma omp taskwait
13              omp_unset_lock( &lock );
14          }
15  omp_destroy_lock( &lock );
```

Example 3. Possible deadlock due to a race on a lock.

4.3   Performance Issues

Because the performance issues named in Figure 1 are not specific to OpenMP programming, we will not include a more detailed specification of them in this work. We do not discourage the usage of critical sections and locks, but recommend that developers consider the amount of work that is done inside synchronization constructs. Depending on this, the other threads will be blocked during that time, or the overhead of synchronization might have a significant impact on the overall runtime. Furthermore, pointless flushing, as well as memory access patterns which will lead to cache trashing or false sharing, will probably lead to bad application performance and are thus best to avoid.

5 Summary

We evaluated each error class in terms of detectability in the above table (2). In this evaluation we distinguished between different methods to detect defects, such as compilers, compiler based static analysis (involving interprocedural analysis), the OpenMP runtime, debuggers and tools which conduct correctness checks at runtime. A cross (•) marks that the tool class is able to detect the defect, a cross in round brackets ((•)) means that the tool class is able to detect the error under special circumstances.

#	Mistake	Compiler	Static Analysis	Runtime	Debuggers	Tools
	Syntactic mistakes					
1.	wrong_directive		•			
2.	wrong_clause	•	•			
	Semantic mistakes					
	Violation of the standard					
3.	uninitialized_locks			•	•	•
4.	barrier_wo_all_threads		•	•		•
5.	violation_sese	(•)	•			
6.	worksharing_wo_all_threads					
7.	invalid_nesting	(•)	•	•		(•)
8.	lock_unlock_nonowner		•	•		•
9.	simd_aligned		(•)		•	
	Conceptual defect					
10.	parallel_inst_parallel_for					
11.	single_prod_wo_worksharing					
12.	number_of_threads					
13.	unallocated_memory	(•)	•	•	•	•
14.	missing_data_mapping	(•)	•			(•)
	Race condition					
15.	host			(•)		•
16.	accelerator			(•)		•
17.	host_accelerator					(•)
	Deadlock					
18.	multiple_locks		(•)			•
19.	single_lock		(•)			•

Fig. 2. Defects and their detectability

6 Conclusion

We developed a classification of OpenMP defects for the OpenMP 4.0 standard. In this classification we distinguished errors by both the defect and the failure. We further summarized many defects we consider common to OpenMP programming and evaluated them in terms of their potential for automatic detection by analysis tools. If we considered the runtime able of handling a failure, we propose a default error handling mechanism that is to be executed when application developers do not specify error handlers of their own. We found that the number of common defects in OpenMP did not decrease with newer versions of the standard, but slowly increased due to new features that were added to the standard. An example of this is the `target` construct which was introduced with OpenMP 4.0.

Future work will explore possible collaborations with developers of specific scientific domains to collect their mistakes and to quantify the frequency of the error classes we listed in this work.

Acknowledgement. Parts of this work were funded by the German Federal Ministry of Research and Education (BMBF) under Grant Number 01IH13008A (ELP).

References

1. Intel Inspector XE (2013),
   https://software.intel.com/en-us/intel-inspector-xe
2. NANOS Project,
   http://www.cepba.upc.edu/nanos/
3. NAS Parallel Benchmarks,
   https://www.nas.nasa.gov/publications/npb.html
4. OpenMP 4.0 specification (July 2013),
   http://openmp.org/wp/openmp-specifications/
5. Oracle Solaris Studio,
   http://www.oracle.com/technetwork/server-storage/
   solarisstudio/documentation/index.html
6. Bull, J.M.: Measuring Synchronisation and Scheduling Overheads in OpenMP. In: Proceedings of First European Workshop on OpenMP, pp. 99–105 (1999)
7. Duran, A., Ferrer, R., Costa, J.J., Gonzàlez, M., Martorell, X., Ayguadé, E., Labarta, J.: A Proposal for Error Handling in OpenMP. In: Mueller, M.S., Chapman, B.M., de Supinski, B.R., Malony, A.D., Voss, M. (eds.) IWOMP 2005/2006. LNCS, vol. 4315, pp. 422–434. Springer, Heidelberg (2008)
8. Petersen, P., Shah, S.: OpenMP Support in the Intel® Thread Checker. In: Voss, M.J. (ed.) WOMPAT 2003. LNCS, vol. 2716, pp. 1–12. Springer, Heidelberg (2003)
9. Serebryany, K., Iskhodzhanov, T.: ThreadSanitizer: Data Race Detection in Practice. In: Proceedings of the Workshop on Binary Instrumentation and Applications, WBIA 2009, pp. 62–71. ACM, New York (2009)
10. Süß, M., Leopold, C.: Common Mistakes in OpenMP and How to Avoid Them: A Collection of Best Practices. In: Mueller, M.S., Chapman, B.M., de Supinski, B.R., Malony, A.D., Voss, M. (eds.) IWOMP 2005/2006. LNCS, vol. 4315, pp. 312–323. Springer, Heidelberg (2008)

11. Wong, M., Klemm, M., Duran, A., Mattson, T., Haab, G., de Supinski, B.R., Churbanov, A.: Towards an Error Model for OpenMP. In: Sato, M., Hanawa, T., Müller, M.S., Chapman, B.M., de Supinski, B.R. (eds.) IWOMP 2010. LNCS, vol. 6132, pp. 70–82. Springer, Heidelberg (2010)
12. Zeller, A.: Why Programs Fail: A Guide to Systematic Debugging. Morgan Kaufmann Publishers Inc., San Francisco (2005)
13. Zheng, M., Ravi, V.T., Qin, F., Agrawal, G.: GMRace: Detecting Data Races in GPU Programs via a Low-Overhead Scheme. IEEE Trans. Parallel Distrib. Syst. 25(1), 104–115 (2014)

Static Validation of Barriers and Worksharing Constructs in OpenMP Applications

Emmanuelle Saillard[1], Patrick Carribault[1], and Denis Barthou[2]

[1] CEA, DAM, DIF
F-91297 Arpajon, France
[2] Bordeaux Institute of Technology, LaBRI / INRIA
Bordeaux, France

Abstract. The OpenMP specification requires that all threads in a team execute the same sequence of worksharing and `barrier` regions. An improper use of such directive may lead to deadlocks. In this paper we propose a static analysis to ensure this property is verified. The well-defined semantic of OpenMP programs makes compiler analysis more effective. We propose a new compile-time method to identify in OpenMP codes the potential improper uses of barriers and worksharing constructs, and the execution paths that are responsible for these issues. We implemented our method in a GCC compiler plugin and show the small impact of our analysis on performance for NAS-OMP benchmarks and a test case for a production industrial code.

1 Introduction

OpenMP is a popular parallel programming model for shared memory machines. While OpenMP aims at making parallel programming easier, there are a number of improper uses of worksharing constructs and barriers that are not statically detected by compilers and may lead to deadlock or unspecified behavior. Indeed, the OpenMP specification requires that all threads of a team must execute the same sequence of worksharing constructs and barriers [16]. However in practice no error occurs when all threads of a team do not execute exactly the same barrier. That is why we authorize threads synchronizations with different barriers and defined two verbosity levels (0 and 1) defining soft and hard barriers verifications. Throughout the rest of the paper, examples are presented with verbosity level 0.

To show the difficulty to enforce this constraint in OpenMP codes, consider the motivating examples in Figure 1. In function `f` of Listing 1.1, each thread may or may not encounter the `single` construct line 9, depending on the control flow (line 6). According to the OpenMP specification, all threads in a team should encounter the same `single`, or none of them. However, compiling this code and executing it does not lead to a syntactic error but to a deadlock. Indeed, if the result of the conditional is not the same among all threads, the first barrier executed will be for some threads the implicit barrier line 12 (end of `single`) while for others, it will be the explicit barrier line 14. Then the first group of

L. DeRose (Eds.): IWOMP 2014, LNCS 8766, pp. 73–86, 2014.
© Springer International Publishing Switzerland 2014

Listing 1.1.

```
1   void f( ){
2     if (...)
3     {
4       #pragma omp parallel
5       {
6         if (...)
7         {
8           /*...*/
9           #pragma omp single
10          {
11            /*...*/
12          }
13        }
14        #pragma omp barrier
15        /*...*/
16      }
17    }
18  }
```

Listing 1.2.

```
1   void f() {
2     /*...*/
3     #pragma omp barrier
4     return;
5   }
6
7   int main(  ) {
8     int r;
9     #pragma omp parallel private(r)
10    {
11      r =...;
12      if( r == 0 )
13        f();
14    }
15    exit(0);
16  }
```

Fig. 1. Examples with Deadlock Situations

threads will stop at the explicit barrier line 14 while the second group will stop at the barrier related to the end of the **parallel** region. Finally, the first set of threads will be released and eventually deadlock at this last barrier. Note that if we modify this example by adding an **else** statement with another **single**, the code is still potentially erroneous since all threads should encounter the same **single**. A more complex case appears Listing 1.2. A deadlock can occur at the end of the parallel region of function **main** because of the conditional line 12. Depending on the control flow the barrier in **f** may be not encountered by all threads. The error is more difficult to detect and an interprocedural analysis is required. This illustrates the fact that the machine state does not help to identify the cause of deadlocks (in these two examples, conditionals).

This paper proposes a new compile-time technique to detect potential improper uses of worksharing constructs and barriers in applications parallelized with OpenMP. The main advantage of our method is to highlight the statements responsible for the execution path potentially leading to future deadlocks or unspecified behaviors. This contribution is an adaptation and transposition of the work presented in [12] for checking MPI applications with respect to barriers. The OpenMP application is checked function per function, using intra-procedural analysis. Each function of a program is said to be correct if all threads of the same team (entering the function or created in the function) have the same sequence of worksharing regions and depending of the verbosity level, the same sequence of barriers (verbosity 1) or the same number of barriers (verbosity 0). An inter-procedural analysis complements the analysis for checking the whole application. This paper makes the following contributions:

- Analysis of barriers and worksharing constructs that may lead to deadlocks, identification of the control-flow that may be responsible for these situations;
- Consideration of the OpenMP specification and the practice through two verbosity levels;

– Full implementation inside a production compiler; experimental results on different benchmarks and applications.

The outline of the paper is the following. Section 2 provides a summary of existing debugging tools for OpenMP programs. Section 3 defines the problem statement, describes the program representation we use and presents our compile-time analysis. Section 4 details experimental results before concluding in Section 5.

2   Related Work

OpenMP applications are prone to concurrency errors such as data races and deadlocks. Debugging tools generally check the correctness of OpenMP programs either at compile-time or during execution of a program, both methods having advantages and inconveniences. This section summarizes some existing tools to detect data races and deadlocks in OpenMP applications.

The well-defined semantics of OpenMP makes static analyses common to check the correctness of OpenMP applications. Several static approaches exist: First we can mention the OpenMP Analysis Toolkit [9] (OAT) that uses symbolic analysis to detect concurrency errors. It relies on the ROSE compiler infrastructure to encode every parallel region into Satisfiability Modulo Theories (SMT) formulae. Those formulae are then solved with a SMT-solver like Yices [17]. OAT terminates its analysis by instrumenting the source code with fault injection technique to confirm the reported errors. OmpVerify [1] is a static tool integrated in Eclipse IDE using the polyhedral model to detect data races in OpenMP parallel loops. This tool is restricted to program fragments called Affine Control Loops but it has the advantage of reporting accurate errors to the user. Lin [8] describes a concurrency analysis technique to detect whether two statements will not be executed concurrently by different threads in a team. The method is an intra-procedural analysis based on phase partitioning using an OpenMP Control Flow Graph (OMPCFG) that models the transfer of control flow in an OpenMP program. Similarly, Zhang et al. [18] use a concurrency analysis to detect unaligned barriers in OpenMP C programs. This inter-procedural method consists in four phases: A CFG construction to model the various OpenMP constructs, a barrier matching to find threads barriers that synchronize together, a program division into phases (sequence of basic blocks separated by barriers) and an aggregation of phases with matching barriers. Any two basic blocks from the same aggregated phase are said to be concurrent. Although quite close to our analysis this work differs from us in several points. Unlike Zhang et al., our analysis is language independent and verifies woksharing-construct placements in a program. To detect possible deadlocks we use the graph representation defined in [8]. Potential errors are automatically returned to the user with the line of the erroneous conditionals by a simple analysis of the OMPCFG. Thus the user knows exactly what can cause a deadlock and correct it. For the verification of the whole program Zhang et al. export a barrier tree when we only need an integer defining the minimal number of possible barriers encountered in a function.

Then a simple callgraph traversal points out the possible sources of deadlocks in the whole program. However both methods could complement each other. Detection can also be done by compilers like GCC when lowering the OpenMP constructs to GOMP function calls [14]. Indeed, GCC issues a warning for wrong nested parallelism, typically a barrier in a single region. Like all static tools, our method has the advantage of not requiring execution of the program but can produce false positives.

Among dynamic tools we can mention the Adaptative Dynamic Analysis Tool [6] (ADAT) and RaceStand [5,10] for focused data races detection and Intel Thread Checker [11,4] and Sun Thread Analyzer [13] for both data races and deadlocks detection. ADAT is a data races detection tool using classification and adaptation mechanisms. The tool creates a pseudo-instrumented source code and an Engine Code Property Selector (ECPS) table and then transforms the pseudo-instrumented source code into an executable by using the ECPS table information. With a C compiler supporting OpenMP, the instrumented source code is compiled and executed to detect data races. RaceStand by GNU utilizes an on-the-fly dynamic monitoring approach to detect data races and has recently improved its check with a dynamic binary instrumentation technique based on Pin software framework. This tool detects the existence of races and locates races between two accesses not causally preceded by other accesses also involved in races (first races) for each shared variable in a program. Intel Thread Checker and Sun Thread Analyzer both require an application instrumentation and trace references to memory and synchronization operations during the application execution. Sun Thread Analyzer necessicates program recompilation with the Sun compilers. To find data races the program must be executed with two or more threads. Unlike Sun Thread Analyzer, Intel Thread Checker does not depend on the number of threads used. It dynamically detects data races using a projection technology which exploits relaxed OpenMP programs. More precisely, the projection technology checks the data dependency of accesses to shared variables using sequentially traced information. But Intel Thread Checker does not consider OpenMP programs specifications and can therefore report false positives. Li *et al.* present in [7] an online-offline model to test the correctness of every OpenMP parallel region. The online correctness testing model is used to find parallel regions with incorrect execution results (not corresponding to serial execution results), identify all places that caused errors (directives used improperly or located wrongly) and correct them. Then the offline correctness testing model tests the correctness of regions with corrected directives. Compared to dynamic tools that detect a deadlock when it occurs, our static analysis prevents programs from deadlocking (the program is stopped whenever a deadlock situation is detected). Moreover our method is not limited to the input dataset of a run. Indeed, even if dynamic tools return no false positive, they can miss errors as they are correlated to one execution of a program.

We proposed in [12] a combining method to detect misuse of MPI collective operations in MPI programs. MPI processes must have the same sequence of collective operations otherwise a deadlock may occur. Restriction on MPI collective operations is the same as restrictions on barriers and worksharing regions in OpenMP programs. Thus we adapted this work to detect potential deadlocks in OpenMP programs. Potential deadlocks due to wrong synchronizations as well as worksharing regions are automatically detected in each function of a program and then errors considering the whole program are reported by an inter-procedural analysis. To our knowledge our analysis is the first intra- and inter-procedural analysis that verifies that all OpenMP tasks encounter the same worksharing regions.

3   Checking OpenMP Directives and Control Flow

In OpenMP programs, the threads of a team can synchronize through the `#pragma omp barrier` directive or at an implicit barrier at the end of worksharing regions (unless a `nowait` clause is specified). Worksharing constructs distribute the execution of the associated region among the threads of a team [16]. Worksharing constructs are loop, sections, single and workshare constructs. The OpenMP specification gives some restrictions to barriers and worksharing constructs. Indeed, each barrier/worksharing region must be encountered by all threads in a team or by none at all, unless cancellation has been requested for the innermost enclosing parallel region ([16] Sections 2.7, p.53 and 2.12.3, p.124). However, due to the control flow inside an OpenMP program, the threads may execute different execution paths with different numbers of barriers and worksharing regions. Such behavior can lead to a deadlock or unspecified behaviors.

The principle of the static analysis we propose is the following. For each function of the code, we check that for all threads entering the function and for all teams created within it, the same number of barriers are executed, whatever the execution path taken by the threads. If the number of barriers may depend on the control flow, the control structures responsible for this are shown with a warning. This is a conservative approach, since we do not check that the conditional of an `if` statement for instance is dependent on the ID of the threads. Moreover, we check that worksharing constructs may not be conditionally executed, potentially leading to unspecified behaviors. This intra-procedural analysis on barriers and worksharing constructs is complemented by a simple inter-procedural analysis: User-defined functions are subsumed by the number of worksharing constructs and barriers executed by the entering threads. This captures all potential improper uses of barriers and worksharing constructs.

The program to analyze is represented using the OMPCFG intermediate representation, briefly described in the following section. Then the intra- and inter-analyses are presented.

3.1   Intermediate Representation: OMPCFG

The *control-flow graph* (CFG) is an intermediate representation of code, used by almost all compilers. The CFG is a directed graph where nodes are basic blocks (straight sequence of code) and edges are potential flow of control between nodes.

Lin [8] extended the notion of CFG to a representation for parallel OpenMP programs, called OMPCFG. Each node of the OMPCFG represents a basic block (basic nodes) or an individual block containing an OpenMP directive (directive nodes). In the OMPCFG, implicit barriers are made explicit and each combined parallel worksharing construct is separated into a `nowait` worksharing construct nested in a parallel region. Moreover the OMPCFG has a single *Entry* and single *Exit* nodes. New edges are inserted between basic nodes and directive nodes according to OpenMP semantics. As a result, the `master` directive is represented as a conditional. Table 1 lists the OpenMP directives and their corresponding directive node in the OMPCFG. Note that Lin also adds edges from the end construct directive to the begin construct directive nodes denoted as construct edges. These edges are not considered here as they do not reflect any control flow.

Table 1. Directive nodes in the OMPCFG

Directive name	Control flow	Worksharing construct
parallel, critical, atomic, section, barrier, ordered, task, taskwait, taskyield	linear	
master	if/else	
for, single	if/else	*
sections, workshare	switch/case	*

Figure 2 shows examples of OMPCFG. All directive nodes containing a `barrier` are represented as thick nodes and all directive nodes containing a worksharing construct are colored in gray. Directive nodes containing a `parallel` construct are considered as barriers but are not considered in our Algorithms. Out of clarity, implicit barriers at the end of worksharing and parallel regions are not designated by barriers but by *region-name* `end`.

This representation is the base of our compiler analysis. GCC uses a graph representation similar to the OMPCFG from version 4.2.

3.2 Intra-procedural Analysis

This section details the static verification of barriers and worksharing constructs for each function of a program. We define two levels of verbosity for barriers verification: level 0 that returns warnings only if there may be an execution error and level 1 that returns warnings in strict accordance with the specification.

For the verbosity level 0, we identify barrier statements that synchronize together. To that purpose, we introduce a number, the *sequential order*, counting the number of barriers traversed before reaching a barrier. This number is assigned to each node in the OMPCFG. Two nodes with different sequential order are sequentially ordered thanks to barriers. This number is 0 for nodes before the first barrier (including the node with the first barrier), 1 for nodes reached

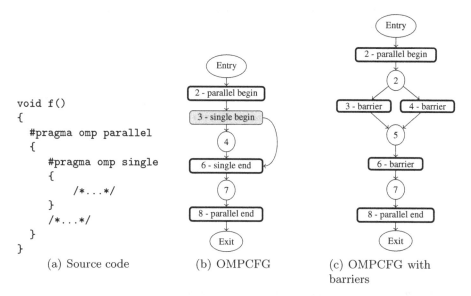

```
void f()
{
    #pragma omp parallel
    {
        #pragma omp single
        {
            /*...*/
        }
        /*...*/
    }
}
```

(a) Source code   (b) OMPCFG   (c) OMPCFG with
                                              barriers

Fig. 2. Example of a simple code (a) with its corresponding OMPCFG (b) and an OMPCFG containing barriers (c)

after one barrier and so on. When multiple paths exist, nodes can have multiple numbers, at most the number of barriers in the function. Loop backedges are removed to have a finite numbering. A function is not correct if there are nodes with multiple orders. These nodes correspond to possible control-flow divergence leading to deadlocks. In Zhang *et al.* [18], this notion of sequential order corresponds to phases, computed through an inter-procedural liveness analysis and a barrier aggregation step. While both methods can be used for our goal, our approach is simpler, more adapted to the verification of barriers. The computation of the execution order uses an algorithm adapted from the algorithm 1 in our previous work [12] on MPI verification. This algorithm detects possible control-flow divergence leading to a deadlock in a MPI barrier. MPI barriers are numbered by so-called *execution ranks* (similar to sequential order here). MPI barriers of same execution rank r are put into a set $C_{r,c}$ as matching MPI barriers. c is used to differenciate MPI collective operations names. In our case, only barriers are considered so the c is useless and only C_r sets are created. Algorithm 1 is an adaptation of this method for OpenMP barriers, from line 6 to line 12. Barriers with multiple sequential orders are put in the set C_r with r corresponding to their maximal sequential order. For example the OMPCFG Figure 2(c) contains three explicit barriers nodes 3, 4 and 6 and one implicit barrier node 8. The sequential order for nodes 3 and 4 is 0, for node 6 , 1 and for node 8, 2. The algorithm computes $C_0 = \{3,4\}$, $C_1 = \{6\}$ and $C_2 = \{8\}$.

For the verbosity level 1, we verify each barrier is encountered by all threads of a team. This is described from line 14 to line 16 in Algorithm 1.

Algorithm 1. OpenMP Intra-procedural Control-flow Analysis

1: **function** FUNCTION_VERIFICATION(f, v)   ▷ f: a function of the application
2:                              ▷ v: level of verbosity
3:      Compute $G = (V, E)$ the OMPCFG of f
4:      $S \leftarrow \emptyset$, $S' \leftarrow \emptyset$ ▷ Output sets: Conditional nodes
5:      **if** $v = 0$ **then**   ▷ level 0 of verbosity
6:          Remove loop backedges in G and Compute sequential order of all nodes
7:          **for** $n = 0..\max($ sequential order $(G))$ **do**
8:              **for** barriers of sequential order n **do**
9:                  $C_n \leftarrow \{u \in V | u$ of order $n\}$
10:                 $S \leftarrow S \cup PDF^+(C_n)$
11:              **end for**
12:          **end for**
13:      **else**   ▷ level 1 of verbosity
14:          **for** $u \in V$ s.t. u contains an explicit barrier **do**
15:              $S \leftarrow S \cup PDF^+(u)$
16:          **end for**
17:      **end if**
18:
19:      **for** $u \in V$ s.t. u contains a worksharing construct **do**
20:          $S' \leftarrow S' \cup PDF^+(u)$
21:      **end for**
22:      Output nodes in S' and S as warnings
23: **end function**

The algorithm takes the OMPCFG of the current function and the verbosity level as input parameters and outputs a message error for conditional nodes that may lead to a deadlock in a barrier (set S). The core of the algorithm is based on the postdominance frontier [2], used in a previous paper in the context of MPI collectives verification [12]: The postdominance frontier of a node u of the OMPCFG (denoted as $PDF(u)$) is the set of all nodes v such that u postdominates a successor of v but does not strictly postdominate v. If $\gg$ denotes the postdominance relation, $PDF(u) = \{v \mid \exists\ w \in SUCC(v), u \trianglerighteq w$ and $u \not\gg v\}$. In other words all paths from w to the exit node go through u. On the contrary v is not postdominated by u so there exists a path from v to the exit node that does not go through u. This concept is extended to a set of nodes N: $PDF(N) = \bigcup_{u \in N} PDF(u)$ and to the notion of iterated postdominance frontier PDF^+ defined as the transitive closure of PDF, when considered as a relation [2]. If barriers with the same sequential order n have a non-empty PDF^+ set, then some threads may not perform the nth synchronization. Due to the representation of all worksharing constructs (as if/else or switch), barriers inside these worksharing constructs are detected as incorrect.

The lines 19 to 21 of the algorithm detect if worksharing constructs may not be executed by all threads of a team. For each node u containing a worksharing construct, we compute the iterated postdominance frontier of u. If the $PDF^+(u)$

is not empty then some threads may execute the construct while others may avoid it. The set of nodes detected are put in the set S' for warnings.

Lemma 1. *Algorithm 1 is correct if it detects all deadlock situations due to* barrier *and worksharing regions.*

Proof. The levels of verbosity enable a strict verification of barriers in compliance with the specification. In that purpose Algorithm 1 detects if all threads of a team have strictly the same sequence of barriers. A soft verification is also possible. The algorithm then verifies all threads of a team encounter the same number of barriers. The proof has been done in [12]. Then Algorithm 1 computes the set S' of control-flow nodes that have execution paths with different number or type of worksharing constructs from the node to the *Exit* node. We prove that nodes in S' correspond exactly to the nodes that lead to a deadlock.

As an example, the first OMPCFG Figure 3 contains one explicit barrier (node 8), two implicit barriers (nodes 7 and 10) and one worksharing construct: `single` (node 5). Algorithm 1 computes sequential orders. Node 7 is of sequential order 0, node 8 is of sequential orders 0 and 1 and finally node 10 is of sequential orders

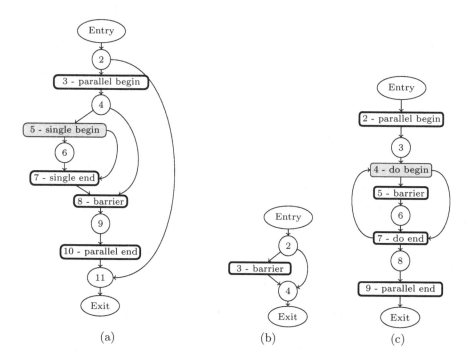

(a)   (b)   (c)

Fig. 3. Function f OMPCFG of the motivating examples ((a) and (b)) and an example of an OMPCFG with a loop ((c))

1 and 2. Thus we have $C_0 = \{7\}$, $C_1 = \{8\}$ (node 8 is in C_1 as it has multiple sequential orders) and $C_2 = \{10\}$. $PDF^+(C_1) = \emptyset$ and $PDF^+(C_2) = \emptyset$ but $PDF^+(C_0) = \{4\}$. Node 4 is the only node in the iterated postdominance frontier of node 7 as the conditional node 2 is outside the parallel region. Then the conditional node 4 is returned as the possible cause of a deadlock in a `barrier`. For node 5, $PDF^+(5) = 4$. To sum up for Listing 1.1, a warning is issued for the conditional located in node 4 as potentially leading to different barriers and worksharing constructs sequence among threads. The OMPCFG Figure3(b) contains one explicit barrier node 5 and one implicit barrier node 7. The algorithm computes $C_0 = \{5\}$, $C_1 = \{7\}$ and $PDF^+(C_0) = \{4\}$. Last, the OMPCFG Figure 3(c) contains one worksharing construct node 4, one explicit barrier node 5, two implicit barriers nodes 7 and 9 and a loop (composed of nodes 4, 5, 6, 7). First Algorithm 1 removes the loop backedge from node 7 to node 4. Then sequential orders are computed: $C_0 = \{5\}$, $C_1 = \{7\}$ and $C_2 = \{9\}$. A warning is issued for the conditional node 4 as $PDF^+(C_0) = \{4\}$. For the loop construct node 4, the iterated postdominance frontier is empty.

3.3   Inter-procedural Analysis

This section describes the analysis for the whole application code. We assume the application is not using recursion, meaning the callgraph of the application has no cycle.

The method iterates through the callgraph, in reverse topological order. It starts with functions that do not call other functions in the code, then callers of these functions, and so forth. After the previous analysis of Algorithm 1, each function retains the minimal number of barriers executed by the team of threads entering the function (excluding the barriers executed by teams created inside the function), as well as the number of worksharing constructs executed by this same team. These numbers are denoted $n_{barrier}$ for the number of barriers, n_d for worksharing constructs (among `for`, `worksharing`, `sections`, `single`). They are obtained through a simple traversal of the OMPCFG of the function. When a function g is called from a function f, g is replaced by as many barriers and worksharing constructs as these values. For worksharing constructs, only the number of constructs matters for the analysis. Indeed, we verify each callee function with worksharing constructs are not depending on the control flow in caller functions. Then the analysis `Function_verification` is called on f. These steps are described in Algorithm 2.

Figure 4 shows callgraphs of Listing 1.2 and BT from the NAS parallel benchmarks OpenMP. Nodes colored in gray are first nodes considered by Algorithm 2. In the example of the Listing 1.2 callgraph, Algorithm 2 computes $n_{worksharing}(f) = 0$ and $n_{barrier}(f) = 0$ which are the minimal numbers of barriers and worksharing constructs in function `f`. Function f is then replaced by these numbers in `main`.

Algorithm 2. OpenMP Inter-Procedural Analysis

1: **function** CODE_VERIFICATION(CG, v)   ▷ CG: call graph   ▷ v: level of verbosity
2:      Sort CG in reverse topological order
3:      **for** $f \in CG$ **do**
4:          **for** g a callee in f **do**
5:              Compute $n_d(g)$ for $d =$**barrier** and worksharing constructs   ▷ n_d:
      minimal number of directives d executed by entering threads
6:              Replace g in f by $n_d(g)$ empty worksharing constructs and $n_{\text{barrier}}(g)$
      barriers.
7:          **end for**
8:          Compute Function_verification(f, v)
9:      **end for**
10: **end function**

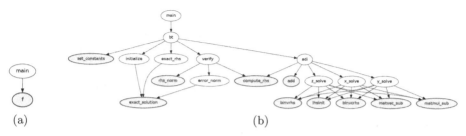

(a)   (b)

Fig. 4. Callgraph of Listing 1.2 (a) and BT from NASPB-OMP (b)

4   Experimental Results

Our analysis is implemented in a GCC 4.7.0 plugin, avoiding the whole compiler recompilation. An adaptation of the plugin is required to work with newer version of GCC. The plugin is located in the middle of the compilation chain as a new pass inserted inside the compiler pass manager after generating CFG informations and before OpenMP directives transformation. The location has the advantage of being language independent allowing a verification of applications written in C, C++ and Fortran. The pass applies Algorithm 1. The implementation of Algorithm 2 is currently under development. This section presents experimental results on the NAS parallel Benchmarks OpenMP (NASPB-OMP) [15] v3.2 using class B and HERA [3], a large multi-physics 2D/3D AMR hydrocode platform. Even if the test case used by HERA is parallelized with MPI+OpenMP, only the correctness of OpenMP barriers and worksharing constructs have been checked. The number of lines and the language of each benchmark is presented Table 2. All experiments were conducted on Tera 100, a supercomputer with a peak performance of 1.2 PetaFlops. Tera 100 hosts 4,370 compute nodes for a total of 140,000 cores. Each compute node gathers four eight-core Nehalem EX processors at 2.27 GHz and 64 GB of RAM. All performance results were computed and averaged with BullxMPI 1.1.16.5.

Our analysis issues warnings for barriers and worksharing constructs potentially not encountered by all threads of a team. The name of the OpenMP directive with potential improper use and the line of the conditional leading to this
situation are returned to the programmer. The following example shows what a
user can read on `stderr` when compiling Listing 1.1 with our plugin.

```
in function 'f':
example.c: warning: STATIC-CHECK: #pragma omp single line 9 is
possibly not called by all threads because of the condition line 6
```

Table 2 shows the number of barriers and worksharing constructs found in
each benchmark and the number of nodes in the sets S and S' generated by
Algorithm 1 with the two verbosity levels. For all these nodes, the control flow
does not depend on thread ID and therefore functions are correct. A data-flow
analysis could be done to complement our analysis to reduce the number of false
positives. Indeed, a check on the conditionals in $S \cup S'$ could help the plugin to
detect control flow not depending on threads ID and avoid false positives. This is
left for future work. The table also presents first results for the inter-procedural
analysis by giving the number of functions executed in parallel with a non null

Table 2. Static Results for each benchmark (F=FORTRAN)

Benchmark	NASPB-OMP											HERA
	BT	CG	DC	EP	FT	IS	LU	LU-HP	MG	SP	UA	
Language	F	F	C	F	F	C	F	F	F	F	F	C++
# lines	3,835	1,204	3,295	294	1,336	940	3,921	3,875	1,497	3,309	8,375	827,739
# explicit barriers	0	0	0	0	0	2	3	0	0	0	0	92
# worksharing	31	18	0	1	8	5	37	37	15	35	77	1,622
# nodes in $S \cup S'$	Verbosity 0											
	0	0	0	0	0	0	0	0	0	0	0	564
	Verbosity 1											
	0	0	0	0	0	0	0	0	0	0	0	587
# functions with $(n_{barrier} + n_d) \neq 0$	3	3	0	0	0	0	8	4	2	3	15	398

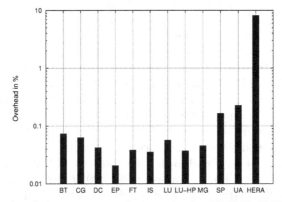

Fig. 5. Overhead of average compilation time for NASPB-OMP and HERA

minimal number of barriers or worksharing constructs. These functions may be replaced by their callee functions in the source code to report errors considering the entire program.

The compile-time overhead obtained when compiling the applications and activating our plugin is shown Figure 5. The overhead remains acceptable as it does not exceed 0.25% for NASPB-OMP and 10% for HERA (caused by the size of the code, it takes 52,3 minutes to compile HERA with the plugin).

5   Conclusion and Future Work

In this paper we propose an adaptation of our previous work on MPI to detect improper uses of barriers and worksharing constructs in OpenMP applications. The method we propose statically detects if all threads entering a function and created in it have the same sequence of barriers (or the same number of barriers) and worksharing constructs. It issues warnings for the statements responsible for the execution path leading to possible deadlocks or unspecified behaviors. Compared to existing work, in particular the method of Zhang *et al.* [18], our technique is fast (introducing little overhead) and able to scale to large applications. For future work, we plan to complement our method by a data-flow analysis, reducing the number of false positives detected by our approach.

Acknowledgments. This work is (integrated and) supported by the PERF-CLOUD project. A French FSN (Fond pour la Société Numérique) cooperative project that associates academics and industrials partners in order to design then provide building blocks for a new generation of HPC datacenters.

References

1. Basupalli, V., Yuki, T., Rajopadhye, S., Morvan, A., Derrien, S., Quinton, P., Wonnacott, D.: OmpVerify: Polyhedral Analysis for the OpenMP Programmer. In: Chapman, B.M., Gropp, W.D., Kumaran, K., Müller, M.S. (eds.) IWOMP 2011. LNCS, vol. 6665, pp. 37–53. Springer, Heidelberg (2011)
2. Cytron, R., Ferrante, J., Rosen, B., Wegman, M., Zadeck, F.: Efficiently computing static single assignment form and the control dependence graph. In: ACM TOPLAS, vol. 13(4), pp. 451–490 (1991)
3. Jourdren, H.: HERA: A hydrodynamic AMR Platform for Multi-Physics Simulations. In: Plewa, T., Linde, T., Weirs, V.G. (eds.) Adaptive Mesh Refinement - Theory and Applications, pp. 283–294. Springer (2003)
4. Kim, Y.J., Daeyoung, K., Jun, Y.K.: An Empirical Analysis of Intel Thread Checker for Detecting Races in OpenMP Programs. In: Lee, R.Y. (ed.) ACIS-ICIS, pp. 409–414. IEEE Computer Societ (2008)
5. Kim, Y.-J., Park, M.-Y., Park, S.-H., Jun, Y.-K.: A Practical Tool for Detecting Races in OpenMP Programs. In: Malyshkin, V.E. (ed.) PaCT 2005. LNCS, vol. 3606, pp. 321–330. Springer, Heidelberg (2005)
6. Kim, Y.J., Song, S., Jun, Y.K.: ADAT: An Adaptable Dynamic Analysis Tool for Race Detection in OpenMP Programs. In: ISPA, pp. 304–310. IEEE (2011)

7. Li, J., Hei, D., Yan, L.: Correctness Analysis based on Testing and Checking for OpenMP Programs. In: Fourth ChinaGrid Annual Conference. IEEE (2009)
8. Lin, Y.: Static Nonconcurrency Analysis of OpenMP Programs. In: Mueller, M.S., Chapman, B.M., de Supinski, B.R., Malony, A.D., Voss, M. (eds.) IWOMP 2005/2006. LNCS, vol. 4315, pp. 36–50. Springer, Heidelberg (2008)
9. Ma, H., Diersen, S., Wang, L., Liao, C., Quinlan, D.J., Yang, Z.: Symbolic Analysis of Concurrency Errors in OpenMP Programs. In: ICPP, pp. 510–516. IEEE (2013)
10. Meng, Y., Ha, O.-K., Jun, Y.-K.: Dynamic Instrumentation for Nested Fork-join Parallelism in OpenMP Programs. In: Kim, T.-h., Lee, Y.-h., Fang, W.-c. (eds.) FGIT 2012. LNCS, vol. 7709, pp. 154–158. Springer, Heidelberg (2012)
11. Petersen, P., Shah, S.: OpenMP Support in the Intel Thread Checker. In: Voss, M.J. (ed.) WOMPAT 2003. LNCS, vol. 2716, pp. 1–12. Springer, Heidelberg (2003)
12. Saillard, E., Carribault, P., Barthou, D.: Combining Static and Dynamic Validation of MPI Collective Communications. In: EuroMPI 2013, pp. 117–122 (2013)
13. Terboven, C.: Comparing Intel Thread Checker and Sun Thread Analyzer. In: Bischof, C.H., Bcker, H.M., Gibbon, P., Joubert, G.R., Lippert, T., Mohr, B., Peters, F.J. (eds.) PARCO. Advances in Parallel Computing, vol. 15, pp. 669–676. IOS Press (2007)
14. GOMP site, http://gcc.gnu.org/projects/gomp
15. NASPB site, http://www.nas.nasa.gov/software/NPB
16. OpenMP API v4.0, http://www.openmp.org/
17. Yices: An SMT solver, http://yices.csl.sri.com
18. Zhang, Y., Duesterwald, E., Gao, G.R.: Concurrency analysis for shared memory programs with textually unaligned barriers. In: Adve, V., Garzarán, M.J., Petersen, P. (eds.) LCPC 2007. LNCS, vol. 5234, pp. 95–109. Springer, Heidelberg (2008)

Loop-Carried Dependence Verification in OpenMP

Juan Salamanca, Luis Mattos, and Guido Araujo

Institute of Computing, University of Campinas
Campinas, São Paulo - Brazil
juan@ic.unicamp.br, ra107822@students.ic.unicamp.br, guido@ic.unicamp.br

Abstract. Data dependence analysis is a very difficult task, mainly due to the limitations imposed by pointer aliasing, and by the overhead of dynamic data dependence analysis. Despite the huge effort to devise improved data dependence analysis techniques, the problem is still far from solved. Efficient methods to reduce memory and time overhead imposed by dynamic instrumentation are thus required to enable fast and correct program parallelization. This paper presents a novel dynamic loop-carried dependence checker integrated as a new extension to OpenMP, the *parallel for check* construct, which can be used to help programmers identify the existence of loop-carried dependences in *parallel for* constructs.

Keywords: Parallel programming, checking, OpenMP, loop-carried dependences, dynamic data dependence analysis, parallelization.

1   Introduction

Tools to support programming correctness are central in any programming model, particularly in parallel programming, in which bugs are typically very hard to detect and reproduce [1].

A fairly common source of bugs in OpenMP and many other parallel programming models shows up when programmers need to evaluate if loops can have their iterations parallelized. In order to do so, programmers have to perform a careful and complex evaluation of the dependence of the loop-body variables across iterations. If such dependences are not present, loops are called DOALL [1], and its iterations can be easily parallelized. Otherwise, they are called DOACROSS [1] loops, which are harder to parallelize and to extract good speedups.

Given that loop-bodies can have complex nested function calls, and pointer aliasing, dynamic cross-iteration dependences can occur at runtime, making the work of the programmer much harder and error prone. Complex loop-bodies can easily produce intricate runtime dependences which cannot be easily detected by the typical programmer at compile time. For this reason, effectively detecting dynamic loop cross-iteration violations is a relevant tool to support parallel programming. In this section we detail the problem of detecting loop cross-iteration violations, and motivate the need to come up with a solution this problem.

L. DeRose (Eds.): IWOMP 2014, LNCS 8766, pp. 87–102, 2014.

A loop (as shown in Fig. 1) has a *loop-carried dependence* if there is a statement *A* dependent on *B* and both statements are executed in different iterations. As mentioned before, loop-carried dependences limit loop iteration parallelization.

#pragma omp parallel for
for (i...) {
    if (rand() % 2) a = b;   // A
    If (rand() % 2) b = i;   // B
}

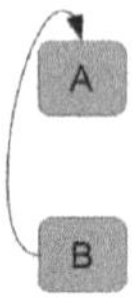

Fig. 1. Loop-carried dependence example

Data-dependence analysis is an important technique to detect loop-carried dependences and to exploit parallelism in programs. It works by detecting if two instructions access the same memory location, and at least one of them is a write operation. A *loop-carried dependence* occurs when these instructions execute in different iterations; otherwise they are called *loop-independent* [1]. As discussed previously, if two instructions are loop-independent, the iterations can be safely executed in parallel without the need of synchronization. Otherwise, if they define a loop-carried dependence, this can not be achieved.

For example, Fig. 2 shows an incorrect execution of the previous loop (Fig. 1), as iteration 2 is executed before iteration 1, so it does not respect the loop-carried dependence between instruction *A* and *B*. Specifically, the read of variable *b* in iteration 2 is incorrect as variable *b* has a loop-carried dependence to the execution of statement B in the previous iteration.

One potential source of bugs, while programming in OpenMP, shows up if a programmer incorrectly evaluates this as a *DOALL* loop, and thus parallelizes it using a *parallel for* construct. By using the *parallel for check* construct, proposed herein, this error could be detected at runtime.

In this paper, we present *parallel for check* (*check*), a new construct to OpenMP, which enables the seamless integration of loop dynamic data dependence verification in OpenMP. This construct makes possible the detection of loop-carried dependences at runtime in OpenMP programs, thus helping programmers to identify potential violations resulting from hard to detect loop-carried dependences. *Checker* was implemented in Pin/GCC-OpenMP and LLVM/Clang-OpenMP. This paper offers the following contributions:

- It presents a novel OpenMP *parallel for check* construct, also named *check* or *checker*, which enables the dynamic detection of loop-carried dependences.
- It does on-the-fly dynamic loop-carried dependence analysis of multithreaded applications, making it possible to detect loop-carried dependences which can not be detected by means of serial or per-thread analysis, as in [3, 4, 6, 7, 9].

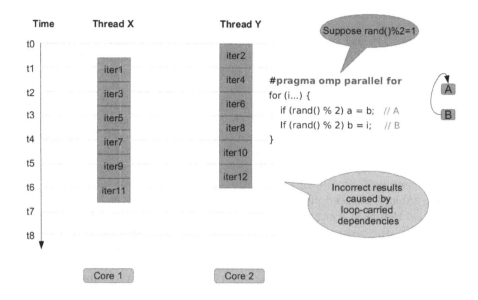

Fig. 2. Possible execution flow of the loop of Fig. 1

This paper is organized as follows. Section 2 analyzes well-known loop-carried dependence checkers and evaluates their disadvantages when compared to our work. Section 3 motivates and describes our *check* construct. Section 4 describes the implementation of *checker* in GCC/Pin and Clang/LLVM. Section 5 shows experimental results, and finally Section 6 concludes the work.

2   Related Work

This section analyzes two techniques used to detect loop-carried dependences. The first one is the *Pairwise* method, which was used in [5]; the second technique is the *Stride-based* method, which was implemented in the SD^3 profiler [4, 6, 7].

Static dependence analysis techniques have been extensively studied in the literature. Approaches like the GCD Test [2] and Banerjee's equality test [17] have been used, for a long time, in the design of parallelizing compiler. These techniques analyze data dependences in array-based memory accesses, and thus are not effective when used in languages which allow pointers and dynamic allocation. Besides, static analysis can become complex in situations when: (a) the bounds of the loop are not known, (b) dynamically created arrays are passed through deep procedure call chains, or (c) the loop-body has a complicated control-flow. In such cases, dynamic loop dependence analysis is an alternative as all memory addresses are resolved at runtime.

2.1   Pairwise Method

The Pairwise Method is still considered the state-of-the-art for loop-carried dependence testing. The basic idea of this method is to store, into a hash table (*pending table*), all memory references (*pending references*) occurring during the current iteration of a loop. When an iteration finishes, the pending table is compared against the *history table*, which stores all memory references (*history references*) of all previous iterations. This method solves nested loops dependences, by having a pending and a history table for each loop. It is important to highlight that our *OpenMP checker* does not target nested loops (yet).

The Pairwise algorithm works as follows. First, memory references are stored into the pending table during an iteration. After of finishing the iteration, the pending table is checked against the history table to discover loop-carried dependences. Before of continuing with the next iteration, the pending references are copied to the history. This process is repeated until the end of all iterations for this loop. If this loop is nested within another loop, the history table of the inner loop is propagated to the pending table of the outer loop. Afterwards, this pending table is checked against the history table of the outer loop (that is initialized empty) to discover loop-carried dependences. This process for the outer loop continues until the end of all its iterations.

Loop-independent dependence does not prevent parallelization; thus, any dependence analyzer must distinguish if a dependence is loop-carried or loop-independent. The Pairwise algorithm, as described in [3, 6, 7], detects loop-independent dependence by implementing *kill addresses* (a technique similar to the notion of *kill sets* in *data-flow analysis*), which marks a memory address as killed once it is written in an iteration. Then all memory references within the same iteration to the killed address are ignored. However, this technique could lead to incorrect results in multithreaded program executions not reporting existing violations of loop-carried dependences between threads as it only works in serial executions or per-thread analysis.

To demonstrate *kill addresses* effectiveness, SD[3] authors analyze the following code from SPEC 179.art [6].

Listing 1. Dependence in pass_flag in 179.art

```
1   void match() {
2       if (condition)
3           pass_flag=1;
4   }
5   void scan_recognize(...) {
6       for (j = starty; j < endy; j += stride)
7           for (i = startx; i < endx; i += stride){
8               ...
9               pass_flag = 0;
10              match();
11              if (pass_flag == 1)
12                  do_something();
13              ...
14          }
15
16  }
```

Assuming that *pass_flag* is a global variable, they argue that a loop-independent flow dependence exists on *pass_flag* as this variable is always initialized at line 9 before any use on every iteration, which should not prevent parallelization, and it is true in a serial execution context. However, in a multithreaded execution this code could have the following problem. Thread X executes line 9 after the same thread executes line 3. Before this thread executes line 11, another thread Y executes line 9. Thus, when thread X reads variable *pass_flag* at line 11, it will be incorrect as the execution does not respect the loop-carried WAR dependence between the write reference at line 9 (executed by thread Y) and the read reference at line 11 (executed by thread X). Thread X will not execute *do_something* when it had to do so.

This problem can be solved with privatization as SD[3] authors argue in [4,6,7]. On the other hand, according to our approach, all violations of loop-carried dependences must be informed to force not omitting corrections of renaming of variables that avoid WAR and WAW loop-carried dependences.

Killed addresses technique is also used by SD[3] [4,6,7] so it could lead to inaccurate results due to multithreaded program executions. Our *OpenMP checker* deals with this problem by storing the thread identifier (*thread ID*) for each memory event within the loop body.

Other problems of Pairwise Method are the time and memory overhead it requires to store all memory references within a loop. These problems can be more complicated when considering nested loops, as the Pairwise Method propagates history references of inner loops to pending tables of outer loops. As explained earlier, nested loops have not been considered in this first implementation of *checker* as we focused on the functionality of the new *check* construct and the integration with GCC and LLVM. On the other hand, we partially addressed the time overhead using pipeline-parallelization of the stages of our implementation.

2.2 Stride-Based Method

This method was proposed in [4, 6, 7] and has the Pairwise Method as a baseline algorithm. It tries to solve the problem of memory overhead by means of compression, and to solve the time overhead by using data-level parallelism.

The compression is achieved by using stride formats. For example, array reference $A[d * i + b]$ generates an address stream that has a stride composed by a base (b), a distance (d), and an induction variable (i). SD[3] [4,6,7] discovers strides dynamically and uses them directly to check loop-carried dependences. Strides are detected by a detector assigned to each PC. If a memory reference is not part of a stride, it is called a *point*.

Stride-based method is implemented using an extension of the Pairwise algorithm defining pending and history *stride* tables. To detect dependences in strides they first do an interval test employing interval trees based on *red-black trees* [11]. They then perform Dynamic-GCD test, as described in [4]. Notice that SD[3] focuses on reducing the memory overhead due to deep nested loops, contrary to this work, which does not consider nested loops as it is more focused on the integration with OpenMP, and to solve the problems with multithreaded executions.

SD^3 solves the problem of time overhead by exploiting data-level parallelism contrary to the task-level parallelism approaches adopted in previous works [12]. It distributes memory references into tasks that perform data-dependence checking with a subset of the entire input. The address space is divided at every 2^k bytes and the subsets are mapped to M tasks on N cores.

As in the previous Pairwise algorithm, this method maintains killed addresses to distinguish between loop-carried and independent dependences. However, as discussed in the previous Section 2.1, this technique could lead to incorrect results for multithreaded application executions. Therefore, SD^3 method can ignore some violations of loop-carried dependences for multithreaded executions as SD^3 analysis is performed sequentially or on a per-thread basis. As explained before, *checker* deals with this problem.

Another problem with SD^3 is that it is more effective for profiling inner loops than outer loops. As data-dependence analysis proceeds to outer loops, irregular strides are more frequent (the compression method will not work), making the cost of detecting dependences extremely expensive. Also, this method requires additional static analysis to recover control flows and loop structures from a binary executable, which is complicated to implement [6]; thus, the selection of loops to analyze is also complicated.

Our solution to these problems is to limit the analyzed loops according to the programmer instructions, while storing memory references in a memory/time efficient data structure as Multilevel Hash Table [11].

3   *Check* Construct in OpenMP

This section presents the new *check* construct, a novel OpenMP construct which can detect loop-carried dependences in OpenMP. It capitalizes on some advantages of both, Pairwise and Stride-based methods; while it tries to minimize their deficiencies.

3.1   Overview of the Algorithm

Pairwise and Stride methods use, for each instrumented loop of the program, one pending table that is flushed at each new iteration of the loop, and one big history table to store all dynamic memory references seen so far along the loop execution. In the case of Stride method, it duplicates the number of tables for managing strides and points. By contrast, our approach uses a single memory efficient data structure per-loop. This implementation feature of *check* considerably reduces the time and memory overhead caused by instrumentation.

To store memory references in *check*, we use a *Multilevel Hash Table (MHT)* [11] which maps references to one bit (*Indicator Function Hash Table*, as shown in Fig. 4). By doing so, the size of the memory footprint required to store iteration addresses is considerably reduced. MHT has a three-level key composed by the

#pragma omp parallel for check
for (i...) {
    if (rand() % 2) a = b; // A   checker activated
    If (rand() % 2) b = i; // B
}

Fig. 3. Usage of *check* construct in the program of Fig. 1

memory address, the thread ID, and the number of iteration, mapping one bit that indicates if this address was written or read in that iteration by that thread. On the average case, search time in this kind of structure is $O(k)$ where k is the number of levels. In our case, $k = 3$ and thus search time is $O(1)$ on average [11].

The detailed algorithm is described in Listing 2 as follows.

Listing 2. OpenMP *checker* Algorithm

1. When a loop with *check* directive, L, starts, the *checker* is activated.
2. On a memory address, R, of L's i-th iteration done by thread X, store 0 (read) or 1 (write) into the bit of the key composed by R, X and i on the Multilevel Hash Table.
3. If the memory reference in R is a read instruction, the *checker* looks for if there is a memory write on this address R, in another thread different from X, from *current_max_iteration* (the maximum number of iteration stored due to a memory reference by any thread at this moment) down to *iteration* $i+1$. If this memory write exists, the *checker* reports a violation of WAR loop-carried dependence. If *warning_option* is activated, the *checker* also looks for if there is a memory write on this address R, in any thread from *current_min_iteration* (the minimum number of iteration stored due to a memory reference by any thread at this moment) to *iteration* $i-1$. If this memory write exists, the *checker* reports a warning of WAR loop-carried dependence.
4. If the memory reference in R is a write instruction, the *checker* looks for if there is a memory write or read on this address R, in another thread different from X, from *current_max_iteration* down to *iteration* $i+1$. If a memory write exists, the *checker* reports a violation of WAW loop-carried dependence. If a memory read exists, it reports a violation of RAW loop-carried dependence. If *warning_option* is activated, the *checker* also looks for if there is a memory write or read on this address R, in any thread from *current_min_iteration* to *iteration* $i-1$. If a memory write exists, the *checker* reports a warning of WAW loop-carried dependence. If a memory read exists, it reports a warning of RAW loop-carried dependence.
5. When L finishes, we flush the Multilevel Hash Table.

The algorithm focuses on detecting violations of loop-carried dependences. Some loop-carried dependences do not cause violations, as the order of execution is respected, and thus *checker* does not report such errors. Nevertheless, in some specific cases the programmer might want to be informed of all existing loop-carried dependences as this information could be useful to understand the causes of violations in future program runs. In order to enable the detection of all loop-carried dependences in *checker*, the programmer should activate an optional parameter called *warning_option*.

Our approach does not need a sophisticated compression algorithm as described in [4,6,7], given that we perform dependence verification for single loops. By combining this with the possibility of selecting the specific loop to analyze and the MHT data structure, we managed to reduce the memory and time overheads of the methods described in Section 2.

As explained in Sections 2.1 and 2.2, previous solutions could have problems with multithreaded executions as they mark an address as killed once the memory address is written in an iteration; besides, they only report dependences per-thread. Thus, they can omit possible violations of loop-carried dependences. Our approach identifies these ignored violations given the analysis is not done on a thread basis but for the whole program. As explained before, we do not use the killed addresses method, as in our approach all violations of loop-carried dependences must be informed to force not omitting corrections of renaming of variables (that avoids WAR and WAW loop-carried dependences). These corrections can generate *privatized variables*. We solve the multithreaded execution problem by using the *thread ID* to do the verification of dependences.

3.2 Parallelization of the Algorithm

Instrumentation is a very time-consuming task because all memory writes and reads are instrumented for each loop as proposed by the Pairwise and Stride

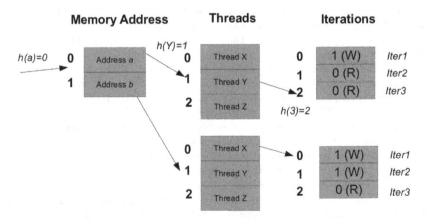

Fig. 4. Multilevel Hash Table mapping to a read in *memory address a, iteration 3* by *thread Y*

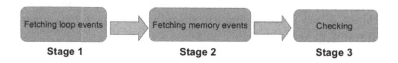

Fig. 5. *OpenMP checker* exploits pipeline level parallelism (*3 stages*)

methods. SD^3 [4, 6, 7] uses data-level parallelism and pipelining to reduce the time overhead. In contrast, our approach uses only pipeline-level parallelism. *Check* is composed by the following stages as shown in the Fig. 5:

- *Fetching loop events.* This stage provides information about the beginning and termination of a loop and corresponds to the *Pass 1* of the algorithm shown in Listing 2.
- *Fetching memory events and storing memory references.* At this stage information about memory addresses, thread ID, number of iteration, and program counter is collected and stored into the MHT. This stage corresponds to the *Pass 2* of the Listing 2.
- *Checking loop-carried dependences.* Here dependence violations are verified as described in *Passes 3, 4 and 5* of the Listing 2.

With pipeline parallelism [13] we parallelize a single task by dividing it into a series of sequential stages as shown in Fig. 5. Parallelism is achieved by pushing succeeding data elements through a consumer-producer pipeline, where stages run simultaneously on different cores [13]. This approach has considerably reduced latency compared to *data-level parallelism*. However, it introduces extra synchronization, because producers and consumers must be tightly coupled; also, it is limited by inter-stage dependences and the duration of the longest stage. In our case, the *third stage* is the most time consuming stage, and thus it will determine the overall speedup of the pipeline; however, we can still hide the latencies of *stages 1 and 2* from pipelining.

4 Implementation

In this section we describe both implementations of *checker* using GCC/Pin and LLVM. First, we present the basic structure of our *checker* and then we detail each implementation.

4.1 Basic Structure

The basic structure of *checker* consists of two modules, a *tracer* (stages 1 and 2 of the pipeline shown in Fig. 5) and an *analyzer* (stage 3 of the pipeline). The first stage instruments the program, fetches loop and memory events at runtime, and stores memory references in a shared memory MHT. The second verifies, on-the-fly, the existence of loop-carried dependences. As *checker* is an online construct, it cannot afford to have large costs of instrumenting all loads and stores of program thus it is very useful an implementation where the programmer chooses which loop wants to verify.

4.2   GCC/Pin

This section describes how the *check* construct was integrated into the GCC compiler. First, we adapted the GCC source code to recognize the *parallel for check* directive into the *#pragma* annotation. This implementation was very challenging as we had to adjust some very critical source files of GCC compiler (e.g. *c-parser.c*) to allow it to accept the new directive and also to delimit which loop will be analyzed.

Basically, when the check directive is inserted, the compiler recognizes it as a token and as part of a correct grammar expression, then inserts two function calls into the IR code: (a) *iterCount*, at the beginning of the chosen loop, which receives the number of the current iteration as parameter and is responsible for marking the beginning of an iteration annotation; and (b) *iterFinish*, at the end of the loop body, which marks the end of the instrumentation region. Finally, the compiler produces an executable file with the identified loops to be analyzed.

The Fig. 6 shows the modifications inserted by the compiler when reflected into the source code.

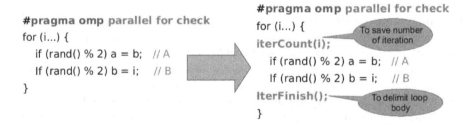

Fig. 6. Imaginary source file with the *check* construct

Tracer module was implemented on top of Pin [14], which is a dynamic instrumentation framework that enables the creation of dynamic program analysis tools. The advantage of using Pin to implement our tracer is that it does not require recompilation for doing the verification, and could be applied to executable files from different compilers. The disadvantages of the Pin tracer, as explained in [7], are: (a) the need of the static analysis to recover control flow graphs and loop structures, and (b) the difficulty of filtering useless loads and stores. In our case, we discriminate loads and stores within a loop by inserting function calls (*iterCount* and *iterFinish*).

The instrumentation is performed at runtime on the compiled binary files. Pin allows a tool to insert code in arbitrary places of the executable, the code is added dynamically while the executable is running. Thus, our tracer walks through the executable files, when it finds an *iterCount* function call, it inserts instrumentation code to store the current iteration. Also, it inserts instrumentation code after every memory reference, be it a read or write, until finding an *iterFinish* function call, after which the instrumentation finishes. At runtime, for every memory reference, the tracer fetches the memory address, the number of the current iteration, and the ID of the thread making the memory reference. Finally, it stores the memory reference into the MHT indexed by memory address, thread ID, and the number of the iteration.

Analyzer module implements the *passes 3, 4, and 5* of Listing 2 and could be used by different tracers (e.g. Pin and LLVM). During its implementation, it was necessary to use many efficient programming techniques and customized data structures to improve the efficiency of the analysis of *checker*. Fig. 7 shows the execution flow of *checker* when implemented using Pin and GCC.

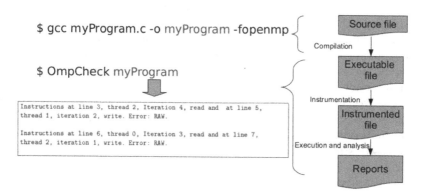

Fig. 7. Flow overview of the *OpenMP checker* with GCC/Pin

4.3   LLVM

As in the previous implementation of *checker* using GCC, we had to adapt the Clang front-end to accept the new *check* directive. The main ideas involved in this implementation are analogous to those used in GCC. We modify the Lexer and Parser files to insert function calls *iterCount* and *iterFinish*. Afterwards, the main issues involved in the LLVM tracer implementation are similar to those used in the Pin Tracer. The GCC/Pin analyzer can be used in LLVM as well.

We implemented the tracer in LLVM by creating an LLVM pass, which provides a very good static-analysis infrastructure. In contrast to Pin, LLVM provided an infrastructure which simplified the task of building control flow and loop structures. Besides, previous LLVM static-analysis passes can considerably decrease instrumentation and analysis overhead by identifying loop-carried dependences, at compile-time, and then ignoring them in the dynamic loop-carried verification, as is described in [10]. On the other hand, the main disadvantage of using an LLVM tracer is the recompilation for each analysis.

5   Experimental Results

This section evaluates the performance of *checker*, when compared to serial and OpenMP executions, using groups of experiments. Our experimental results were obtained on machines with Ubuntu 13.10 (64-bit), Intel i7 4-core with hyper-threading technology, and 8 GB main memory. We use 8 *Parboil benchmarks* [16] to report time and memory overheads by running the most executed loops (hottest loops) one at a time with *check*.[1] [2] [3]

Fig. 8 and Fig. 9 show the memory footprint for serial, OpenMP, and *checker* executions of the hottest loops of 8 Parboil benchmarks using the Parboil Datasets. As shown in Fig. 8 and Fig. 9, the memory overhead of *checker* is considerably smaller for most selected programs. The *OpenMP checker* verified all the benchmarks successfully as shown in Fig. 10, requiring not more than 400 MB of memory. Thus, selection of loops by the programmer and the data structure used in *checker* are effective techniques to avoid large memory overheads.

Fig. 10 shows the verification results of executing 8 Parboil benchmarks with *checker*. The checker reports 4 loops with violations of loop-carried dependences, and the column *Verified* explains the reasons. Notice that, if the operation involves updating a shared variable by means of a commutative operation the violation does not correspond to an error.

The time overhead results are presented in the Fig. 11 and Fig. 12. As shown, some executions with *check* are still faster than serial, with speedups of about 1.6x. This indicates that, although *check* adds instrumentation overhead it can, for some cases, still keep part of the performance resulting to the *parallel for* parallelization.

The largest slowdowns against *OpenMP execution* are about 20x and 8x as shown in Fig. 13, corresponding respectively to the *cutcp*1 *loop* of *Cutcp* benchmark and the *kernels*1 *loop* of *Stencil* benchmark. The largest slowdowns against *serial execution* are about 56x and 36x, corresponding to the *main*1 *loop* of the *Histo* benchmark and the *model*1 *loop* of the *Tpacf* benchmark respectively. However, the *OpenMP* time executions are larger than the *serial* executions, as this two benchmarks have been poorly parallelized in the original distribution. Thus, only the slowdowns against *OpenMP* are valid (*OpenMP* execution times would be smaller than *serial* using methods as *privatization*). We can conclude that *check* offers a reasonably smaller overhead when compared to the serial and OpenMP executions. This has been achieved due to the pipeline parallelization and the *OpenMP checker* algorithm described in Section 3.

---

[1] Our results are from GCC/Pin, but LLVM shows a similar performance.

[2] The remaining three benchmarks of Parboil were ignored as they do not have OpenMP *parallel for* constructs, or they were not programmed in C.

[3] The charts shown below are for different loops for each benchmark. For example, *lbm*1 is the lbm parboil benchmark but with its *loop1* modified to use the *checker*. Thus, all variants of *lbm* have the same serial and OpenMP time/memory overhead.

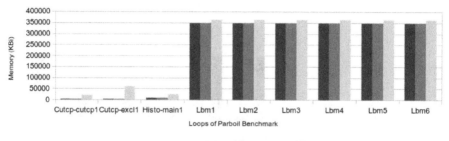

Fig. 8. Memory footprint of 3 Parboil Benchmarks (*Cutcp*, *Histo* and *Lbm*) executed *serially*, with *OpenMP*, and with *check* modifying different hottest loops

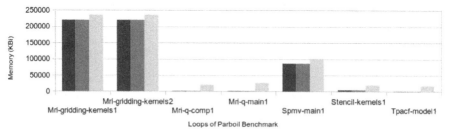

Fig. 9. Memory footprint of 5 Parboil Benchmarks (*Mri-gridding*, *Mri-q*, *Spmv*, *Stencil* and *Tpacf*) executed *serially*, with *OpenMP*, and with *check* modifying different hottest loops

Benchmark	Program	Loop	Violation	Verified
Cutcp	cutcp.c	1	✔	Ok. + is commutative on pg.
	excl.c	1	✔	Ok. All threads writing the same value on pg.
Histo	main.c	1	✔	Ok. + is commutative on histo.
Lbm	lbm.c	1		Ok.
		2		Ok.
		3		Ok.
		4		Ok.
		5		Ok.
		6		Ok.
Mri-gridding	CPU_kernels.c	1		Ok.
		2		Ok.
Mri-q	ComputeQ.c	1		Ok.
	main.c	1		Ok.
Spmv	main.c	1		Ok.
Stencil	kernels.c	1		OK.
Tpacf	model_comput e_cpu.c	1	✔	Ok. + is commutative on data_bins.

Fig. 10. Verification of 8 Parboil executed with *check* modifying different hottest loops

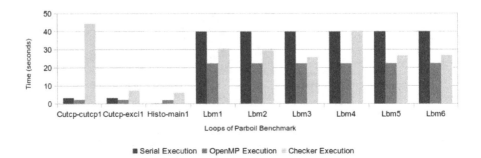

Fig. 11. Execution time of loops of Parboil benchmarks

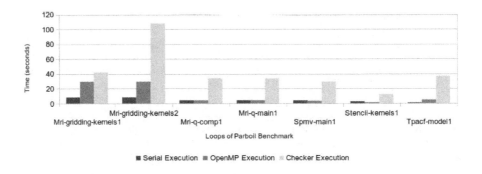

Fig. 12. Execution time of loops of Parboil benchmarks

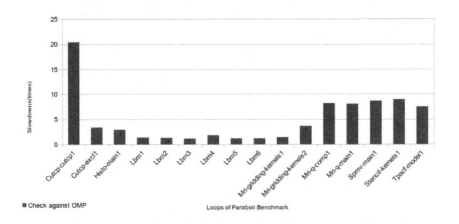

Fig. 13. Execution time of loops of Parboil benchmarks

6   Conclusions and Future Work

This paper proposes the *check* OpenMP extension (i.e. *parallel for check* construct), a novel implementation of a dynamic loop-carried dependence *checker* in OpenMP. It enables on-the-fly dynamic loop-carried dependence analysis of multithreaded applications, making it possible to detect hidden loop-carried dependences which can result in hard to detect parallel execution bugs. Some of these bugs can not be detected even by means of serial analysis or per-thread analysis as in previous works [4, 6, 7] described in Section 2. In order to reduce memory overhead, *OpenMP checker* analyzes only the loops that the programmer wants and uses a memory/time efficient data structure (Multilevel Hash Table) to store 1 bit per memory address. To reduce the time overhead, we used a three-stage Pipeline: (1) fetching loop events; (2) fetching memory events and storing memory references; and (3) checking loop-carried dependences. Furthermore, we showed how to integrate the *check* construct into GCC/Pin and LLVM.

As next steps in our work, we are going to research novel efficient techniques to deal with the overhead problem in nested loops. Also, we are going to consider static analysis to decrease the number of memory address candidates which require verification. Finally, we are going to use other benchmark suites such as SPEC OMP2001 or SPEC OMP2012.

Acknowledgments. We thank the IWOMP 2014 referees for their very constructive comments. We also would like to thank Samsung and CNPq for their support to this work.

References

1. Wolfe, M.J.: High Performance Compilers for Parallel Computing. Shanklin, C., Ortega, L. (eds.). Addison-Wesley Longman Publishing Co., Inc., Boston (1995)
2. Muchnick, S.S.: Advanced Compiler Design and Implementation. Morgan Kaufmann (1997) ISBN 1-55860-320-4
3. Yu, H., Li, Z.: Fast loop-level data dependence profiling. In: Proceedings of the 26th ACM International Conference on Supercomputing (ICS 2012), pp. 37–46. ACM, New York (2012), http://doi.acm.org/10.1145/2304576.2304584, doi:10.1145/2304576.2304584
4. Kim, M., Kim, H., Luk, C.-K.: SD3: A scalable approach to dynamic data- dependence profiling. Technical Report TR-2010-001, Atlanta, GA, USA (2010)
5. Larus, J.R.: Loop-level parallelism in numeric and symbolic programs. IEEE Transactions on Parallel and Distributed Systems 4(7), 812 (1993), doi:10.1109/71.238302.
6. Kim, M., Kim, H., Luk, C.-K.: SD3: A Scalable Approach to Dynamic Data-Dependence Profiling. In: 2010 43rd Annual IEEE/ACM International Symposium on Microarchitecture (MICRO), December 4-8, pp. 535–546 (2010), doi:10.1109/MICRO.2010.49.

7. Kim, M., Lakshminarayana, N.B., Kim, H., Luk, C.-K.: SD3: An Efficient Dynamic Data-Dependence Profiling Mechanism. IEEE Transactions on Computers 62(12), 2516–2530 (2013), doi:10.1109/TC.2012.182

8. Kim, M., Kim, H., Luk, C.-K.: Prospector: A dynamic data-dependence profiler to help parallel programming. In: 2nd USENIX Workshop on Hot Topics in Parallelism, HotPar 2010 (2010)

9. Ketterlin, A., Clauss, P.: Profiling Data-Dependence to Assist Parallelization: Framework, Scope, and Optimization. In: 2012 45th Annual IEEE/ACM International Symposium on Microarchitecture (MICRO), December 1-5, pp. 437–448 (2012), doi:10.1109/MICRO.2012.47

10. Vanka, R., Tuck, J.: Efficient and accurate data dependence profiling using software signatures. In: Proceedings of the Tenth International Symposium on Code Generation and Optimization (CGO 2012), pp. 186–195. ACM, New York (2012), http://doi.acm.org/10.1145/2259016.2259041, doi:10.1145/2259016.2259041

11. Cormen, T.H., Leiserson, C.E., Rivest, R.L., Stein, C.: Introduction to Algorithms, 2nd edn. The MIT Press (September 2001)

12. Moseley, T., Shye, A., Reddi, V.J., Grunwald, D., Peri, R.: Shadow Profiling: Hiding Instrumentation Costs with Parallelism. In: International Symposium on Code Generation and Optimization, CGO 2007, March 11-14, pp. 198–208 (2007), doi:10.1109/CGO.2007.35

13. Gordon, M.I., Thies, W., Amarasinghe, S.: Exploiting coarse-grained task, data, and pipeline parallelism in stream programs. SIGOPS Oper. Syst. Rev. 40(5), 151–162 (2006), http://doi.acm.org/10.1145/1168917.1168877, doi:10.1145/1168917.1168877

14. Bach, M.M., Charney, M., Cohn, R., Demikhovsky, E., Devor, T., Hazelwood, K., Jaleel, A., Luk, C.-K., Lyons, G., Patil, H., Tal, A.: Analyzing parallel programs with pin. Computer 43(3), 34–41 (2010)

15. Pacheco, P.: An Introduction to Parallel Programming, 1st edn. Morgan Kaufmann Publishers Inc., San Francisco (2011)

16. Stratton, J.A., et al.: Parboil: A Revised Benchmark Suite for Scientific and Commercial Throughput Computing (2012)

17. Kong, X., Klappholz, D., Psarris, K.: The I test: An improved dependence test for automatic parallelization and vectorization. IEEE Transactions on Parallel and Distributed Systems 2(3), 342–349 (1991), doi:10.1109/71.86109.

18. Zhang, X., Navabi, A., Jagannathan, S.: Alchemist: A Transparent Dependence Distance Profiling Infrastructure. In: International Symposium on Code Generation and Optimization, CGO 2009, March 22-25, pp. 47–58 (2009), doi:10.1109/CGO.2009.15

An OpenMP Extension Library for Memory Affinity

Dirk Schmidl, Tim Cramer, Christian Terboven, Dieter an Mey, and Matthias S. Müller

IT Center, RWTH Aachen University, D - 52074 Aachen
Chair for High Performance Computing, RWTH Aachen University, D - 52074 Aachen
JARA - High-Performance Computing, Schinkelstraße 2, D - 52062 Aachen
{schmidl,cramer,terboven,anmey,mueller}@itc.rwth-aachen.de

Abstract. OpenMP 4.0 extended affinity support to allow pinning of threads to places. Places are an abstraction of machine locations which in many cases do not require extensive hardware knowledge by the user. For memory affinity, i.e. data initialization and migration on NUMA systems, support is still missing in OpenMP. In this work we present an extension library for OpenMP which implements round-robin memory initialization over places and memory migration, either explicitly or implicitly. The latter is presented with an implementation based on a *next-touch* algorithm for Linux. We study the overhead of our methods with a simple model that allows to predict if migration is beneficial or not for a certain use case and we demonstrate the correctness of the migration methods and the correctness of our model prediction with the STREAM benchmark and an implementation of a CG method. Finally, we discuss how memory affinity could be integrated in future OpenMP versions.

1 Introduction

Non uniform memory access (NUMA) architectures are the standard system architecture even for commodity servers, nowadays. In shared memory programming for High Performance Computing (HPC) this needs to be taken into account in order to reach good scalability on such a system. OpenMP, the most widely used standard for shared memory parallel programming in HPC, recently improved the affinity support by adding easy-to-use thread placement mechanisms. These facilities provide an abstraction layer, called place list, as a model of the system topology, and strategies to pin threads to the places, where a place is a set of execution units, see [12]. This basic support can help to write efficient programs for NUMA architectures if the data placement can be performed in an optimal manner at the time when the data is initialized, by using the first-touch data placement policy of the operating system. If the data is badly placed at the beginning or if the data access pattern changes over runtime, data migration is needed to adjust the data placement with the intent to maximize local memory accesses over all threads. Data migration mechanisms exist for many operating systems, including Linux, but they are complex to use and require detailed knowledge of the hardware and the thread placement, which contradicts the idea of OpenMP to have an abstract hardware description with the place list.

In this work we will investigate the usefulness and overhead of standard mechanism for explicit memory migration under the Linux operating system, as well as self developed semi-automatic memory migration, where data is migrated to the thread that

L. DeRose (Eds.): IWOMP 2014, LNCS 8766, pp. 103–114, 2014.

touches the data next. Furthermore we provide an easy mechanism for round robin memory allocation based on OpenMP places. Round robin memory allocation can be a good compromise for memory allocation, if the data access pattern is random which prevents local memory placement in advance. We implement these functionality in the RWTH OpenMP extension library libr_ompx.

We compare the performance of these mechanisms to each other and to serial and parallel memory allocation on a standard 2- and 4-socket server equipped with Intel processors. Through measurements of the overhead and access time we will predict break-even points indicating for how many memory accesses migration is beneficial in advance and when accepting the remote accesses results in better performance.

The rest of this work is structured as follows: After we discuss related work and the current status of affinity support in OpenMP in sec. 2, we introduce the functionality of our RWTH OpenMP extension library in sec. 3. In sec. 4 we analyze the overhead of these mechanisms and introduce a simple model to understand when the migration is useful and when not, before we show examples in which these optimizations have been applied in sec. 5. Afterwards we discuss how memory affinity could be integrated in future OpenMP versions in sec. 6 and finally draw our conclusion in sec. 7.

2   Related Work

OpenMP 4.0 [12] introduced the concept of places and thread binding strategies. A place is defined as a set of hardware execution units that is targeted by OpenMP as one unit of location when dealing with thread binding. The place list is defined as an ordered list of places, specified by the user of an OpenMP program either as an abstract name (i.e. cores: each place corresponds to a single core) or as an explicit list of places described by logical processor IDs as they are used in the operating system. The thread affinity policies (i.e. close and spread) are used to control the binding of threads over the places in the place list. With spread, the user requests to spread the threads evenly within the places of the system, while with close, the runtime should pack the threads close together.

Beside the placement of threads the placement of data is as well important for optimal performance on NUMA systems. Therefore, memory affinity and migration for shared memory programming has been investigated in several studies before. Already in early NUMA machines, hardware and operating system support for automatic page migration was provided [7,11]. Here the operating system of the SGI Origin uses TLB miss statistics and remote memory reference counters to identify pages for an automatic migration [7], while the Sun WildFire tracks the number of times that cache lines from a given page are retrieved in the same sharing state [11]. For the Linux operating system kernel patches for automatic page migration mechanisms exist, like AutoNUMA [4], where statistics on remote accesses are collected and threads, processes or data is migrated to establish a good thread to data locality. Nikolopoulos et al. [10] presented an integrated compiler / runtime / OS migration framework for user-level dynamic page migration. They use compiler instrumentation and a sampling approach which improves the locality of the memory pages.

None of these mechanisms works well for all sorts of applications and that is why other approaches try to allow users to initiate data migration. The advantage is that a user can have more insight knowledge of the application which can help to make better migration decisions. An extension of OpenMP for memory migration on NUMA machines was implemented in Compaq's OpenMP compiler in [1]. With the help of a set of additional OpenMP Fortran directives the programmer had the possibility to specify user-directed page migration and user-directed data layout. In our library we provide a similar compiler independent functionality for today's standard Linux distributions. Another study about future OpenMP runtime perspectives was made in [2]. Their results suggest that there is a need to extend OpenMP for mixed solutions (thread and data migration) to transmit affinity relations to the underlying runtime. An application-driven study for the benefit of *affinity-on-next-touch* mechanisms in user space was done by Löfer et al. [8].

While the idea to migrate data in this way has already been implemented under the Solaris operating system before, no operating system support for migration on next touch exists for Linux. In our previous work [13] we already sketched a mechanism for *affinity-on-next-touch* for the Linux operating system. A kernel-level implementation for the same purpose with a higher bandwidth is presented by Lankes et. al. [6], the downside is that a kernel patch is required, so this approach cannot be used on arbitrary HPC production systems. In addition, Goglin and Furmento [3] compared a similar memory migration mechanism in user space with an approach in kernel space. Furthermore, they improved the move_pages call for big memory chunks. We benefit from this improvement as well since it is included in the kernel we used for our tests. Although the kernel-based implementation is 30 % faster than the user-space model we think our extended OpenMP library is an adequate tool to evaluate *affinity-on-next-touch* support for future OpenMP runtime implementations.

3 The RWTH OpenMP Extension Library

In this section we describe the functionality of our OpenMP extension library named libr_ompx. The purpose of this library is to provide easy-to-use functionality to improve the memory affinity of programs. The implementation is based on *libnuma* [5] which provides NUMA support for the Linux operating system, therefore at the time of this writing our library is limited to Linux as well.

The most-common way to handle NUMA machines in OpenMP programs is to use the *first-touch* memory initialization strategy provided by all operating systems to the extent of our knowledge, to place memory pages at the NUMA node where the page is first used. During computation the data then should be used in the same way as the initialization was done, otherwise local memory access is not guaranteed. If this approach is applicable because the data access pattern is known a priori, does not change over time and initialization is done in the user code and not in any non NUMA-aware library, OpenMP programs can reach good performance on NUMA machines with this simple strategy.

Our library aims to improve cases, in which these preconditions are not fulfilled, meaning the data access pattern is unknown or unpredictable, changes over time or the memory initialization is not in the hand of the user. We therefore implemented the following four functions with the interface shown in listing 1.

```
void* r_ompx_interleave_alloc( size_t  size );
int r_ompx_migrate( void* addr , size_t  size , int  node );
int r_ompx_fetch( void* addr , size_t  size );
int r_ompx_next_touch( void* addr , size_t  size );
```

Listing 1. Interface of all functions of the r_ompx library

r_ompx_interleave_alloc. If the memory access pattern of an application is unpredictable, it is impossible to place the data in advance on the NUMA-node where it is used later on. In such cases distributing the data evenly across the NUMA-nodes of the system in a round-robin fashion does not reduce the average number of remote accesses. However, it distributes these accesses evenly over all NUMA-nodes, which is still better than when all remote accesses occur on a single NUMA-node. The functions numa_alloc_interleave and numa_alloc_interleave_subset provided by libnuma allow to allocate data in a round-robin fashion already. In contrast to those functions r_ompx_interleave_alloc distributes the data round robin across all places specified in the OpenMP place list. In this way the user only uses the memory attached to the NUMA-nodes used by the program without the need to manually figure out which nodes actually were chosen by the OpenMP runtime system for execution.

r_ompx_migrate and r_ompx_fetch. If the memory is badly placed because of dynamically changing access patterns or because the allocation was done by a library not respecting the NUMA architecture, memory migration is a way to re-establish good thread to memory affinity. The function r_ompx_migrate provides functionality to migrate a chunk of memory to a specified node and the function r_ompx_fetch migrates data to the node where the calling thread is currently running. The first function allows a master thread to distribute data for a team of threads in advance, whereas the latter function allows all threads to fetch data to the local NUMA-node. This can be done without the need to find out which cores and NUMA-nodes have been chosen by the OpenMP runtime for which thread. A migration mechanism to OpenMP places would be desirable as well but since OpenMP does not provide an API function to identify the currently used places from within a program, this is not possible.

r_ompx_next_touch. This function is useful when the data access pattern is repetitive but not known exactly in advance or when it is hard to divide the data into consecutive chunks, e.g. when the data is accessed indirectly through pointers. One thread can flag a chunk of memory to be moved when it is accessed the next time. The page is then moved to the thread which tried to access the page. This allows to distribute pages during computation without the need to explicitly specify the distribution pattern.

We already provided a sketch of an algorithm for next_touch migration working in user space under Linux in [13]. Although implementations in kernel space exist with lower overhead, as discussed in sec. 2, we used the user level approach in order to run on standard HPC installations without kernel patches. Our algorithm is fully

```
1   function r_ompx_next_touch(addr,size)
2       foreach page p from addr to (addr+size)
3           lock p for read and write access;
4       end foreach
5       install sigh() as signal handler for SIGSEGV;
6   end function
7
8   function sigh()
9       p = page causing the SIGSEGV;
10      n = NUMA-node of the current thread;
11      migrate p to n;
12      release the read/write lock on p;
13  end function
```

Listing 1.2. Pseudo-Code illustrating the next_touch algorithm

implemented in the RWTH OpenMP Extension Library and can be used on any Linux kernel supporting libnuma.

The algorithm, outlined in code 1.2, works in two phases. First, all pages of the user specified memory chunk are protected for read/write access and a signal handler for the signal SIGSEGV is installed. Second, when a SIGSEGV signal occurs this means a thread has tried to access the page. The installed signal handler then migrates the page to the NUMA-node of this particular thread and releases the read/write lock on the page. Then the library returns to the user program where the page is now accessible and located on the local NUMA-node.

4   Overhead Analysis

After the migration methods have been presented, we will analyze the overhead of these methods and compare it to the benefit of the improved memory access pattern. For our tests we used a 2-socket system equipped with 3.07 GHz Intel Westmere processors and a 4-socket system with 2.20 GHz Intel SandyBridge processors. Both machines run Linux kernel 2.6.32 and we used 4k pages for all test. The tests perform a daxpy operation on three vectors and measure the access time of all threads and then compute a per page average access time for all threads. The tests use one thread per core on both systems. We further investigate the following cases:

- **serial_init:** The data is initialized by a single thread (in serial) and thus all data is placed on only one of the NUMA-nodes.
- **parallel_init:** The data is initialized in parallel so that the data is distributed across all NUMA-nodes and the daxpy operation works on local data.
- **interleaved_init:** The data is distributed round robin across the NUMA-nodes using r_ompx_interleave_alloc. During the daxpy operation the data is still used with a static schedule, so the number of remote accesses is not reduced compared

to serial_init. However, the advantage is that the remote accesses are now evenly
distributed across the nodes.

- **migrate:** Here the data is initialized serially and then the data is migrated to the
  thread that will use it later on. We use the function r_ompx_fetch for this purpose, but r_ompx_migrate has similar overhead, since it uses the same mechanism internally.
- **next_touch:** The data is also initialized serially and then migrated, but in contrast
  to the former case, the function r_ompx_next_touch is used to flag the data for
  migration and to move it in the first iteration of the daxpy kernel.

Table 1. Average page access time and overhead to migrate a page in μs on the 2-socket Westmere
and 4-socket SandyBridge system

Strategy	serial_init	parallel_init	interleaved_init	migrate	next_touch
2-socket Westmere					
Access time	0.204	0.102	0.141	-	-
Migration Overhead	-	-	-	1.295	15.593
Access time after migration	-	-	-	0.102	0.102
4-socket SandyBridge					
Access time	0.334	0.048	0.095	-	-
Migration Overhead	-	-	-	14.458	73.939
Access time after migration	-	-	-	0.047	0.047

Table 1 shows the average time to access all variables of a complete page as well
as the overhead for the migration of a page. In the serial_init case all pages lay on one
NUMA-node whereas they lay perfectly distributed across both NUMA-nodes in the
parallel_init case. In the latter case on the Westmere system this leads to an average
access time of about 0.1 μs which is 2x faster than the 0.2 μs when the data is serially
initialized. Since two memory controllers are used instead of one this is as expected.
When the pages are initialized interleaved, the access time is 0.141 μs. Both migration
strategies deliver the same good access time as the parallel_init strategy after migration,
but they introduce overhead of 1.3 μs for explicit migration and 15.6 μs for next_touch.

Since the overhead is much higher than a single remote access of the data, it is
only useful if the data is needed multiple times. Given the overhead (O) and access
time (A) of table 1 the total access time for x memory accesses (T) can be calculated
as $T = O + x \times A$. Figure 1 shows the access time for the investigated memory
initialization and migration mechanisms. The intersection points of the straight lines
indicate the break-even point where the migration starts to be beneficial. For example
on the Westmere system the lines of serial_init and migrate intersect at 12.7
(50 on SandyBridge). This means if the data is initialized serially it is beneficial to
migrate it in advance if all the data of the complete page is used 13 (50) or more times.
Migration with the next_touch mechanism is beneficial for 154+ or 258+ accesses
on the Westmere system or SandyBridge system, respectively. If only a fraction of the
data on a page is used, e.g. only one variable, migration will of course pay off only for
a higher number of accesses.

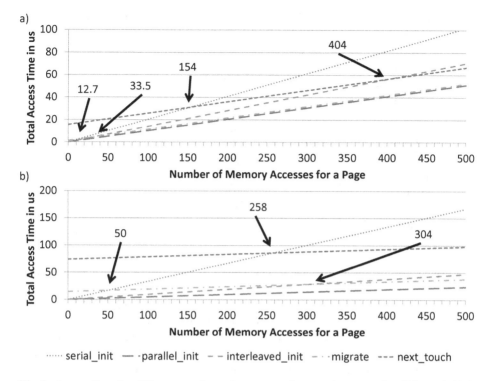

Fig. 1. Access time for different numbers of accesses of a complete page for different initialization and migration strategies on the 2-socket Westmere a) and 4-socket SandyBridge b) system. The points of intersection indicate when migration is beneficial over serial_init or interleaved_init.

5   Evaluation

In this section we will show that the presented mechanisms deliver the expected behavior in practice. First, we look at the STREAM benchmark to investigate the achievable memory bandwidth for all mechanism. Second, we take an implementation of an iterative conjugate gradient method to verify our predictions when migration is useful.

5.1   STREAM

The STREAM benchmark [9] is a standard benchmark to investigate the memory bandwidth of a system. It runs several vector-vector operations, measures the time and calculates the achieved bandwidth. We modified the data allocation and initialization and added our migration mechanisms to the code in different versions in order to prove that the presented data migration strategies lead to a good data distribution. Table 2 shows the achieved bandwidth for all investigated methods. As for the tests in section 4 we initialized the data serially before the migration strategies were applied in the cases migration and next_touch. The benchmark ignores the first iteration to avoid

Table 2. Bandwidth in GB/s measured with the stream benchmark after different memory allocation or migration strategies on the 2-socket Westmere and 4-socket SandyBridge system

	serial_init	parallel_init	interleaved_init	migration	next_touch
2-socket Westmere					
Copy	18	40	27	40	40
Scale	19	40	25	40	40
Add	18	40	29	40	40
Triad	18	40	29	40	40
4-socket SandyBridge					
Copy	11	83	41	83	83
Scale	11	80	41	80	80
Add	12	86	43	87	86
Triad	12	86	43	87	85

measuring warm-up phases for caches. Since our next_touch mechanism happens in the very first iteration it is ignored as well.

On the 2-socket (4-socket) system we reach 18 to 19 GB/s (11 to 12 GB/s) bandwidth if one local memory is used by serial initialization and about 40 GB/s (80 GB/s) in the parallel initialization case. On both systems the interleaved initialization delivers performance roughly in the middle between these two mechanisms with 25 - 29 GB/s and 41 - 43 GB/s respectively. Both migration strategies deliver basically the same good performance as the parallel initialization strategy on both systems. This shows that the memory distribution after migration is as good as with optimal manual initialization.

5.2   Conjugate Gradient Method

We did further tests with an implementation of a conjugate gradient method (CG) for sparse linear equation systems. The CG algorithm is an iterative method which allows us to stop after a certain number of iterations for our performance measurements. The algorithm is dominated by exactly one sparse matrix vector multiplication per iteration. The matrix used is about 3.2 GB in size (in memory) and is stored in compressed row storage (CRS) format. A matrix in CRS format is stored in three vectors, the first vector containing all values, the second one containing all column indices and the third one with the start index of every row of the matrix. It follows from this storage format, that the memory access pattern is consecutive for the matrix vector product since all of these vectors are accessed consecutively. We again implemented several versions with serial, parallel and interleaved allocation as well as with serial initialization followed by explicit migration and next_touch migration. At the boundary between two thread a page might contain data for more than one thread. In this case the page is migrated to the lower numbered thread in the case of explicit migration. In the next_touch case the page is migrated to the thread accessing the page first. Most probably this is the thread with the higher number, because it is the first page for this thread whereas it is the last page for the thread with the lower thread number. Figure 2 shows the average run-time of an iteration for different numbers of total iterations. The different initialization strategies have some warm-up effects, so a very small number of iterations is slightly slower but after 5-10 iterations they reach a constant time per iteration. The parallel initialization is the fastest, followed by interleaved allocation with the serial initialization being the slowest version as expected, since the kernel is known to be memory bound. The `migrate` and `next_touch` version have a much higher runtime for one iteration, since the migration overhead is completely mapped to this iteration if only one iteration is done. For more iterations the overhead is still the same, but the algorithm profits from the higher bandwidth after migration for all following iterations. On the Westmere system the `serial_init` curve intersects the `migrate` curve between 10 and 20 and the `next_touch` curve at about 160. We predicted the migration strategies to be beneficial for 12.7 and 154 memory accesses, so the CG fits well into these predictions. The `interleaved_init` curve is intersected at about 40 and 400 iterations, where 33.5 and 404 were predicted, so the model also works fine for this case.

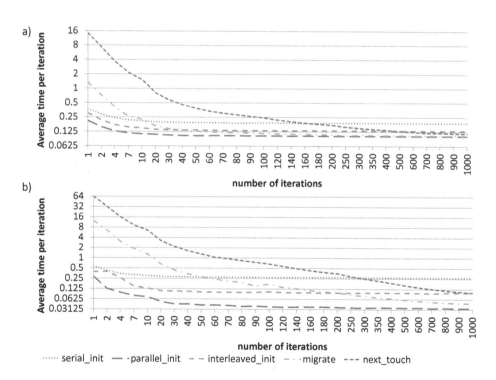

Fig. 2. Average runtime of an iteration of a conjugate gradient method with increasing numbers of iterations on a) the 2-socket Westmere and b) the 4-socket SandyBridge system

We conclude that memory migration with `r_ompx` is beneficial if enough accesses occur after the migration. On the investigated systems these were about 10 - 30 accesses for explicit migration whereas the overhead was larger for `next_touch` where 150 - 260 accesses were necessary to reach the break-even point.

6 Possible Integration into OpenMP

The previous sections presented the necessary concepts to support memory affinity in OpenMP as well as our library-based implementation for Linux. Our library and the corresponding source code will soon be made publically available[1] under FreeBSD license. The intent of this release is to make the functionality available to an interested audience of HPC developers and to gather usage experiences with a broader application range, and hopefully to demonstrate the general suitability of our proposed concepts. If sufficient interest is shown, there are various options of integrating this functionality into OpenMP, ranging from memory access advice constructs to extensions to the (target) data construct, which would then be discussed within the OpenMP Language Committee.

6.1 Consideration of OpenMP Tasks

As already discussed in Section 3 the first touch mechanism can be used in OpenMP worksharing constructs if the data access pattern is known, predictable or does not change over time. For the OpenMP tasking model additional aspects have to be considered. When the data is allocated inside the task during its execution, locality is achieved automatically due to the first-touch strategy of the operating system, because the data is allocated by the thread executing the task. Only untied tasks can be migrated between different threads during execution, which might lead to remote data accesses. To the best of our knowledge no production runtime implements migration of untied tasks during execution, which makes this issue negligible in practice. However, if the data is allocated outside the task region locality behavior is undefined, because the OpenMP runtime selects a thread for executing of the particular tasks without considering data affinity. Hence, tasks might be scheduled to threads far away from where the data has been allocated.

In [14,15] we showed that for some implementations it is beneficial to use a parallel-producer pattern. This means that the *loop* worksharing construct is used to generate the tasks in parallel. The Intel OpenMP runtime, which is available as open source, allows to examine the implementation details. Tasks are managed in per-thread task queues, newly created tasks are enqueued at the tail of these queues while task processing and task stealing is performed from the head. Task stealing is only performed, if the thread local task queue is empty. Consequently, generating tasks with the parallel-producer pattern reduces overhead incurred by per-thread locks and also allows to achieve data locality, if the same thread allocated the data and then generates and executes the corresponding tasks.

However, if tasks are employed to avoid load imbalances at some point in time threads have to steal tasks from a remote thread's task queue, remote data accesses might be unavoidable. Then, data locality and load balancing are conflicting optimization goals. In this case it would be an opportunity for an OpenMP runtime to not only steal tasks, but also to migrate the corresponding data. As seen in Section 4 migrating data is only beneficial if the data is accessed often enough. Since neither the compiler

---

[1] https://bitbucket.org/rwth-itc-hpc/ompx

nor an OpenMP runtime can reliably analyze and predict the data access within a task, a specification of the data access by the programmer is necessary.

7 Conclusion

We have shown different methods for memory allocation and memory migration which work well together with the current OpenMP support for affinity. All methods were implemented in r_ompx, an extension library for memory affinity support in OpenMP. Our implemented initialization or migration strategies provide easy-to-use support for cases where data locality cannot easily be established at initialization time, e.g. because the memory access changes over runtime or is unpredictable. We measured basic performance results for good and bad memory accesses and overhead for migration and formed a simple model to calculate break-even points which indicate when memory allocation is beneficial on modern HPC systems. If the data is local on one socket explicit migration is useful if the data is used 13 or more times on the 2-socket Intel Westmere system. Our presented algorithm for migration on next_touch is more expensive (154+ accesses needed) but it is very user friendly because it can be applied without any explicit description of how to distribute the memory which is hard to figure out and specify for some algorithms.

We have proven with the STREAM benchmark, that the distribution of memory after our migration strategies is as good as the standard parallel initialization within STREAM. This means that we can achieve good memory locality even in cases were parallel initialization is not possible or where the data access pattern changes over runtime, e.g. in adaptive algorithms. For the iterative CG algorithm we have proven, that our model predictions hold in real applications, since the migration strategies were beneficial nearly after the predicted number of memory accesses. Finally we discussed ideas and challenges about how to integrate memory affinity support in OpenMP.

Acknowledgement. Some of the tests were performed with computing resources granted by JARA-HPC from RWTH Aachen University under project jara0001. Parts of this work were funded by the German Federal Ministry of Research and Education (BMBF) under Grant Numbers 01IH11006D(LMAC), 01IH13001D(Score-E) and 01IH13008A(ELP).

References

1. Bircsak, J., Craig, P., Crowell, R., Cvetanovic, Z., Harris, J., Nelson, C.A., Offner, C.D.: Extending OpenMP for NUMA Machines. In: Proceedings of the 2000 ACM/IEEE Conference on Supercomputing, SC 2000. IEEE Computer Society, Washington, DC (2000)
2. Broquedis, F., Furmento, N., Goglin, B., Namyst, R., Wacrenier, P.-A.: Dynamic Task and Data Placement over NUMA Architectures: An OpenMP Runtime Perspective. In: Müller, M.S., de Supinski, B.R., Chapman, B.M. (eds.) IWOMP 2009. LNCS, vol. 5568, pp. 79–92. Springer, Heidelberg (2009)
3. Goglin, B., Furmento, N.: Enabling high-performance memory migration for multithreaded applications on LINUX. In: IEEE International Symposium on Parallel Distributed Processing, IPDPS 2009, pp. 1–9 (May 2009)

4. Corbet, J.: AutoNUMA: The other approach to NUMA scheduling, http://lwn.net/Articles/488709/ (last visited on Sepetmber 05, 2014)
5. Kleen, A.: A NUMA API for LINUX. Technical linux whitepaper, Novell (April 2005)
6. Lankes, S., Bierbaum, B., Bemmerl, T.: Affinity-on-next-touch: An Extension to the Linux Kernel for NUMA Architectures. In: Wyrzykowski, R., Dongarra, J., Karczewski, K., Wasniewski, J. (eds.) PPAM 2009, Part I. LNCS, vol. 6067, pp. 576–585. Springer, Heidelberg (2010)
7. Laudon, J., Lenoski, D.: The SGI Origin: A ccNUMA Highly Scalable Server. In: Proceedings of the 24th Annual International Symposium on Computer Architecture, ISCA 1997, pp. 241–251. ACM, New York (1997)
8. Löf, H., Holmgren, S.: Affinity-on-next-touch: Increasing the Performance of an Industrial PDE Solver on a cc-NUMA System. In: Proceedings of the 19th Annual International Conference on Supercomputing, ICS 2005, pp. 387–392. ACM, New York (2005)
9. McCalpin, J.D.: STREAM: Sustainable Memory Bandwidth in High Performance Computers (1995)
10. Nikolopoulos, D.S., Papatheodorou, T.S., Polychronopoulos, C.D., Labarta, J., Ayguadé, E.: Leveraging Transparent Data Distribution in OpenMP via User-Level Dynamic Page Migration. In: Valero, M., Joe, K., Kitsuregawa, M., Tanaka, H. (eds.) ISHPC 2000. LNCS, vol. 1940, pp. 415–427. Springer, Heidelberg (2000)
11. Noordergraaf, L., van der Pas, R.: Performance experiences on sun's wildfire prototype. In: Proceedings of the 1999 ACM/IEEE Conference on Supercomputing, SC 1999. ACM, New York (1999)
12. OpenMP ARB, OpenMP Application Program Interface, v. 4.0, http://www.openmp.org (last visited on September 05, 2014)
13. Terboven, C., an Mey, D., Schmidl, D., Jin, H., Reichstein, T.: Data and Thread Affinity in OpenMP Programs. In: Proceedings of the 2008 Workshop on Memory Access on Future Processors: A solved Problem? MAW 2008, pp. 377–384. ACM, New York (2008)
14. Terboven, C., Schmidl, D., Cramer, T., an Mey, D.: Assessing OpenMP Tasking Implementations on NUMA Architectures. In: Chapman, B.M., Massaioli, F., Müller, M.S., Rorro, M. (eds.) IWOMP 2012. LNCS, vol. 7312, pp. 182–195. Springer, Heidelberg (2012)
15. Terboven, C., Schmidl, D., Cramer, T., an Mey, D.: Task-Parallel Programming on NUMA Architectures. In: Kaklamanis, C., Papatheodorou, T., Spirakis, P.G. (eds.) Euro-Par 2012. LNCS, vol. 7484, pp. 638–649. Springer, Heidelberg (2012)

On the Algorithmic Aspects of Using OpenMP Synchronization Mechanisms: The Effects of Transactional Memory

Barna L. Bihari[1], Michael Wong[2], Bronis R. de Supinski[1], and Lori Diachin[1]

[1] Lawrence Livermore National Laboratory
[2] IBM Corporation
{bihari1,bronis,diachin2}@llnl.gov,
{michaelw}@ca.ibm.com

Abstract. In this paper we analyze the effects of using different OpenMP synchronization mechanisms in iterative mesh optimization algorithms run on the IBM Blue Gene/Q system. We perform a systematic study of a threaded Laplacian mesh smoothing method on Cartesian meshes of different sizes that have been initially perturbed by a factor that is random, but within a controlled range. We consider three different run modes, two of which are OpenMP synchronization mechanisms: (hardware) transactional memory (TM), OpenMP critical, and "none". We find that TM typically outperforms the other two modes in terms of its convergence characteristics. Because of the algorithmic simplicity and light operation count, the raw runtime performance was not our focus in this work; however, we present some results on TM scaling. We also show the TM rollback and conflict probabilities, and conclude that mesh optimization codes are good candidates for using TM when the more general "time-to-convergence" criterion is considered.

1 Introduction

Transactional memory (TM) [9] has long promised ease of use similar to coarse-grained locks, complemented by scaling comparable to fine-grained locks. TM also provides composability, leading to safe and scalable composition of software modules that can overcome the potential incomposability of locks. However, TM has suffered from being viewed as a panacea that can reduce the complexity in programming multicore systems and even to reduce energy consumption, especially for embedded devices.

TM has passed through the typical Gartner hype cycle for emerging technology [1]. Previously, TM reached a peak of inflated expectations that it would solve all difficulties of locked-based programming because of its usability promise. Subsequently, it descended into a trough of disillusionment as many realized that it cannot be used in all cases; like any promising technology, it has its inappropriate use cases. Recently, TM has risen through a slope of enlightenment with realization that it provides benefits for some use cases. Soon, it should approach a plateau of productivity, with hardware implementations on IBM's BG/Q, Power 8 and Intel's Haswell. Over the past two decades, TM has become progressively more efficient under the primary metric of runtime performance compared to serial code as well as other synchronization mechanisms such as OpenMP `atomic` and `critical`.

L. DeRose (Eds.): IWOMP 2014, LNCS 8766, pp. 115–129, 2014.
© Springer International Publishing Switzerland 2014

The first available hardware transactional memory (HTM), in IBM®'s Blue Gene/Q (BG/Q) [8,4], provided real evidence of significant gains in performance over software transactional memory (STM). For the first time, elegance, scalability and speed appeared to be within reach for OpenMP threaded code [15,16,4,20]. However, TM continues to be a non-standard OpenMP extension on the IBM Blue Gene/Q system. Other software language implementations exist for Intel's STM compiler [10], as well as an older IBM's Alphaworks STM compiler [17] . More recently, GNU 4.7 [5] included STM support based on the Draft C++ Software Transactional Memory Specification [7]. While C++ is likely to adopt TM as a non-normative specification [18], TM is unlikely to be part of C++ officially for at least another five years. Even then, it would not be available for Fortran or C.

While experimentation continues, to our knowledge no major scientific code has adopted TM, partly because it is still considered a new and exotic feature of many-core systems that takes time to take hold in industrial grade codes which are unlikely to adopt techniques that are not widely supported. However, commercially TM's use has taken off especially, in the Haskell community [14]. We expect TM usage to become much more common with the commercial availability of Intel's Haswell and IBM's Power8 support of HTM.

This paper explores a different aspect of synchronization or data sharing at thread boundaries. In our prior work [20,2,4,3], we used well-defined and exact measures of what happens when synchronization is absent and what the "right" answer should be. In the current work, however, we have an iterative scheme that will most likely converge to the correct answer even with no synchronization. Thus, we explore three synchronization choices in order to achieve the fastest overall solution of a simple Laplacian mesh smoothing algorithm. We use different mesh sizes and two different synchronization methods (TM and OpenMP `critical`) as well as not using any synchronization at all. We also vary the number of threads between 1 and 64. While the current prototype code does not have sufficient operation count to allow for a fair evaluation of raw performance, our preliminary studies are quite encouraging for TM when success is measured in terms of "time-to-quality" or "time-to-convergence."

The rest of this paper is organized as follows. Section 2 provides a status update on and general motivation for TM, while Section 3 gives a brief overview of the relatively unchartered territory of TM for scientific computing. Section 4 presents the algorithm that we use in this study, and Section 5 details our experimental results, including several runs that contrast existing OpenMP constructs with our proposed solution, with emphasis on our new performance measurement. Finally, Section 6 reviews our results and points to future possibilities for applying the ideas described in this work.

2   Why High-Level TM Support Is Needed

A transaction is an atomic sequence of steps that is intended to replace locks and condition variables. In contrast with compare-and-swap (CAS) and load-linked store-conditional (LL/SC), which at best can access contiguous memory atomically, transactions can operate on non-contiguous memory and, thus, better suit lock-free data structures and algorithms. Transactions also offer the promise of software composability to parallel programming, which is functionality that libraries require. TM will clearly be supported in some form by most of the major systems manufacturers in the near future.

TM has recently become more than research. Significant development has occurred in commercial HTM, from IBM's BG/Q (2011), to Intel's TSX code named Haswell (2012) and IBM's Power8 (2013). Production compilers that support this hardware include:

- IBM Alphaworks STM for BG
- IBM xlC z/OS V1R13 compiler,

while others provide a pure software implementation:

- Intel STM C/C++ compiler V12.2
- GNU 4.7 .

Most of these compilers use their own high-level language to create TM regions, or supply low-level built-in functions to access TM directly.

Similar to the birth of OpenMP, unified high-level language support for TM is clearly needed, given the many incompatible attempts by multiple vendors to supply it. In 2008, IBM, Intel, and Sun started joint teleconference discussions every other week to design this common support. This group has since been joined by HP, RedHat and academia. In 2009, a Version 1.0 of this support was released and was followed by version 1.1 in 2011, which added support for exceptions for C++. C++ was chosen as the base language because it has the most complex language features, in terms of polymorphism, exceptions, and memory model.

In 2012, this proposal was brought to the C++ Standard, which agreed to prepare for its adoption after examining many of the use cases, usability and performance claims. Thus, the C++ Standard formed Study Group 5 (SG5), led by one of our co-authors, to develop a complete proposal. In 2014, after two more years of collaboration to improve TM's fit into the C++ language, an official New Proposal (NP) has started and official Standard wording will soon follow. However, even with this progress, official TM language support in C++ will likely arrive at least five years from now. Support in C or Fortran is even further off. In fact, the ISO process still requires two years for an NP to become a *Technical Specification* then another 2-5 years for it to become a Standard. OpenMP could provide TM support much sooner because it can move much faster and get implementation status even earlier as it is moving toward a two-year ratification cycle with technical reports issued during the interim years.

OpenMP currently includes four synchronization mechanisms that serve as TM alternatives: locks, barriers, atomics and critical sections. However, they are limited in their performance and applicability or are difficult to use correctly in large and realistic programs such as a Quake server or a multi-physics simulation.. TM provides greater flexibility and ease of use. Our results show it can also provide performance advantages.

Using locks for synchronization on a per construct basis leads to fine-grained locking that can produce complex associations between data and synchronization as multiple locks are held and released through intersecting lifetimes. A failure to acquire and release these locks in the correct order can lead to deadlocks and data races. They are not composable and, thus, break modular programming. Alternatively, developers can use coarse-grained locking strategies. However, using few locks can lead to unnecessary convoying of execution and loss of performance. Developers can synthesize more directed synchronization mechanisms from OpenMP atomics. However, these techniques usually remain low level and suffer from problems similar to locks. Thus, we must use more advanced abstractions as OpenMP programs increase in size and complexity.

OpenMP barriers and critical sections provide higher level abstractions. However, barriers enforce synchronization across all threads in a team, which is frequently a much larger scope than the programmer requires. OpenMP critical sections provide a directed, high-level synchronization mechanism. However, the OpenMP specification precludes nesting of critical sections. Further, named critical sections allow additional complexity that is often unnecessary and undesirable. Overall, a shortcoming of the OpenMP specification is that it lacks a composable concurrency mechanism. None of the existing TM alternatives, or even lock elision, can offer composability without potential deadlocks.

Parallel programming is complex, whether it is developing the program, reasoning about the program or looking for bugs. TM provides a higher level of abstraction than existing OpenMP synchronization mechanisms without unnecessary restrictions or complexities. TM results in simpler design, simpler reasoning, and maintenance, while allowing specialized synchronization support for different platforms. Above all, it enables simple lexical or dynamic nesting and is composable across library interfaces.

This paper uses the IBM XL TM compiler for BG/Q, which is described extensively in various manuals such as [6] as well as studied in papers (see e.g. [4], [15], [16], among others). Since in our current work we are using the BG/Q hardware exclusively, we provide a brief summary here of its salient features. Each BG/Q compute node (A2 chip) has 16 cores, each of which can execute up to four hardware threads. The transactional memory conflict detection itself is implemented in hardware through the L2 cache which consists of 16 banks of 2MB each across a full crossbar from all the cores. Final synchronization is therefore achieved in the L2 cache. Conflict resolution, on the other hand, is achieved through the TM software stack which has several tuning parameters all described in [6]. This is a sophisticated piece of code that handles numerous fall-back scenarios with heuristics that aim to guarantee progress among all threads – if necessary, by serialization – while optimizing performance subject to user inputs via environmental variables. This is a unique strategy which is different from, for example, that of Intel's Haswell processor (see e.g. [21]). While the latter also uses a form of cache coherence protocol to detect conflicts, there is no inherent guarantee that the transaction will ever commit successfully. In fact, applications must actually provide a non-transactional fall-back mechanism which usually reverts to locks. It would certainly be a worthwhile exercise to compare IBM's and Intel's approaches in terms of convergence, scaling, as well as performance and user effort, but it is, at least for now, beyond the scope of the current work which focuses largely on a new proposed way to rethink performance itself for a class of numerical algorithms.

3   Transactional Memory for Scientific Computing

The arrival of multi- and many-core computer architectures brought about a renewed interest in TM as a possible avenue for threading new, and retrofitting legacy codes in the scientific computing arena. Indeed, the promise of simplicity, efficiency and guarantee of correctness was quite appealing. Our prior work in this area [2,15,4,3] as well as most of [16,21] emphasized a rigorous measure of correctness. In fact, we are not aware of any published bodies of work that even studied the applicability of TM to large scale high-performance numerical simulations; therefore existing definitions of correctness, beyond the obvious, are difficult to find. As a consequence, one typically reverts to the classic rigor of the "ACID" test as described by [13] and others. Of course, even this well-defined test is not always satisfied by most TM implementations, but at least it provides a baseline against which one may compare and contrast.

For BUSTM [2,4,3], for example, we clearly defined what "correct" meant, to which we could compare the results in both the deterministic and probabilistic running modes. We could precisely measure the difference between "correct" and "incorrect" either by a mathematical norm or by counting the wrong number of updates. Such comparisons turned out to be useful when we analyzed the TM statistics and the performance in both the TM and unsynchronized modes, as well as when using the OMP `atomic` and `critical` constructs.

However, several large classes of scientific computing problems have a *steady-state* to which the goal is to *converge* rather than to compute a one-step final answer or a multi-step time-accurate solution. These iterative schemes typically work on a computational domain discretized by a mesh, or a matrix, or some other finite list of computational elements that are ordered in some way. Threading iterative schemes is known to be non-trivial because of possible data dependencies as well as order-dependence. One of the greatest challenges is the non-reproducibility or non-serializability of the results in the exact sense. However, most of these schemes still *converge*, albeit at possibly very different rates. On the other hand, depending on the method, the "correctness" problem may still be present: sometimes in insidious ways and possibly leading to convergence to the wrong answer or even divergence. In any case, correctness now becomes a more difficult concept to quantify.

In the current work we consider a relatively large class of iterative problems: mesh optimization (e.g. [11,12]). Within this realm, much work has been done over the past couple of decades, but almost all codes step through some type of an iterative process, even if for only a few steps. Many codes exist for both structured and unstructured meshes and many different strategies are used for meshes of all types. These methods almost always try to use the "latest" information in a *Gauss-Seidel* fashion, versus "old" data that would correspond to a *Jacobi* iteration (analogies and terminology borrowed from iterative matrix methods). Therefore, the ordering of the mesh points or elements can make a huge difference, since that will also dictate the direction in which the information propagates. Reverting to a Jacobi iteration would remove this dependence, but would also double the memory requirements and greatly slow convergence due to stale neighbor information.

One can now quickly see the challenge of parallelizing such a highly order-dependent algorithm. First, the effect (positive or negative) of the parallelization on the ordering itself is unclear. Also, if threading is used either by itself or in addition to domain decomposition, the effect of how and when the mesh point updates are done is unclear and can be highly unpredictable. To our knowledge, TM has never been used in this

```
1
2 #pragma omp parallel for
3        for(int i=0; i < numFreeVerts; i++) {
4            int vertexID = freeVertexIDs[i];
5
6 // get attached vertex ids:
7            std::vector<Point2D*> &myAttachedVertices = attachedVertices[vertexID];
8
9            Point2D newX={0.0,0.0};
10           size_t numAttachedVertices = myAttachedVertices.size();
11
12 #pragma tm_atomic
13           {
14
15 // Step 1:  take average of neighbors
16           for(int j=0;j<numAttachedVertices;j++){
17             newX.x += myAttachedVertices[j]->x;
18             newX.y += myAttachedVertices[j]->y;
19           } // end for (over neighbor vertices)
20           newX.x = newX.x/numAttachedVertices;
21           newX.y = newX.y/numAttachedVertices;
22
23 // Step 2:  update current coordinates:
24           x[vertexID].x = newX.x/numAttachedVertices;
25           x[vertexID].y = newX.y/numAttachedVertices;
26           }       // end tm_atomic
27        }          // end for (over all vertices)
```

Fig. 1. Simple Laplacian mesh smoothing algorithm

context. In order to determine its effects, we use a relatively simple mesh smoothing code that currently works on 2-D unstructured meshes that have been converted from their corresponding structured Cartesian counterparts, as explained in the next section.

4   The Laplacian Mesh Smoother

4.1   The Algorithm

The code that we use in our experiments is a relatively simple C++ mesh smoothing algorithm that takes an initial (input) mesh and produces a final mesh as its output. The main for-loop visits each of the non-boundary interior mesh points and replaces its coordinates with the average of the coordinates of its neighbors:

$$\mathbf{x}_i^{(n+1)} = \frac{1}{N_i} \sum_{j=1}^{N_i} \mathbf{x}_j^{(m)} \tag{1}$$

where $\mathbf{x}$ is a 2- or 3-D vector, n is the current (old) iterate, $n + 1$ is the latest (new) iterate, N_i is the number of connected vertices for grid point i, and m can refer to either n or $n + 1$ depending on whether or not that point has already been updated or not. Figure 1 shows the relevant code section.

The #pragma tm_atomic directive is a non-standard OpenMP extension that is specific to the compiler used in our experiments. The associated brackets delimit a *transaction.* In our comparative experiments, we comment out this directive (the *unsync* mode) or replace it with an OpenMP `critical` construct (the *critical* mode).

If we restrict the "transaction" in Figure 1 to the coordinate update in "Step 2", no conflicts exist since each thread only updates the points that it owns. However, the neighboring coordinates might change during "Step 1" so the result could depend significantly on whether old or new data is used. In other words, we have a write-after-read (WAR) transaction for which we cannot use `#pragma omp atomic`. Thus, we will not compare *TM* to *atomic* as we did in our prior experiments of [4]. As alluded to in Section 2, atomics may be faster, but are not as versatile and composable as TM is.

4.2   The Role of Transactional Memory

While the algorithm of the previous section appears to be quite simple, the WAR-type update makes it unique in the way transactions are typically used. Often times the same variable is read from and written to within the same transaction, which is a simpler model than WAR, and which, at least for a single variable, is equivalent to the already existing `#pragma omp atomic` OpenMP standard and against which we compared, for example, in [4] where this was possible. In this code section, however, this is not possible. On the other hand, in theory it should be possible to use an array of locks, atomic reads and writes, domain decomposition for threads, various coloring schemes or cell-renumbering to achieve the same effect as TM offers. However, each of these alternatives would require a substantial amount of coding or even research to accomplish. When it comes to a comparable "human effort," `#pragma omp critical` is the only real alternative in this case.

Indeed, the way the TM hardware detects memory access conflicts has a profound influence on its overall behavior; the hardware is briefly reviewed in Section 4. Fortunately, the BG/Q implementation of TM offers two detection schemes: "eager" and "lazy." Among the many tuning parameters offered by the system in the form of environmental variables, the runtime variable `TM_ENABLE_INTERRUPT_ON_CONFLICT` informs the system whether or not threads receive interrupts immediately upon WAW, WAR, and RAW conflicts. Conflict arbitration is then based upon the age of the transactions and favors the survival of the older one. The default mode is *lazy*, which can be overwritten by setting this environmental variable rendering it an *eager*-type detection, which is precisely what we had to do in all subsequent numerical experiments to get the desired results. With this configuration, transactional memory will play a key role in altering the convergence characteristics of the mesh smoothing scheme itself and adding algorithmic aspects of its own to the overall performance of the method.

4.3   The Test Mesh

We keep the test mesh for our experiments simple as well. We start with an equal spaced, 2-D Cartesian-like mesh which is then distorted by a random, but bounded factor at each mesh point. Figure 2 shows an example where the original, randomized, and smoothed (converged) meshes are put in sequence. Relatively large disturbances are allowed as long as the mesh remains untangled (all elements have positive volume/areas). We then

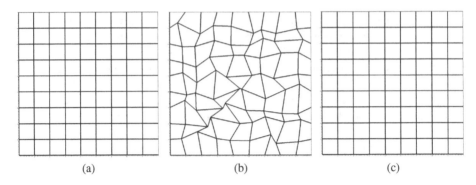

Fig. 2. (a) Original, (b) randomly distorted (input), and (c) converged (output) 10×10 mesh

apply the smoothing algorithm to this synthetically randomized mesh with the expectation that after a sufficient number of cycles the smoothed mesh will converge to the undistorted regular Cartesian grid, which is, in essence the same as the "original" mesh in Figure 2. That is, we know the "exact" solution precisely, so we can measure convergence. For convergent methods (and infinite series in a mathematical context) the residual and error, defined as "distance-to-exact", are equivalent measures in the sense that both either converge or diverge. However, the actual numerical values of these error functions will not necessarily decrease at the same rate. When the solution is known, as in the present case, the actual errors are more accurate and are therefore what we use in all subsequent figures.

5   Experimental Results

We now present several sets of computational experiments for our algorithm and test mesh. In each case, the original Cartesian mesh cells were 1×1 non-dimensional units in size, which are then disturbed by a random factor in the range of $(-0.5, 0.5)$ which is the largest distortion that still guarantees positive cell-areas as an initial condition. During the runs we vary the number of threads (1, 2, 4, 8, 16, 32, and 64) and use the two coarse-grain synchronization modes *TM* and *critical*, as well as *unsync*. Strictly speaking, the latter is not a valid OpenMP synchronization protocol, but nevertheless is very useful for comparison purposes. All run-modes start from the same initial conditions (i.e. same random seed); therefore, the sensitivity of convergence to this random parameter does not have to be taken into account.

We now analyze the convergence, the scaling, as well as the TM-specific characteristics of the results.

5.1   Convergence

We compute the l_1 norm of the distance between the current mesh point iterate and the ideal (exact) solution via:

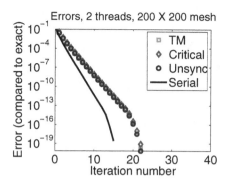

Fig. 3. Convergence on 2 threads

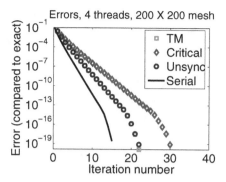

Fig. 4. Convergence on 4 threads

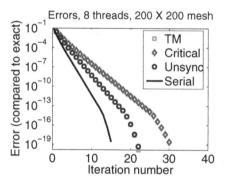

Fig. 5. Convergence on 8 threads

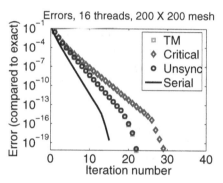

Fig. 6. Convergence on 16 threads

$$e^{(n)} = \frac{1}{M} \sum_{i=1}^{M} |\mathbf{x}_i^{(exact)} - \mathbf{x}_i^{(n)}| \qquad (2)$$

where (n) denotes the current iterate, M is the number of interior (non-boundary) vertices, and $\mathbf{x}_i$ is the coordinate vector of point i. The $(exact)$ supersript denotes the solution of the mesh optimization problem, which is known for our simple problem and which is the leftmost mesh on Figure 2. In all cases and run-modes we show next the mesh converged to the exact solution (to machine zero.)

As expected, on one thread all three modes yield identical answers to that of the serial version. We use that result as our reference solution in all plots. Figure 3 shows that convergence rates with 2 threads exhibit little difference, an expected result. However, Figures 4, 5 and 6 reveal that while with 4, 8 and 16 threads *TM* and *unsync* are still very close to each other, we can already see some differences showing between them and the *critical* versions. It may not be obvious at first, but the serial version should have the least error since each grid point has the most recent information from its neighbor. With more than one thread, the smoothing process starts from more than one grid point, each of which will have older information, on the average. In the limiting case with as

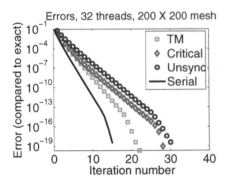
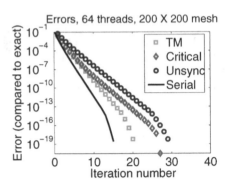

Fig. 7. Convergence on 32 threads   **Fig. 8.** Convergence on 64 threads

many threads as interior mesh points (say a 10×10 mesh with 64 interior points run on 64 threads), the mesh smoother would be identical to a Jacobi iteration assuming that they would all be synchronized at the beginning of the outer for-loop of Figure 1 so they would all proceed in lock-step.

As we increase the thread count to 32 (Figure 7) and 64 (Figure 8), we find an interesting trend: *TM* has much lower error than *critical*, which, in turn, has lower error than *unsync*. This difference arises from how TM and OpenMP critical synchronize threads: TM uses WAR type conflict resolution (as explained briefly in Section 4.2), and thereby has "fresher" information than *critical*, which, on a large number of threads, makes a significant difference.

5.2   Transactional Memory Statistics

We now present results obtained from the tm_print_stats() utility provided by the TM runtime on the BG/Q. At each iteration we observe the number of rollbacks that have occurred, as well as the total at the end of the run, including on a per-thread basis. In Figure 9, we see a relatively large (one order of magnitude) spread in the number of conflicts from iteration to iteration on low to moderate thread counts (2 to 8 threads). This range gradually decreases as we increase the thread count to 64 threads, which shows a high volatility (non-reproducability) in terms of TM rollbacks with low thread count. The volatility probably arises because the subdomain (loop index set) "owned" by each thread becomes smaller as we increase the number of threads. Thus, the chance of new collisions occuring at the iterate that did not occur at the previous one is reduced. We also find that on larger meshes the convergence trends are very similar, thus the results are not shown separately.

The results for conflict-prone threaded code in general, and with TM in particular, are always timing-sensitive. The number of rollbacks depends on the iteration or time step. Therefore, as in all of our previous work where we analyzed the behavior of TM for different representative workloads (e.g. [2,4,3], we typically repeat the same outer loop hundred(s) of times, both to get some statistical average, as well as to get an idea of the variation from iteration to iteration, as in Figure 9.

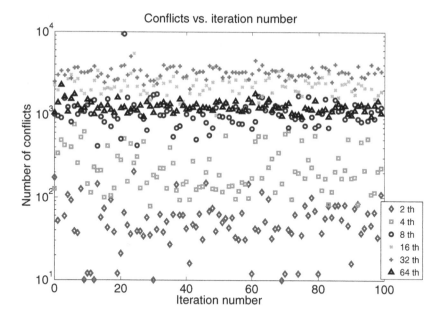

Fig. 9. Rollbacks per iteration on a 200×200 mesh on 2 through 64 threads

As we break down the total number of rollbacks for each thread (reported when the run ends) in Figure 11, the number of conflicts per specific threads is within the same order of magnitude when we run on a different number of threads, except for 64 threads, for which it is much lower. The cause of this exception may have to do with the unique, and quite regular mesh topology since the mesh was converted to unstructured bookkeeping from its structured counterpart. At 64 threads we may have also fallen below a threshold of "false conflicts" which may have been triggered with lower thread counts. False conflicts can occassionally be caused by many of the memory reads/writes falling on the same L2 cache line of 128 Bytes. The lower conflict volatility at 64 threads mentioned earlier may also play a role in the overall lower number of conflicts at the highest thread count.

Figure 10 shows the total number of conflicts for all thread counts. We observe a monotonic increase in the number of total conflicts (over all iterations) as the number of threads increases to 32, with a significant drop at 64 threads. The overall number of conflicts per transactions was between $0.27\% - 4.1\%$, attaining its maximum at 32 threads (see Figure 10); this satisfies the requirement of non-zero but low conflict probabilities that we typically pose for algorithms that are good use cases for TM.

5.3 A New Measure of Performance

As a recurring theme throughout this paper, performance of transactional memory has had varying levels of success. While our small test code and mesh are not intended to measure raw timings, they do provide an efficient tool to perform a systematic study for scaling, and, more importantly, to introduce another concept of *performance*: that

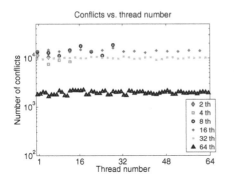

Fig. 10. Rollbacks per thread number on a 200 × 200 mesh on 2 through 64 threads

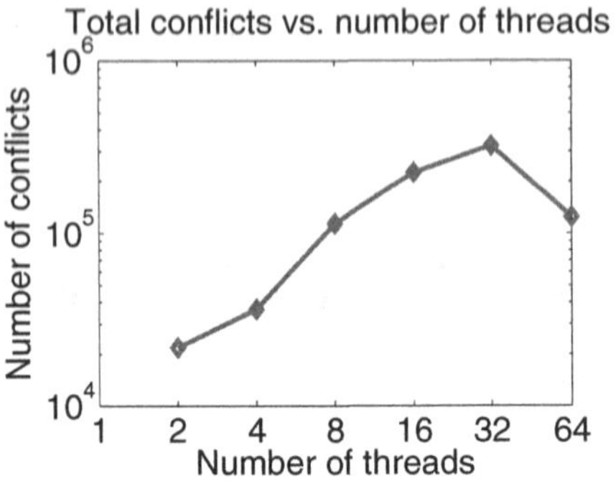

Fig. 11. Total number of rollbacks on a 200 × 200 mesh on 2 through 64 threads

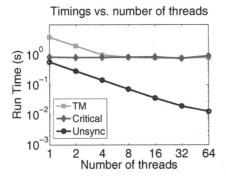
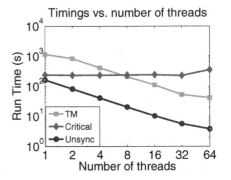

Fig. 12. Timings on a 200 × 200 mesh

Fig. 13. Timings on a 3200 × 3200 mesh

defined by the (run) time it takes to get an answer of a certain quality. Since iterative schemes are expected to yield successively "better" solutions at each iterate, we should not only measure the runtime to get to a certain iterate, but also the "quality" obtained by iterating a given number of steps. If we define quality $q^{(n)}$ at iterate n as the inverse of the error $e^{(n)}$ defined in equation (2), then the "run time per quality" $t_q^{(n)}$ becomes:

$$t_q^{(n)} = \frac{t^{(n)}}{q^{(n)}} = t^{(n)} e^{(n)}. \tag{3}$$

For purposes of comparison with this new measure, we first show (Figure 12) the traditional timing performance on a seconds vs. number of threads log-log plot for 1 through 64 threads for all modes: *TM*, *critical* and *unsync*. We stopped and timed the entire calculation at iteration 20; as shown on all of Figures 4 - 8 the salient iteration number appeared to be 20 where most calculations were about to converge, but the errors where still non-zero.

The message of Figure 12 is simple and expected. Not being burdened by any over-head or locking bottlenecks, *unsync* outperforms the other two in terms of runtime, as well as scaling. *TM* stops improving past 4 threads, and on fewer than 4 threads it

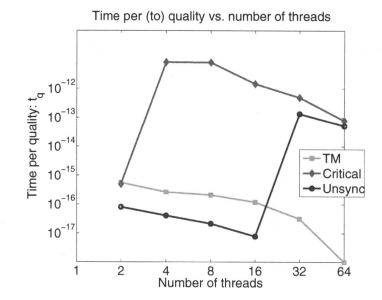

Fig. 14. Time per quality on a 200 × 200 mesh on up to 64 threads

is slower than even *critical*. Given the small mesh and a code with few floating point operations, this result is expected.

We demonstrate that the *TM* version can scale well by using a mesh that was two orders of magnitude larger: 3200 × 3200. Figure 13 shows the results. The plots confirm good scaling for both *TM* and *unsync*, with the latter being consistently faster by about an order of magnitude. On the other hand, *critical* does not scale and it does not exhibit any qualitative change from Figure 12. As before, *critical* becomes slightly worse as the thread count increases, but it is, in absolute terms, faster than *TM* on up to 4 threads.

However, when we actually weigh the total runtime spent by how much we gain in terms of reducing the error and plot t_q as defined in equation (3) instead of t, we find that *TM* outperforms *critical* by several orders of magnitude on all except 2 threads, and scales well all the way up to 64 threads (Figure 14). Moreover, *TM* yields significantly better time-per-quality at 32 and 64 threads than even *unsync*. At the highest thread count, *TM* is superior to even *unsync* at *any* thread count, probably because of its unique synchronization method, which is typically more accurate than *critical* at all thread counts and usually also faster at the higher thread counts. Note that the data in Figure 14 is, in some sense, a compilation of snapshots of Figures 4 - 8 convolved with those of Figure 12.

It must also be re-emphasized that, while in this simple case all three modes of running eventually converge to the right answer, the *unsync* version is, strictly speaking, non-conforming OpenMP code since it completely ignores memory conflicts and has data races. We include the unsynchronized results in this paper for the mere purpose of a baseline performance comparison to the other two "correct" synchronization mechanisms.

6 Conclusions and Future Work

We studied different OpenMP synchronization mechanisms using an iterative Laplacian mesh-smoothing algorithm on Cartesian-like meshes, but connected via unstructured bookkeeping. Since the exact solution was known, we could make quantitative measurements of the error, or "distance to exact" and, in turn, use it to define a new measure of performance, which takes into account not just the elapsed cpu-time but the quality that is obtained by iterating during that time. By comparing TM to OpenMP `critical` and a completely unsynchronized version of the code, we find that *TM* always outperforms *critical*, and in some cases even the unsynchronized version.

While more studies are needed, this iterative mesh smoothing scenario appears to be a good use case for TM, and along with [2,4,19] can be considered another small step towards adoption of TM into the OpenMP standard. To this end, we plan to experiment with more complicated unstructured mesh types as well as extend this work to production quality mesh optimizers such as that of [12]. As different hardware implementations of TM become available from more commercial vendors, we also hope to test our codes on the new and emerging TM platforms as well.

Acknowledgments. The authors wish to thank Pat Knupp of Dihedral LLC for many fruitful discussions.

This article (LLNL-CONF-654956) has been authored in part by Lawrence Livermore National Security, LLC under Contract DE-AC52-07NA27344 with the U.S. Department of Energy. In addition, this material is also based upon work supported by the U.S. Department of Energy, Office of Science, Office of Advanced Scientific Computing Research (ASCR). Accordingly, the United States Government retains and the publisher, by accepting the article for publication, acknowledges that the United States Government retains a non-exclusive, paid-up, irrevocable, world-wide license to publish or reproduce the published form of this article or allow others to do so, for United States Government purposes.

References

1. Gartner Hype Cycle (May 2014), http://www.gartner.com/technology/research/methodologies/hype-cycle.jsp
2. Bihari, B.L.: Applicability of transactional memory to modern codes. In: Conference Proceedings of International Conference on Numerical Analysis and Applied Mathematics (ICNAAM 2010), Rodos, Greece, pp. 1764–1767. APS (2010)

3. Bihari, B.L.: Transactional Memory for Unstructured Mesh Simulations. J. Sci. Comput. 54, 311–332 (2012)
4. Bihari, B.L., Wong, M., Wang, A., de Supinski, B.R., Chen, W.: A Case for Including Transactions in OpenMP II: Hardware Transactional Memory. In: Chapman, B.M., Massaioli, F., Müller, M.S., Rorro, M. (eds.) IWOMP 2012. LNCS, vol. 7312, pp. 44–58. Springer, Heidelberg (2012)
5. GNU. TM in GCC (May 2014),
   https://gcc.gnu.org/wiki/TransactionalMemory
6. IBM Compiler Group. IBM XL C/C++ for Blue Gene/Q, V12.1 Compiler Reference (2012)
7. TM Specification Drafting Group (May 2014),
   https://sites.google.com/site/tmforcplusplus/,
   https://sites.google.com/site/tmforcplusplus/
8. Ruud Haring and the IBM BlueGene Team. The IBM Blue Gene/Q Compute Chip. In: Hot Chips 24: A Symposium on High Performance Chips, Palo Alto, CA (2011)
9. Herlihy, M., Moss, J.E.B.: Transactional memory: Architectural support for lock-free data structures. SIGARCH Comput. Archit. News 51(2), 289–300 (1993)
10. Intel. Intel C++ STM Compiler, Prototype Edition (May 2014),
    https://software.intel.com/en-us/articles/
    intel-c-stm-compiler-prototype-edition
11. Knupp, P.: Hexahedral and Tetrahedral Mesh Shape Optimization. Intl. J. Numer. Meth. Engr. 58, 319–332 (2003)
12. Knupp, P.: Introducing the Target-matrix Paradigm for Mesh Optimization via Node-Movement. In: Proceedings of the 19th International Meshing Roundtable, pp. 67–83. Springer (2010)
13. Larus, J.R., Kozyrakis, C.: Transactional memory: Is TM the answer for improving parallel programming? Communications of the ACM 51(7), 80–88 (2008)
14. Haskell Community Page. Software Transactional Memory (May 2014),
    http://www.haskell.org/haskellwiki/
    Software_transactional_memory
15. Schindewolf, M., Gyllenhaal, J., Bihari, B.L., Wang, A., Schulz, M., Karl, W.: What Scientific Applications Can Benefit from Hardware Transacional Memory? In: Int. Conf. for High Perf. Computing, Networking, Storage and Analysis, SC 2012 (2012)
16. Wang, A., Gaudet, M., Wu, P., Ohmacht, M., Amaral, J.N., Barton, C., Silvera, R., MIchael, M.: Evaluation of Blue Gene/Q Hardware Support for Transactional Memories. In: PACT (2012)
17. Wong, M.: IBM XL C/C++ for Transactional Memory for AIX. 2008 (August 2009),
    http://www-949.ibm.com/software/rational/cafe/blogs/
    ccpp-parallel-multicore/2009/08/11/
    ibms-alphaworks-software-transactional-memory-compiler
18. Wong, M.: C++14: The New Standard, Through the Looking Glass: The View from the Feb 2014 C++ Standard meeting (May 2014), http://tinyurl.com/mzs22qw
19. Wong, M., Ayguade, E., Gottschlich, J., Luchangco, V., de Supinski, B.R., Bihari, B.L.: Towards Transactional Memory for OpenMP. In: IWOMP 2014 Conference Proceedings, Salvador, Brazil (to appear June 2014)
20. Wong, M., Bihari, B.L., de Supinski, B.R., Wu, P., Michael, M., Liu, Y., Chen, W.: A case for including transactions in OpenMP. In: Sato, M., Hanawa, T., Müller, M.S., Chapman, B.M., de Supinski, B.R. (eds.) IWOMP 2010. LNCS, vol. 6132, pp. 149–160. Springer, Heidelberg (2010)
21. Yoo, R., Hughes, C., Lai, K., Rajwar, R.: Performance Evaluation of Intel Transactional Synhcornization Extensions for High-Performance Computing. In: Int. Conf. for High Perf. Computing, Networking, Storage and Analysis, SC 2013 (2013)

Towards Transactional Memory for OpenMP

Michael Wong[1], Eduard Ayguadé[2],
Justin Gottschlich[3], Victor Luchangco[4], Bronis R. de Supinski[5], Barna Bihari[5],
and other members of the WG21 SG5 Transactional Memory Sub-Group

[1] IBM
[2] BSC
[3] Intel
[4] Oracle
[5] LLNL

Abstract. The OpenMP specification lacks a composable shared memory concurrency mechanism: the current OpenMP concurrency mechanisms, such as OMP critical, locks, or atomics, do not support composition. In this paper, we motivate the need for transactional memory (TM) in OpenMP. The chief reason is to support composition of realistic programs, but we also consider whether TM is easier to program than locks, the use case for TM, and whether a software-only TM can outperform traditional locking through a survey of recent publications. This paper advances upon previous proposals of OpenMP TM by introducing a new construct specifically to handle irrevocable actions, which is also composable. It also proposes a pure atomic transaction construct as well as the concept of transaction safety. Further, we examine how our proposed construct integrates with current OpenMP constructs.

1 Introduction

Locks and atomics are often described as not being *composable*: using locks or atomics to synchronize access to shared data makes it difficult to construct large programs out of smaller pieces. Thus, these synchronization mechanisms do not support modular programming [1]. As multithreaded programs increase in size and complexity, more advanced abstractions are needed to mitigate the programming complexity that arises from frequent use of synchronization in large-scale software systems. We propose transactional memory (TM) for OpenMP and show that TM provides stricter correctness guarantees than other OpenMP concurrency techniques and may be easier to use.

2 Limitations of OpenMP Concurrency Techniques

OpenMP V4.0 [2] (the latest release) includes four synchronization mechanisms: locks, barriers, atomics and critical sections [3]. These mechanisms synchronize objects in shared memory but unnecessarily limit performance or can be challenging to use properly. TM provides greater flexibility and ease of use and in the case of template programming, or callback-style programming, TM offers correctness, which none of the other constructs offer.

L. DeRose (Eds.): IWOMP 2014, LNCS 8766, pp. 130–145, 2014.

Mutual exclusion, implemented as critical sections, is perhaps the most common form of concurrency control for shared memory parallel programming. In general, mutual exclusion ensures program correctness by limiting access to shared memory variables to one thread at a time. This restriction is achieved in OpenMP using mutually exclusive locks, also known as OpenMP locks or critical sections. To access a shared memory variable, a thread must first acquire the lock that protects the shared memory variable. When the thread has completed its access to the shared memory variable, it releases the lock. Although mutual exclusion may seem to be straightforward and easy to apply, it is notoriously challenging to write both correct and efficient large-scale multithreaded software using mutual exclusion [4].

A less common way to synchronize access to shared data is to write nonblocking algorithms using nonblocking atomic primitives, such as compare-and-swap (CAS), or load-linked and store-conditional (LL/SC), or more recently, C++ and OpenMP atomic types. This is how most OpenMP barriers or atomics are implemented. Although it can often yield substantial concurrency, using these kinds of synchronization primitives to correctly build even simple data structures, such as queues, can be challenging [4]. Thus, their nontrivial use is typically limited to expert parallel programmers.

Lock elision is another possible speculative technique that has been proposed [5], in which locks are not acquired (i.e., they are elided) when there are no conflicts on the data they protect. By reducing unnecessary synchronization, lock elision may increase throughput without changing the programming interface. Although this is an advantage for backward compatibility, it means that lock elision does not reduce the challenge of writing multithreaded software: programmers must still write correct locking schemes for their multithreaded software.

3 Motivation for Transactional Memory in OpenMP

The synchronization types available in OpenMP are OpenMP critical section, barrier, mutex (or lock), and atomic, as discussed in prior work [6,7]. Locks and atomics are basic abstractions used to control the reading and writing of shared memory [4]. Threads communicate using shared memory, which is synchronized using locks or atomics to ensure the threads see a consistent view of such shared memory. However, locks and atomics are notoriously difficult to use [8]. Simple coarse-grained locking strategies, which protect all program data using one or few locks, lead to unnecessary serialization of program execution and generally degrade performance. Sophisticated fine-grained locking or the use of atomics usually results in a complex (and unenforced) association between data and the synchronization constructs (e.g., locks) used to protect access to that data. Because these associations are typically complex and unchecked, a programmer can easily use them incorrectly, leading to concurrency errors such as data races and deadlocks. Moreover, synchronization strategies designed to work well on one platform often perform poorly on a platform with a different number of hardware threads or a different cost for synchronization primitives.

Another serious deficiency with current synchronization mechanisms is that they do not support *composition*, that is, combining multiple operations into a single compound operation. For example, in a system that uses locks to synchronize data access, when two functions, $A()$ and $B()$, that acquire and release the appropriate locks internally are called in sequence by one thread, other threads can generally observe $A()$ and $B()$ as individual operations. To ensure that other threads observe $A()$ and $B()$ as a single atomic operation, that is, to *compose* $A()$ and $B()$, a programmer must use some kind of external synchronization. Typically, the program acquires the locks of both $A()$ and $B()$ before either is called, and holds these locks until both $A()$ and $B()$ complete. This exposes the internals of these functions, violating modularity. Furthermore, this approach may lead to deadlock. For example, one thread may acquire the locks for $A()$ and then attempt to acquire those for $B()$, while another thread acquires the locks for $B()$ and then attempts to acquire those for $A()$, resulting in deadlock. The usual way to prevent deadlock is for all threads to agree on an order in which locks must be acquired (i.e., a lock does not be acquired while a "later" lock is held). But enforcing this order is difficult, if not impossible, in large software systems. In *The Problem with Threads* [9], Edward Lee illustrates this problem with a simple practical example (the observer pattern) in the context of Java; similar examples can be constructed in C++. Implementing this pattern with locks turns out to be nearly impossible. The article's title notwithstanding, the problem lies not with threads, but with locks: With transactions, this pattern can be written almost as easily for a multithreaded program as for a single-threaded one.

When atomics are used to synchronize access to shared memory, the situation is no better. Indeed, it is arguably worse: there is no simple generic technique (i.e., analogous to two-phase locking) for composing functions that use atomics to perform shared memory operations into a single large atomic operation.

In general, the use of fine-grain mechanisms makes concurrent programs more difficult to write, debug and reason about, and this increases exponentially with the complexity of the program. On the other hand, traditional coarse-grain mutual exclusion inhibits parallel execution, which is necessary to achieve good performance on modern multiprocessors. Using transactions rather than locks avoids the need to associate shared data with their metadata (e.g., the lock that protects each piece of data), remember this association, and use it appropriately when accessing the data. By leaving these tasks to the system, a programmer can write relatively simple code (akin to using coarse-grain locks) while the system may use fine-grain mechanisms to achieve high performance. The resulting programs are likely to be simpler, and thus easier to write, debug, maintain and reason about, and the underlying systems can be specialized for different platforms, and can be improved without requiring changes to application code.

For these reasons, we propose that OpenMP be extended to include transactional language constructs, or for short, transactional memory (TM). Our proposal and its integration into OpenMP are described in detail in Section 4. Some key benefits of TM compared to locks are discussed in our paper [10] that motivated the C++ Standards Committee to start a new Work Item and form Study Group 5 (i.e., SG5: Transactional Memory). Extending OpenMP to include TM will improve the modularity of concurrent libraries, make OpenMP easier to teach and learn, and supply a programming model for architectures based on IBM's Blue Gene/Q and Power8, and Intel's Haswell RTM. This is especially important as OpenMP moves further into the commercial development space as well as remaining relevant for scientific workloads.

3.1 Background

Several studies have investigated the trade-off between programmability and performance with TM compared to locks, looking at programs for Delaunay triangulation [11], minimum spanning forest of sparse graphs [12], Lee's routing algorithm [13], and the Quake game server, such as QuakeTM [14], Atomic Quake [15] (based on a lock-based version of Quake [16]), and SynQuake [17], among others. Many of these works use software implementations of transactional memory (STM), where TM is implemented entirely in software, which tend to execute transactions more slowly than systems that execute transactions in hardware (HTM) or that use hardware and software jointly (Hybrid TM, or HyTM for short). There has also been an effort to create benchmark suites for STM, including STMBench7 [18], STAMP [19] and RMS-TM [20], all of which include several applications that represent a variety of domains.

As several of these studies demonstrate, STM *can* be faster than locks in real world applications, not just toy laboratory benchmarks. For example, SynQuake [17] reimplements a lock-based Quake game server using STM, to examine the performance and scalability of TM without hardware support. Scaling a game server by parallelizing multi-player game code is difficult because game code is typically complex and includes the use of spatial data structures for collision detection, as well as other dynamic artifacts that require conservative synchronization. Player actions usually include dynamically evolving sub-actions: a person may move while shifting items in their backpack, throwing an object at a distance, grabbing a nearby object, and/or shooting, which together constitute a single player action. Since the terrain within the potentially affected area may contain mutable objects, all sub-actions must be processed as an atomic, consistent unit when detecting collision with other player actions. This code may induce substantial contention due to both false and true sharing between threads, in a parallel lock-based game implementation [16]. Thus, conservatively acquiring locks at the beginning of the action and holding these locks until the end of the action induces unnecessary conflicts by locking more objects, and holding these locks for longer, than necessary. Fine-grain locking of the action sequence led to problems with deadlocks and inconsistent views. In contrast, by implementing player actions with transactions, the atomicity and consistency of the player action is provided by the underlying TM, which tracks accesses to shared and private data and detects and resolves conflicts automatically: the transaction simply commits if there is no conflict with another player, or rolls back if conflict occurs. In this work, STM support reduced the number and duration of conflicts due to false sharing. The result was that the STM-based implementation was about 33% faster than the lock-based one with 4–8 threads under medium contention, and it scales better in all cases of low, medium and high contention.

Other studies have investigated the usability of TM, trying to assess the claim that concurrent programming with transactional memory is easier than using other alternatives such as locks. For example, Rossbach et al. [21] asked students to program in three different ways: with coarse-grain locks, fine-grain locks or TM. In this study, programs using fine-grain locking were more likely to contain errors than those using coarse-grain locks or TM. The most common error was acquiring a lock and never releasing it. Students reported that TM was harder to program (in part because of the lack of TM documentation) than coarse-grain locks but easier than fine-grain locks. Another study [22] created separate teams working on locks and on TM to implement a search application. Although the average lines of code (LOC) for the whole program was not strongly correlated with the use of locks or TM, the TM teams had fewer LOC with parallel constructs. The TM teams spent more time thinking sequentially about their code, and less time on parallelizing their code before moving on to performance testing. Nonetheless, a TM team had the first working parallel version, even though they subjectively believed they advanced slowly. By the project deadline, all of the teams except for one TM team (the team with the least experience) had executable parallel search engines, though only one (a lock team) was able to handle all the test queries, and one of the TM teams was deemed to have the best overall performance. This mixed result suggests that TM still is not a panacea for parallel programming: it still requires good programmers. But it does suggest that TM has promise compared to fine-grain locking for large and complex parallel programming tasks.

Two proposals for adding transactional memory support within the OpenMP programming interface were presented around the same time in 2007 [23,7]. The topic has reborn with a more recent proposal [3], presenting results using hardware transactional memory, which can significantly reduce the complexity of shared memory programming while retaining efficiency. This work extended a previous work [6] that demonstrated that even with the relatively high overheads of software implementations, transactions could outperform OpenMP critical sections.

Gottschlich and Boehm [24] demonstrate that locks are an insufficient synchronization mechanism for generic (i.e., template) programming in C++. They argue that because the locking order required by a client program cannot be known when a programmer is creating his or her template library, which may eventually call-back into client code that uses locks, it is not possible to guarantee that any such program will not deadlock. They then show that TM naturally solves this problem because transactions do not impose ordering constraints and because they are composable.

In conclusion, they debunk the popular notion that an enforced lock ordering is guaranteed to avoid deadlock, showing that such an approach is essentially impossible in C++ template programming. This is a form of callback-style programming that exists in C and Fortran and ignores the question of whether TM is useful for performance and programmability, and instead demonstrates that TM may actually be necessary for correctness for multithreaded programs that use shared memory.

Gottschlich and Boehm further argue that what makes generic programming different from prior examples is that many of the function and operator calls used within C++ templates are type-dependent, and are likely to be user-defined, meaning, in many cases, such calls are essentially callback functions. These callbacks may include operations like C++ assignment operators, constructors, and syntactically invisible destructors, and possibly even syntactically invisible constructors and destructors of expression temporaries. In all cases, such operations are likely to acquire locks if, for example, an object requires access to a shared resource, which is usually needed at least at construction, assignment, and destruction time. In order to enforce a lock ordering, the author of any generic function acquiring locks (or that could possibly be called while holding a lock) would have to reason about the locks that could potentially be acquired by any of these operators, in any order, which appears thoroughly intractable as these types do not even exist when the generic programmer is writing his or her template code. With all of this in mind, Gottschlich and Boehm conclude that locks should be forbidden in templates and callbacks, and that transactions should be used instead.

3.2 Transactional Language Constructs and C++

In 2008, IBM, Intel, and Sun Microsystems (later acquired by Oracle) began work on "The Draft Specification of Transactional Language Constructs for C++" which aimed to design a set of language interfaces for TM in C++ [25]. In August 2009, version 1.0 of their specification was released to the public. The group subsequently expanded its membership to include representatives from HP and Red Hat and, in February 2012, released version 1.1 of their specification, which included support for exceptions. In February of 2012, they presented their specification to the Standard C++ Committee. In July of 2012, after several months of examining use cases, usability, and performance claims of TM, the Standard C++ Committee requested that the TM group form a Standard C++ Study Group, called Study Group 5: Transactional Memory (SG5, for short) [26], which is now working with the C++ Standards Committee with the goal of creating an acceptable set of transactional language constructs for Standard C++.

SG5 chose the C++ Programming Language for a variety of reasons. Firstly, Intel and Sun Microsystems were, at the time, working on adding TM support to their respective C++ compilers and wanted to enable cross-compiler support for TM. Secondly, the group wanted to add TM support to a language that was used by a large, active community where its integration into the language would naturally align with the language's future direction. C++11 was on the horizon when the C++ TM group formed in 2008, and it was well known that multithreaded support for C++ was being seriously considered; in this sense, C++ was nearly an ideal fit for TM. Moreover, C++ was a language where the majority of members of the TM group were comfortable, if not extremely well versed.

The proposal we present in this paper lifts certain aspects from the C++ SG5 proposal [27], merges with the BSC OpenMP proposal [7], while using the experience from IBM's BG/Q HTM design [28] and adapts it to the existing OpenMP Language to offer an initial design for TM in OpenMP for the future integration with C, C++, and Fortran.

4 A Proposal for an OpenMP Transactional Memory Technical Report

We introduce two kinds of blocks to exploit transactional memory: *synchronized blocks* in Section 4.2 and *atomic blocks* called *OMP transaction* (as a keyword placeholder) in Section 4.1. Synchronized blocks behave as if all synchronized blocks were protected by a single global recursive mutex. Atomic blocks (also called *atomic transactions*, or just *transactions*) appear to execute atomically and not concurrently with any synchronized block (unless the atomic block is executed within the synchronized block).

Some operations are prohibited within atomic blocks because it may be impossible, difficult, or expensive to support executing them in atomic blocks; such operations are called *transaction-unsafe*. An atomic block also specifies how to handle an exception thrown but not caught within the atomic block. User cancellation can be supported through the OpenMP cancellation feature.

Some noteworthy points about synchronized and atomic blocks:

Data races. Operations executed within synchronized or atomic blocks do not form data races with each other. However, they may form data races with operations not executed within any synchronized or atomic block. As usual, programs with data races have undefined semantics.

Exceptions. When an exception is thrown but not caught within an atomic block, the effects of operations executed within the block may take effect or be discarded, or terminate may be called. This behavior is specified by an additional keyword in the atomic block statement, as described in Section 4.1. An atomic block whose effects are discarded is said to be *canceled*. An atomic block that completes without its effects being discarded, and without calling terminate, is said to be *committed*.

Transaction-safety. As mentioned above, transaction-unsafe operations are prohibited within an atomic block. As a practical matter, some code is considered transaction-unsafe because we do not know effective ways to execute it atomically without special hardware support. This restriction applies not only to code in the body of an atomic block, but also to code in the body of functions called (directly or indirectly) within the atomic block. To support static checking of this restriction, we introduce pragmas to declare that a function or function pointer is transaction-safe, and augment the type of a function or function pointer to specify whether it is transaction-safe. We also introduce a pragma to explicitly declare that a function is *not* transaction-safe.

To reduce the burden of declaring functions transaction-safe, a function is assumed to be transaction-safe if its definition does not contain any transaction-unsafe code and it is not explicitly declared transaction-unsafe. Furthermore, unless declared otherwise, a non-virtual function whose definition is unavailable is assumed to be transaction-safe. (This assumption does *not* apply to virtual functions because the callee is not generally known statically to the caller.) These assumptions are checked at link time.

4.1   Atomic Blocks

This is a pure form of a transaction and is based on combining the C++ SG5 [29] proposal and BSC's OpenMP TM extension proposal [7].

An *atomic block* can be written in one of the following forms:

#pragma omp transaction *[clause[[,] clause]...]* { *body* }

The clause following *transaction* can specify the atomic block's *exception specifier*. It specifies the behavior when an exception escapes the transaction or an OpenMP cancel occurs within the TM region:

  – noexcept: This is undefined behavior and is not allowed; no side effects of the transaction can be observed.

- `commitonesc`: The transaction is committed and the exception is thrown.
- `cancelonesc`: If the exception is transaction-safe (defined below), the transaction is canceled and the exception is thrown. Otherwise, it is undefined behavior. In either case, no side effects of the transaction can be observed.

Code within the body of a transaction must be *transaction-safe* (i.e. it must not be transaction-unsafe). Code is *transaction-unsafe* if:

- it contains an initialization of, assignment to, or a read from a volatile object;
- it is a transaction-unsafe `asm` declaration (the definition of a transaction-unsafe `asm` declaration is implementation-defined); or
- it contains a call to a transaction-unsafe function, or through a function pointer that is not transaction-safe

While we have pragma syntax to allow declaring and defining functions for transaction safety, we do not show it here due to space constraints.

Synchronization via locks and atomic objects is not allowed within atomic blocks (operations on these objects are calls to transaction-unsafe functions in the current proposal).

Jumping into the body of an atomic block using `goto` or `switch` is prohibited.

The body of an atomic block appears to take effect atomically: no other thread sees any intermediate state of an atomic block, nor does the thread executing an atomic block see the effects of any operation of other threads interleaved between the steps within the atomic block.

The evaluation of any atomic block synchronizes with every evaluation of any atomic or synchronized block by another thread, so that the evaluations of non-nested atomic and synchronized blocks across all threads are totally ordered by the synchronizes-with relation. Thus, a memory access within an atomic block does not race with any other memory access in an atomic or synchronized block. However, a memory access within an atomic block may race with conflicting memory accesses not within any atomic or synchronized block. The exact rules for defining data races are defined by the memory model Section 4.5.

As usual, programs with data races have undefined semantics.

Although it has no observable effects, a canceled atomic block may still participate in data races.

This proposal provides "closed nesting" semantics for nested atomic blocks.

Use of atomic blocks. Atomic blocks are intended in part to replace many uses of mutexes for synchronizing memory access, simplifying the code and avoiding many problems introduced by mutexes (e.g., deadlock). We expect that some implementations of atomic blocks will exploit hardware and software transactional memory mechanisms to improve performance relative to mutex-based synchronization. Nonetheless, programmers should still endeavor to reduce the size of atomic blocks and the conflicts among atomic blocks and with synchronized blocks: poor performance is likely if atomic blocks are too large or concurrent conflicting executions of atomic and synchronized blocks are common.

The following code illustrates with a bank account example the atomicity of atomic blocks.

```
1 class Account {
2    int bal;
3  public:
4    Account(int initbal) { bal = initbal; };
5
6    void deposit(int x) {
7      #pragma omp transaction noexcept {
8        this.bal += x;
9      }
10   };
11
12   void withdraw(int x) {
13     deposit(-x);
14   };
15
16   int balance() { return bal; }
17 }
18
19 void transfer(Account a1, a2; int x;) {
20   #pragma omp transaction noexcept {
21     a1.withdraw(x);
22     a2.deposit(x);
23   }
24 };
25
26 Account a1(0), a2(100);
27
28 Thread 1                    Thread 2
29 ──────                      ──────
30
31 transfer(a1, a2, 50);       #pragma omp transaction noexcept {
32                               r1 = a1.balance() + a2.balance();
33                             }
34                             assert(r1 == 100);
```

The assert cannot fire, because the transfer happens atomically and the two calls to `balance` happen atomically.

Example demonstrating need for transaction_cancelonesc. Here, we extend the above example slightly so that transactions are logged by a function that may throw an exception, for example due to allocation failure.

```
1 void deposit(int x) {
2   #pragma omp transaction cancelonesc {
3     log_deposit(x);          // might throw
4     this.bal += x;
5   }
6 }
7
8 void withdraw(int x) {
9   deposit(-x);
10 }
11
12 void transfer(account a1, a2; int x;) {
13   try {
14     #pragma omp transaction cancelonesc {
15       a1.withdraw(x);
16       a2.deposit(x);
17     } catch (...) {
18       printf("Transfer_failed");
19     }
20   }
21 }
```

If the call from `transfer()` to `a2.deposit()` throws an exception, we should not simply commit the transaction, because the withdrawal has happened but the deposit has not. Canceling the transaction provides an easy way to recover to a good state, without violating the invariant the transaction in `transfer()` is intended to preserve. In this simple example, an error message is printed indicating that the transfer did not happen.

Default behavior. The default for atomic transactions without any of the three clauses (`noexcept`, `commitonesc`, `cancelonesc`) is as if the user wrote `cancelonesc`. This offers a pure transaction that rolls back. The other two optional clauses (`noexcept` and `commitonesc`) do not rollback and therefore offer no invariance protection. But they do still offer advanced synchronization ability. However, they are still limited in that they cannot have any transaction unsafe actions. We show in the next section how to handle transactions with transaction unsafe actions.

4.2 Synchronized Blocks

The synchronized blocks variant is a simple replacement for locks that is composable and offers only a synchronization ability with no invariance protection. Furthermore, synchronized blocks can become irrevocable in the presence of unsafe actions and that distinguishes it from an atomic transaction.

A *synchronized block* has the following form:

    #pragma omp synchronized { *body* }

The evaluation of any synchronized block synchronizes with every evaluation of any synchronized block (whether it is an evaluation of the same block or a different one) by another thread, so that the evaluations of non-nested synchronized blocks across all threads are totally ordered by the synchronizes-with relation as defined by C++ and Java memory model. That is, the semantics of a synchronized block is equivalent to having a single global recursive mutex that is acquired before executing the body and released after the body is executed (unless the synchronized block is nested within another synchronized block). Thus, an operation within a synchronized block never forms a data race with any other operation within a synchronized block (the same block or a different one).

Entering and exiting a nested synchronized block (i.e., a synchronized block within another synchronized block) has no effect.

Jumping into the body of a synchronized block using `goto` or `switch` is prohibited.

Use of synchronized blocks. Synchronized blocks are intended in part to address some of the difficulties with using mutexes for synchronizing memory access by raising the level of abstraction and providing greater implementation flexibility [24] With synchronized blocks, a programmer need not associate locks with memory locations, nor obey a locking discipline to avoid deadlock: Deadlock cannot occur if synchronized blocks are the only synchronization mechanism used in a program.

Although synchronized blocks can be implemented using a single global mutex, we expect that some implementations of synchronized blocks will exploit recent hardware and software mechanisms for transactional memory to improve performance relative to mutex-based synchronization. For example, threads may use speculation and conflict detection to evaluate synchronized blocks concurrently, discarding speculative outcomes if conflict is detected. Programmers should still endeavor to reduce the size of synchronized blocks and the conflicts between synchronized blocks: poor performance is likely if synchronized blocks are too large or concurrent conflicting evaluations of synchronized blocks are common. In addition, certain operations, such as I/O, cannot be executed speculatively, so their use within synchronized blocks may hurt performance.

Example

The following example illustrates synchronized blocks and non-races between accesses within transactions (including synchronized blocks). Suppose we add the following method to the `Account` class shown in Section 4.1.

```
1 void print_balances_and_total (account a1, a2) {
2   #pragma omp synchronized {
3     printf("First_account_balance:_%ld", a1.balance());
4     printf("Second_account_balance:_%ld", a2.balance());
5     printf("Total:_%ld", a1.balance() + a2.balance());
6   }
7 }
```

Observations:

- This program is data-race-free: all concurrent accesses are within transactions.
- The synchronized block cannot be replaced with an atomic block, as I/O is not transaction-safe (due to calls to `printf`, which is a transaction-unsafe function).
- Balances will be consistent and total will equal sum of balances displayed.
- If we eliminate the synchronized block from this example (so the calls to `balance()` in `print_balances_and_total()` are not in transactions), then this program is racy.

4.3   Nesting of OpenMP Parallel Regions and Transaction Blocks

In the common case of a TM region nested inside an OpenMP parallel region, the outer OpenMP region is run in parallel and the TM region is run speculatively. In the opposite case where an OpenMP parallel region is nested inside a TM region, there are several choices which needs to be debated within the community.

Currently on IBM's Blue Gene/Q system [28], an OpenMP region running in parallel inside the speculative TM region causes the TM region to be stopped. The stopped transaction is then rolled back and run nonspeculatively. The inner OpenMP region is run nonspeculatively by multiple threads. This is considered to be quite restrictive and heavy weight. An alternative is where the transaction could be executed *as if* the OpenMP portion was serialized. This could have complication with hardware and if the user create a race condition inside the transaction, it would be caveat emptor.

Another choice is that the parallel region inside the TM region can be executed with one thread. This solution will often be better than restarting the transaction and running it non-speculatively. There will be complication if the OpenMP region do some undesirable action such as checking for the number of threads being more than one. But these are details that can be worked out in committee.

4.4   Interaction between OpenMP Worksharing/Tasking Constructs and Transaction Blocks

We also intend to introduce interaction of TM with existing OpenMP constructs. These are now called composite constructs as they enable additional semantics. Starting with the workshare constructs, we propose the following where each iteration of the loop constitutes an atomic transaction with the usual clauses available.

```
1 #pragma omp for transaction
2 for (   ;   ;   )
3 { ... }
```

Similar for an OpenMP section construct where each section is an atomic transaction.

```
1 #pragma omp sections transaction
2 #pragma omp section
3 { ... }
4 #pragma omp section
5 { ... }
```

We also plan to support TM with OpenMP tasks. Tasks are defined as deferrable units of work that can be executed by any thread in the thread team associated to the active parallel region. Task can create new tasks and can also be nested inside work-sharing constructs. In this scenario, data access ordering and synchronization based on locks will be even more difficult to express, so transactions appear as an easy way to express intent and leave the mechanisms to the TM implementation. For tasks we propose tagging a task as a transaction, using the same clause specified above.

```
1 #pragma omp task transaction
2 { ... }
```

We will also need consideration of the interaction with cancellation constructs. These are details to be explored in future proposals and in committee.

4.5   Memory Model and Race Free Semantics

Transactions impose ordering constraints on the execution of the program. In this regard, they act as synchronization operations similar to the synchronization mechanisms defined in the C++11 standard [30] (i.e., locks and C++11 atomic variables). The C++11 standard defines the rules that determine what values can be seen by the reads in a multi-threaded program. Transactions affect these rules by introducing additional ordering constraints between operations of different threads.

In C++11, an execution of a program consists of the execution of all of its threads. The operations of each thread are ordered by the *sequenced before* relationship that is consistent with each thread's single threaded semantics. The C++11 library defines a number of operations that are specifically identified as synchronization operations. Synchronization operations include operations on locks and certain atomic operations (that is, operations on C++11 atomic variables). In addition, there are memory_order_relaxed atomic operations that are not synchronization operations. Certain synchronization operations synchronize with other synchronization operations performed by another thread. (For example, a lock release *synchronizes with* the next lock acquire on the same lock.)

The *sequenced before* and *synchronizes with* relationships contribute to the *happens before* relationship. The *happens before* relationship is defined by the following rules:

1. If an operation A is *sequenced before* an operation B then A *happens before B*.
2. If an operation A *synchronizes with* an operation B then A *happens before B*.
3. If there exists an operation B such that an operation A *happens before B* and B *happens before* an operation C then A *happens before C*.

Two operations conflict if one of them modifies a memory location and the other one accesses or modifies the same memory location. The execution of a program contains a data race if it contains two conflicting operations in different threads, at least one of which is not an atomic operation, and neither *happens before* the other. Any such data race results in undefined behavior. A program is race-free if none of its executions contain a data race. In a race-free program each read from a non-atomic memory location sees the value written by the last write ordered before it by the *happens before* relationship. It follows that a race-free program that uses no atomic operations with memory ordering other than the default memory_order_seq_cst behaves according to one of its sequentially consistent executions.

Outermost transactions (that is, transactions that are not dynamically nested within other transactions) appear to execute sequentially in some total global order that contributes to the *synchronizes with* relationship. Conceptually, every outermost transaction is associated with *StartTransaction* and *EndTransaction* operations, which mark the beginning and end of the transaction. A *StartTransaction* operation is *sequenced before* all other operations of its transaction. All operations of a transaction are *sequenced before* its *EndTransaction* operation. Given a transaction T, any operation that is not part of T and is *sequenced before* some operation of T is *sequenced before* T's *StartTransaction* operation. Given a transaction T, T's *EndTransaction* operation is *sequenced before* any operation A that is not part of T and has an operation in T that is *sequenced before A*.

There exists a total order over all *StartTransaction* and *EndTransaction* operations called the *transactional synchronizaton order*, which is consistent with the *sequenced before* relationship. In this order, transactions executed by different threads do not interleave. In other words, *transactional synchronization order* is such that a *StartTransaction* operation executed by one thread does not occur in between a matching pair of *StartTransaction* and *EndTransaction* operations executed by another thread.

The *transactional synchronization order* contributes to the *synchronizes with* relationship defined in the C++11 standard. In particular, each *EndTransaction* operation *synchronizes with* the next *StartTransaction* operation in the *transactional synchronization order* executed by a different thread.

The definition of the *synchronizes with* relation affects all other parts of the memory model, including the definition of the *happens before* relationship, visibility rules that specify what values can be seen by the reads, and the definition of data race freedom. Consequently, including transactions in the *synchronizes with* relation is the only change to the memory model that is necessary to account for transaction statements. With this extension, the C++11 memory model fully describes the behavior of programs with transaction statements.

The C++11 memory model has consequences for compiler optimizations. Sequentially valid source-to-source compiler transformations that transform only code between synchronization operations (which include *StartTransaction* and *EndTransaction* operations), and which do not introduce data races, remain valid. Source-to-source compiler transformations that introduce data races (e.g., hoisting load operations outside of a transaction) may be invalid depending on a particular implementation.

5 Future OpenMP Recommendation

We propose an OpenMP Transactional Memory Technical Report (TR), to enable early implementation experience and obtain feedbacks from the community. Transactional Memory forms a key cornerstone of tools for synchronization that enables composability whereas critical sections, mutexes, locks, atomics, even lock elision cannot. It enables functional correctness in C and Fortran call back programming style and C++ generic programming. Recent surveys have some data point showing it is easier to use than fine-grained locks, and some real-world tests have shown even an STM implementation can scale and perform better than fine-grained locks. As such, it enables and simplifies support for large scale programs that contain complex locking semantics.

This proposal is agnostic to hardware and can be entirely implemented in software, hardware, some hybrid or adaptive form of TM.

Our next goal is to provide an implementation using BSC's Mercurium OpenMP compiler [7] or GNU compiler (which already has a reduced form of this proposal in 4.7) to demonstrate the concept and confirm the performance capability.

References

1. Sutter, H.: The pillars of concurrency. Dr. Dobbs (July 2007)
2. OpenMP ARB.: OpenMP Application Program Interface, v. 4.0 (June 2013)
3. Bihari, B.L., Wong, M., Wang, A., de Supinski, B.R., Chen, W.: A case for including transactions in OpenMP II: Hardware transactional memory. In: Chapman, B.M., Massaioli, F., Müller, M.S., Rorro, M. (eds.) IWOMP 2012. LNCS, vol. 7312, pp. 44–58. Springer, Heidelberg (2012)
4. Herlihy, M., Shavit, N.: The Art of Multiprocessor Programming. Elsevier, Inc. (2008)
5. Rajwar, R., Goodman, J.R.: Speculative lock elision: Enabling highly concurrent multithreaded execution. In: 34th International Symposium on Microarchitecture, MICRO (2001)
6. Wong, M., Bihari, B.L., de Supinski, B.R., Wu, P., Michael, M., Liu, Y., Chen, W.: A case for including transactions in OpenMP. In: Sato, M., Hanawa, T., Müller, M.S., Chapman, B.M., de Supinski, B.R. (eds.) IWOMP 2010. LNCS, vol. 6132, pp. 149–160. Springer, Heidelberg (2010)
7. Milovanović, M., Ferrer, R., Unsal, O.S., Cristal, A., Martorell, X., Ayguadé, E., Labarta, J., Valero, M.: Transactional memory and OpenMP. In: Chapman, B., Zheng, W., Gao, G.R., Sato, M., Ayguadé, E., Wang, D. (eds.) IWOMP 2007. LNCS, vol. 4935, pp. 37–53. Springer, Heidelberg (2008)
8. Sutter, H.: The trouble with locks. Dr. Dobbs (March 2005)
9. Lee, E.A.: The problem with threads. Technical report, Electrical Engineering and Computer Sciences University of California at Berkeley (January 2006)

10. Wong, M., Boehm, H., Gottschlich, J., Shpeisman, T.: Transactional Language Constructs for C++ (January 2012),
    `http://www.open-std.org/jtc1/sc22/wg21/docs/papers/`
    `2012/n3341.pdf`
11. Scott, M.L., Spear, M.F., Dalessandro, L., Marathe, V.J.: Delaunay triangulation with transactions and barriers. In: Proceedings IEEE International Symposium on Workload Characterization (2007)
12. Kang, S., Bader, D.A.: An efficient transactional memory algorithm for computing minimum spanning forest of sparse graphs. In: Proceedings of the 14th ACM SIGPLAN Symposium on Principles and Practice of Parallel Programming, PPoPP 2009, pp. 15–24 (2009)
13. Ansari, M., Kotselidis, C., Watson, I., Kirkham, C., Luján, M., Jarvis, K.: Lee-TM: A nontrivial benchmark for transactional memory. In: Bourgeois, A.G., Zheng, S.Q. (eds.) ICA3PP 2008. LNCS, vol. 5022, pp. 196–207. Springer, Heidelberg (2008)
14. Gajinov, V., Zyulkyarov, F., Unsal, O.S., Cristal, A., Ayguade, E., Harris, T., Valero, M.: QuakeTM: Parallelizing a complex sequential application using transactional memory. In: Proceedings of the 23rd International Conference on Supercomputing, ICS 2009, pp. 126–135 (2009)
15. Zyulkyarov, F., Gajinov, V., Unsal, O.S., Cristal, A., Ayguade, E., Harris, T., Valero, M.: Atomic Quake: Using transactional memory in an interactive multiplayer game server. In: Proceedings of the 14th ACM SIGPLAN Symposium on Principles and Practice of Parallel Programming, pp. 25–34 (2009)
16. Abdelkhalek, A., Bilas, A.: Parallelization and performance of interactive multiplayer game servers. In: Proceedings of the 18th International Parallel and Distributed Processing Symposium, IPDPS (2004)
17. Lupei, D., Simion, B., Bogdan, P.D., Misler, M., Burcea, M., Krick, W., Amza, C.: Transactional memory support for scalable and transparent parallelization of multiplayer games. In: Proceedings of the 5th European Conference on Computer Systems, EuroSys 2010, pp. 41–54 (2010)
18. Guerraoui, R., Kapalka, M., Vitek, J.: STMBench7: A benchmark for software transactional memory. In: Proceedings of the 2Nd ACM SIGOPS/EuroSys European Conference on Computer Systems, EuroSys 2007, pp. 315–324 (2007)
19. Minh, C.C., Chung, J., Kozyrakis, C., Olukotun, K.: STAMP: Stanford transactional applications for multi-processing. In: Proceedings of The IEEE International Symposium on Workload Characterization, IISWC 2008, pp. 315–324 (2008)
20. Kestor, G., Stipic, S., Unsal, O., Cristal, A., Valero, M.: RMS-TM: A transactional memory benchmark for recognition, mining and synthesis applications. In: Proceedings 4th ACM SIGPLAN Workshop on Transactional Computing TRANSACT (2009)
21. Rossbach, C.J., Hofmann, O.S., Witchel, W.: Is transactional programming actually easier? In: Proceedings of the 15th ACM SIGPLAN Symposium on Principles and Practice of Parallel Programming, PPoPP 2010, pp. 47–56 (2010)
22. Pankratius, V., Adl-Tabatabai, A.: A study of transactional memory vs. locks in practice. In: Proceedings of the Twenty-third Annual ACM Symposium on Parallelism in Algorithms and Architectures, SPAA 2011, pp. 43–52 (2011)
23. Baek, W., Minh, C.C., Trautmann, M., Kozyrakis, C., Olukotun, K.: The opentm transactional application programming interface. In: Proceedings International Conference on Parallel Architectures and Compilation Techniques, PaCT 2007, pp. 376–387 (2007)
24. Gottschlich, J.E., Boehm, H.J.: Generic programming needs transactional memory. In: The 8th ACM SIGPLAN Workshop on Transactional Computing, TRANSACT (2013)
25. Transactional Memory Specification Drafting Group: Transactional language constructs for C++ (May 2014), `https://sites.google.com/site/tmforcplusplus/`

26. Wong, M., Gottschlich, J.: SG5: Software Transactional Memory (TM) Status Report (September 2012),
http://www.open-std.org/jtc1/sc22/wg21/docs/papers/2012/n3422.pdf
27. Luchangco, V., Wong, M.: Transactional Memory Support for C++ (February 2014),
http://www.open-std.org/jtc1/sc22/wg21/docs/papers/2014/n3919.pdf
28. IBM: IBM XL C/C++ for Transactional Memory for AIX, V0.9 Language Extensions and Users Guide (May 2008),
http://dl.alphaworks.ibm.com/technologies/xlcstm/xlcstm-whitepaper.pdf
29. Sutter, H.: (May 2014), https://isocpp.org/std/status
30. ISO C++ Standard: C++ Standard, aka C++11 (November 2011)

Integrated Measurement for Cross-Platform OpenMP Performance Analysis

Kevin A. Huck[1], Allen D. Malony[1], Sameer Shende[1], and Doug W. Jacobsen[2]

[1] University of Oregon, Eugene, OR 97403, USA
[2] Los Alamos National Laboratory, Los Alamos, NM 87545, USA

Abstract. The ability to measure the performance of OpenMP programs portably across shared memory platforms and across OpenMP compilers is a challenge due to the lack of a widely-implemented performance interface standard. While the OpenMP community is currently evaluating a tools interface specification called OMPT, at present there are different instrumentation methods possible at different levels of observation and with different system and compiler dependencies. This paper describes how support for four mechanisms for OpenMP measurement has been integrated into the TAU performance system. These include source-level instrumentation (Opari), a runtime "collector" API (called ORA) built into an OpenMP compiler (OpenUH), a wrapped OpenMP runtime library (GOMP using ORA), and an OpenMP runtime library supporting an OMPT prototype (Intel). The capabilities of these approaches are evaluated with respect to observation visibility, portability, and measurement overhead for OpenMP benchmarks from the NAS parallel benchmarks, Barcelona OpenMP Task Suite, and SPEC 2012. The integrated OpenMP measurement support is also demonstrated on a scientific application, MPAS-Ocean.

1 Introduction

Any parallel language system based on compiler interpretation of parallel syntax, code transformation, and runtime systems support introduces the question of how external tools can observe the execution-time performance of the generated program code. In general, the parallel language observability problem is one of *performance visibility* coupled with *semantic context*. Performance visibility is the means by which a tool can gain access to and can acquire information about the parallel execution performance. Because the parallel program is being transformed during compilation and is utilizing a runtime environment for execution, there are different levels where visibility can be made operative. However, it is precisely for this reason that performance data must be augmented with semantic information about the context in which the data was acquired, in order to understand its relevance and be able to link performance behavior across levels. The coupling between visibility and context can be implicit (e.g., an instrumented event could carry semantics) or explicit (e.g., the compiler or runtime allows certain state to be queried). The key point is that observing parallel language performance requires both types of capabilities and with support across different levels of program generation and execution.

L. DeRose (Eds.): IWOMP 2014, LNCS 8766, pp. 146–160, 2014.
© Springer International Publishing Switzerland 2014

OpenMP [2] is a widely supported and commonly used programming specification for multi-threaded parallelism in which performance observability has been an important consideration as well as a challenge to provide in a portable manner. It is a pragma-based language extension for C/C++ and Fortran plus a user-level library that relieves the programmer from the burden of creating, scheduling, managing, and destroying threads explicitly. Compilers supporting OpenMP hide this complexity by generating code that supports the (user facing) concurrency semantics in the OpenMP language, but interfaces with a runtime environment that is free to build (system facing) thread-level operation in whatever way is desired. Thus, available OpenMP compilers, both open source (e.g., GNU, OpenUH/Open64) and vendor supplied (e.g., IBM, Microsoft, Intel, PGI, Cray), offer alternative implementations on different platforms.

How can portable OpenMP performance measurement and analysis be provided across compilers and platforms given this situation? The OpenMP community discussed performance observability requirements early on in its history and there has been a strong interest in defining a tools API as part of the OpenMP standard. Efforts are underway by the OpenMP Tools Working Group in this regard. In the meantime, various techniques have been created to enable OpenMP performance analysis. This paper presents the present landscape and looks at the integration of different OpenMP observation techniques with a common measurement infrastructure, the TAU Performance System® [31].

The main contribution of this work is the creation of a robust, cross-platform OpenMP performance measurement system that utilizes the available support for observing OpenMP runtime system behavior. Four different approaches were integrated with TAU serving as the core measurement framework, including a portable tool for GCC OpenMP performance analysis. The overall goal is to provide significant coverage across OpenMP environments and parallel systems to allow portable performance evaluation of OpenMP applications.

2   Background

As described by Mohsen et al. [24], several performance tools can perform thread-specific measurement of an OpenMP application. In some cases, vendor-supplied tools such as the Intel Thread Profiler [12] provide specific details about one particular OpenMP compiler by utilizing proprietary instrumentation in the OpenMP runtime. On the other hand, portable performance tools such as TAU [31], ompP [5], Kojak [23], Scalasca [6] and Vampir [14] provide thread-specific measurements that can include the OpenMP static and runtime context, such as the parallel region location or synchronization operation (barrier, lock, atomic, critical), but only if that information is available. Typically, to access the OpenMP context these performance tools rely on either instrumentation of the application code or the OpenMP runtime itself, if it is available.

Two early efforts to define a tools interface for OpenMP performance observation were *POMP* [22] and the Sun/Oracle OpenMP Runtime API (ORA), better known as the *Collector API* [13]. The POMP interface was intended to be used by a source code instrumentation system which would insert POMP calls within in an application that was rewritten to expose OpenMP execution events. The Opari [22] OpenMP rewriting tool supported the POMP interface. In contrast, the Collector API was intended to be implemented by an OpenMP runtime. It exposed certain runtime events and information about OpenMP state to measurement tools.

Neither of these two approaches gained enough traction to be widely adopted, resulting in various approaches being used in both portable and proprietary compilers. Recently, there has been a resurgence of effort by the OpenMP Tools Working Group towards an OpenMP API standard for tools, called *OMPT* [3]. This work shows strong signs of a broader commitment from multiple compiler vendors and has a good chance of being included in the OpenMP standard. The availability of the GCC OpenMP runtime library (GOMP) [9] and the recent open-sourcing of the Intel OpenMP runtime system [11] makes other performance observability support possible.

The integration of all of these methods can significantly extend the coverage and cross-platform portability of an OpenMP measurement and analysis tool. What is necessary is a parallel performance system robust enough to implement the different techniques being used and already portable across parallel programming environments and platforms. TAU is an example of a portable profiling and tracing toolkit for performance analysis of parallel programs written in languages supporting OpenMP and running on a variety of shared and distributed memory parallel architectures. TAU provides different means for instrumentation (source, library, binary) and is capable of gathering performance information (time, hardware counters) about functions, methods, basic blocks and statements as well as periodic sampling. TAU is distributed with profile and trace analysis tools, a performance database, and a data mining package.

Given a performance system like TAU, the opportunity is there to integrate multiple OpenMP observation techniques with a common measurement and analysis infrastructure. Doing so will enable both cross-platform performance analysis coverage and means to evaluate OpenMP performance for different compiler and system environments.

3   Approach

Our strategy to integrate different approaches for performance observation of OpenMP runtime behavior has the goal of cross-compiler / cross-platform performance analysis and evaluation. Figure 1 shows how each approach is integrated with the TAU system. First, source code instrumentation uses the POMP interface and the Opari [22] tool. Second, the

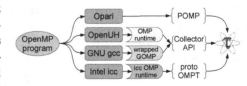

Fig. 1. Instrumentation flow for OpenMP programs with different measurement approaches

OpenMP Collector API [13], as implemented in the OpenUH [17] compiler and associated runtime, is interfaced with TAU. The third approach wraps the GNU OpenMP runtime library, GOMP [9], with a measurement interface that implements the Collector API. Finally, the proposed OpenMP Tools API (OMPT) [3] is supported in TAU and we tested it with a modified version of the recently open-sourced Intel OpenMP runtime combined with the Intel compiler suite.

3.1 POMP and Opari

The *OpenMP Pragma And Region Instrumentor (Opari)* [22] is a source-to-source code transformation utility to parse C/C++ and Fortran source code, locate Open-MP pragmas, insert instrumentation via the POMP [21] interface, and write out instrumented application code. Opari has been the OpenMP instrumentation tool for TAU [31], Kojak [23], and Scalasca [6] for several years. However, because Opari relies entirely on source transformation and instrumentation, by choice it constrains what can be observed of runtime operations. Instead, it attempts to provide a performance view with respect to program semantics only, including raising the awareness of certain runtime behavior (e.g., synchronization) to a higher level for observation. Interestingly, in doing so, Opari is able to potentially provide more context for performance events, but with no insight into the OpenMP runtime implementation or uninstrumented OpenMP libraries.

Opari is highly portable and compatible with all OpenMP compilers and runtimes. Unfortunately, there are some drawbacks. First, the user application must be passed through the Opari instrumentor, which modifies the original source code. Automated source instrumentation can be problematic if the source code includes complex preprocessor macros or language features that are not well supported by the parser in the instrumentation framework. In addition, the instrumentation of lightweight work sharing and tasking regions at the source level can introduce significant overhead in performance measurements. Source instrumentation can also prevent compiler and/or runtime optimizations. Secondly, applications typically rely on uninstrumented libraries that cannot be re-compiled. These libraries may have OpenMP parallel regions in them, but are a blind spot to any performance measurement. In fact, the OpenMP runtime itself is also a blind spot. Lastly, there are some OpenMP features that are hard to support with a purely source rewriting approach, such as untied tasks.

3.2 OpenMP Runtime API (Collector API)

In an attempt to encourage OpenMP compiler developers to integrate a performance tool interface into their runtime systems, Itzkowitz et al. [13] proposed an *OpenMP Runtime API (ORA)* for profiling, commonly known as the *Collector API*. The external API consists of a single function call to interact with the runtime system, whose purpose is to manage the *collector* (initialize, pause, resume, terminate), register a callback function for a predefined set of significant event transitions in the runtime, or query an executing thread's state through a signal safe request. The callback function is particularly useful for profiling and tracing tools that use timer probes for measurement. The state query feature provides support for sampling-based performance tools. Altogether, the API provides relatively good coverage of the internal performance of an OpenMP runtime implementation. In the original specification, there are 11 mutually exclusive states (for sampling support) and 22 defined callback events, representing the entry and exit for OpenMP 2.0 pragmas. additional events and states have been proposed [27] to include task support in OpenMP 3.0. For a performance measurement library to take advantage of ORA, only a few features need to be implemented. The measurement library needs to implement and register one or more event handlers to process the events as they are encountered. Alternatively, a sampling measurement library can request the state of a thread when the execution is interrupted and sampled by the measurement library. The TAU implementation provides full support for ORA, including both events and states. For sampling, when an application thread is interrupted, the OpenMP runtime is queried using the API to get the state of the thread after the thread source code location is determined using *libbfd* [8] and optionally, *libunwind* [33].

However, encouragement of a performance tool API and actual adoption are two different things. Even though the OpenMP ARB sanctioned the Collector API interface specification, it has only been implemented in the the OpenUH compiler [18] and the Oracle Solaris Studio compiler [26]. While there have been several evaluations of the Collector API as implemented in the OpenMP runtimes of OpenUH [10,1] and Solaris Studio [19], previously only Oracle's Solaris Studio Performance Tool and OpenUH's profiling tool use ORA.

3.3   GOMP Wrapper

The GNU Compiler Collection (GCC) [7] is a widely used open-source compiler suite for C/C++ and Fortran that has provided support for OpenMP since version 4.2. The runtime library for GCC is called *libgomp*, or more commonly, *GOMP*. GOMP consists of approximately 60 API calls which GCC compilers, other compilers, or source transformation tools can use to implement an OpenMP runtime. For instance, the Rose transformation tool [28,29] uses GOMP as one of its OpenMP runtime targets. The open source availability of GOMP provides us with a means to interpose performance instrumentation at the library interface. TAU includes a utility for generating a measurement wrapper around external libraries that cannot be or simply are not instrumented [32]. Using the function declarations for the library (in the form of one or more header files), TAU will generate a new shared object library which replaces the wrapped symbols with proxy functions that provide ORA support and call the real library functions during execution. The wrapper interposition library can be preloaded before application execution. For statically linked executables (which do not support dynamic symbol loading), a similar functionality is also available at link time.

The result of our work is that TAU now has Collector API runtime support for all GCC compilers and the GOMP runtime. Our wrapper library will work with any GCC compiled OpenMP application on any platform where it is supported. However, a library wrapping approach comes with certain limitations, namely none of the GOMP internals are visible for performance measurement. As we shall see in the next section, though, visibility within the runtime is key to understanding cause-and-effect relationships within threading synchronization.

3.4 OpenMP Tools API

Based on experiences with Opari and ORA, a broader group of interested parties has been working on extending the OpenMP specification to include a formal performance and debugging tool interface. The proposed specification is called *OMPT: OpenMP Tools Application Programming Interfaces for Performance Analysis* [4]. Like ORA, OMPT includes support for events and states. Unlike ORA, OMPT has broad support from several compiler vendors as well as tool developers. The OMPT draft specification is complete and is available as a Proposed Draft Technical Report at the OpenMP Forum website [25]. The key OMPT design objectives are to provide low overhead observation of OpenMP applications and the runtime in order to collect performance measurements, provide stack frame support for sampling tools and incur minimal (near zero) overhead when not in use. OMPT specifies support for a larger set of events and states, and can therefore be considered a superset of ORA. In addition, OMPT specifies additional insight into the OpenMP runtime in the form of data structures populated by the runtime itself. These data structures include the parallel region and task identifiers, wait identifiers and stack frame data. Finally, OMPT specifies interfaces for applying *blame shifting* logic to resource synchronization [20]. From a tool developer perspective, the broad support and large set of events and states makes OMPT the most attractive approach of those tested.

There are two known OMPT runtime implementations. In April 2013, Intel open-sourced their OpenMP runtime[11] and members of the OMPT draft committee implemented a first version of support for Intel compilers. We have contributed to this effort, adding the event callbacks to key locations in the Intel runtime. In addition, IBM has prototyped support in an experimental limited release version of the XL compilers. There are plans to implement OMPT support within the GOMP library for the GNU compiler runtime as well.

Support for OMPT in TAU is similar to that for ORA, with some key differences. First, each event in OMPT is registered to different handlers, and not all events are fully supported yet. All OMPT states are supported, but TAU does not yet take advantage of the blame shifting support. However, because ORA and OMPT are conceptually very similar, the integration of OMPT support in TAU reuses much of the ORA infrastructure, including the use of libbfd.

3.5 Comparison of Measurement Support

Table 1 shows the coverage for the different OpenMP measurement approaches. We have separated ORA into three columns: the specified support, the extended task support in the OpenUH compiler, and the support provided by our GOMP wrapper. Note that because the GOMP wrapper and Opari have no access to the runtime internals, they cannot report on all implicit barriers or task preemption. Task preemption is somewhat of a moot point for the GOMP runtime – as of v4.8.2 it does not perform any preemption or migration of tasks.

Table 1. OpenMP pragma / event coverage using different measurement techniques

OpenMP Feature	Opari	ORA	OpenUH ORA	GOMP ORA	OMPT
Parallel Region	enter/exit, begin/end	Yes	Yes	Yes	Yes
Thread create/exit	pthread create/exit	No	No	No	Yes
Work Sharing	enter/exit, begin/end	Yes	Yes	Yes	Yes
Atomics	enter/exit	waiting state	waiting state	waiting state	Yes
Barriers	explicit only	Yes	Yes	explicit, some implicit	Yes
Critical	enter/exit, begin/end	waiting state	waiting state	waiting state	Yes
Master	begin/end	Yes	Yes	Yes	Yes
Ordered	enter/exit, begin/end	Yes, wait state	wait state	wait state	Yes
Sections	enter/exit, begin/end	No	No	No	Yes
Single	begin/end	Yes	Yes	Yes	Yes
Locks	lock wrappers	waiting state	waiting state	waiting state	Yes
Task Creation	begin/end	Yes	Yes	Yes	Yes
Task Schedule	No	No	Yes	No	Yes
Task Wait	begin/end	Yes	Yes	Yes	Yes
Task Execution	begin/end	Yes	Yes	Yes	Yes
Task Completion	No	No	Yes	No	Yes
Task Yield	No	No	Yes	No	Yes

Table 2. OpenMP profile timer events captured by each method for the cfft1 function in the NPB 3.2.1 FT.B benchmark. GOMP ORA and OpenUH ORA are similar.

Opari		
0.898		paralleldo (loop body) [OpenMP location: file:FT/ft.f <556, 575>]
	0.073	paralleldo (barrier enter/exit) [OpenMP location: file:FT/ft.f <556, 575>]
	7.1E-4	paralleldo (parallel fork/join) [OpenMP location: file:FT/ft.f <556, 575>]
	2.4E-4	paralleldo (parallel begin/end) [OpenMP location: file:FT/ft.f <556, 575>]

ORA		
0.89		OpenMP_PARALLEL_REGION: [OPENMP] cffts1_ [{FT/ft.f} {557}]
	0.098	OpenMP_IMPLICIT_BARRIER: [OPENMP] cffts1_ [{FT/ft.f} {557}]

OMPT		
0.879		OpenMP_LOOP: [OPENMP] cffts1 [{FT/ft.f} {556}]
	0.013	OpenMP_BARRIER: [OPENMP] cffts1 [{FT/ft.f} {556}]
	6.5E-4	OpenMP_PARALLEL_REGION: [OPENMP] cffts1 [{FT/ft.f} {556}]

Table 2 shows a selection of profile timers from each of the event-based measurement methods for benchmark code. The profile views are from *ParaProf*, the interactive TAU profile visualization and analysis tool. All methods show the parallel region and barrier timers in the `cffts1` function. The Opari measurements refer to code locations only by source code line numbers rather than by function name. The Opari measurement adds more timers to the profile, which can potentially increase measurement overhead, as we shall see in Section 4. The GOMP and OpenUH measurements are very similar, as they both use the same ORA support in TAU. It should be noted that like Opari, OMPT provides separate events for work sharing loops, whereas ORA attributes productive time in those loops to the enclosing parallel region.

4   Experiments

4.1   Benchmark Measurements

In order to evaluate the OpenMP measurement methods and the TAU integration, we first compared the measurement capability and overhead added to applications under different scenarios. We used three compilers in our study, GNU GCC versions 4.4.7 and 4.8.0, OpenUH 3.0.26 with prototype extensions to the Collector API for task events, and Intel 13.1.2. As described in Section 3, OpenUH includes Collector API support built-in. Collector API support for libGOMP is provided by our wrapper library. The Intel-compiled experiments replaced the standard OpenMP runtime library with the modified open-source version with OMPT support. It should be strongly noted that our experiments are *not* intended to demonstrate the comparative performance differences between compilers and runtimes with benchmark applications. Rather, our experiments are intended to show broad measurement coverage with various compilers under various scenarios, and measure the overhead of performance measurement with TAU linked in. The main purpose of the experiments is to demonstrate that using various OpenMP performance measurement techniques is possible with a single measurement system.

For each compiler, we generated baseline executables of the applications and compared the execution time to each of two different types of OpenMP performance measurement. The baseline compilation used the highest available (and stable) optimization (-O3 for most cases, -Ofast for OpenUH in the BOTS benchmarks). The baseline executables were executed and the runtimes collected. The applications were then instrumented with Opari and recompiled using each of the compilers with the same optimization settings. In these experiments, the applications were built with TAU compiler wrappers that manage the instrumentation and compilation process. Because Opari does not support untied tasks, the BOTS benchmarks were executed as tied tasks. For two sets of benchmarks (NPB, BOTS), each of the baseline executables were then also executed using tau_exec, a utility that preloads TAU measurement libraries and enables the Collector API tool support. The GOMP library wrapper was also preloaded for GCC executables. Similarly, the modified Intel OpenMP runtime library was also preloaded for Intel executables. Because the SPEC 2012 build framework was not amenable to using tau_exec to execute the SPEC benchmarks, those applications were minimally instrumented (main only) with TAU prior to compilation and the required TAU and OpenMP measurement libraries were used.

In all, three variants for each compiler were tested with 31 benchmark applications. The applications tested include well known OpenMP benchmarks from three different OpenMP benchmark suites - the NAS Parallel Benchmarks v3.2.1, SPEC 2012 OpenMP Benchmarks, and The Barcelona OpenMP Task Suite (BOTS) version 1.1.2. Three pairs of benchmarks (BT and 357.bt331, LU and 371.applu331, MG and 370.mgrid331) are in both NPB and SPEC, although they do represent different versions of the codes. The applications were compiled and executed on a single "fatnode" node of the ACISS cluster at the University of Oregon [34] with four Intel X7560 2.27GHz 8-core CPUs and 384GB of memory. For all experiments, OMP_NUM_THREADS was set to 32 prior to execution. All other OpenMP runtime parameters used the runtime default settings. Each experiment variant was executed 10 times, and the fastest execution of the 10 is reported in the results. Over 2790 executions were generated. The self-reported execution

Table 3. Overhead measurements for 32 threads on ACISS

	GNU			INTEL			OPENUH		
NPB 3.2.1 Benchmark	Baseline	Opari	ORA	Baseline	Opari	OMPT	Baseline	Opari	ORA
BT.B	17.92	19.96	22.42	16.18	16.56	16.80	18.58	18.85	19.37
CG.B	7.49	7.68	7.51	7.31	7.96	7.63	8.02	8.93	9.39
EP.B	2.92	2.99	2.96	1.40	1.42	1.40	1.47	1.51	1.51
FT.B	3.17	3.13	3.13	3.21	3.27	3.29	3.60	3.57	3.65
IS.B	0.75	0.74	0.74	0.75	0.75	0.75	0.81	0.83	0.82
LU.B	12.37	**17.43**	12.38	12.25	**26.71**	13.22	13.31	**26.37**	14.32
LU-HP.B	22.00	**42.86**	**31.26**	19.24	**51.74**	**30.93**	23.13	**86.17**	**39.04**
MG.B	1.21	1.61	1.30	1.08	1.27	1.13	1.16	1.51	1.31
SP.B	16.02	16.10	16.53	14.55	15.53	15.59	16.61	18.07	19.62
BOTS 1.1.2 Benchmark	Baseline	Opari	ORA	Baseline	Opari	OMPT	Baseline	Opari	ORA
alignment.single 1000	70.59	73.99	70.77	48.85	48.90	48.86	56.19	56.44	56.20
fft 134217728	**132.55**	124.93	127.94	3.57	5.52	4.61	11.69	13.05	13.78
fib 30	**23.91**	27.11	28.89	0.10	1.71	1.33	0.97	4.16	3.18
floorplan 15	**226.58**	225.71	234.35	0.70	**11.44**	**6.06**	18.95	**24.09**	21.38
health small	**38.78**	37.04	29.47	0.46	1.78	0.98	2.41	2.70	2.72
nqueens 12	**120.18**	134.28	156.44	0.13	**5.14**	**3.87**	10.17	11.92	11.18
sort 134217728	**20.76**	26.83	22.73	2.44	2.49	2.55	2.90	3.15	3.17
sparselu.single 100x100	4.11	4.19	4.10	11.49	11.52	11.60	3.82	3.85	3.83
strassen 8192	0.02	0.02	0.03	0.03	0.03	0.04	0.01	0.04	0.03
uts small	53.54	**212.57**	**218.78**	11.00	**64.84**	**34.26**	*segv*	n/a	n/a
SPEC 2012 Benchmark	Baseline	Opari	ORA	Baseline	Opari	OMPT	Baseline	Opari	ORA
351.bwaves	23.99	24.38	24.18	*segv*	n/a	n/a	*segv*	n/a	n/a
352.nab	24.00	25.85	29.41	20.40	22.96	21.40	35.13	35.80	35.68
357.bt331	20.69	n/a	21.44	18.27	22.49	18.75	21.41	n/a	n/a
358.botsalgn	1.07	1.21	3.65	1.07	1.25	1.07	1.05	1.08	1.15
359.botsspar	2.67	2.97	2.87	2.78	2.31	1.88	2.87	1.12	2.89
360.ilbdc (test)	**502.76**	**282.18**	**313.58**	13.33	13.47	13.48	14.16	14.36	15.65
362.fma3d	14.31	15.05	47.73	13.15	13.58	13.16	19.88	24.74	24.57
363.swim	10.18	11.13	10.21	10.26	10.97	10.29	22.36	n/a	23.00
367.imagick	19.40	19.44	19.52	5.84	5.86	6.04	145.97	145.85	146.06
370.mgrid331	0.72	1.37	0.86	0.65	1.85	1.10	0.75	2.71	2.57
371.applu331	3.82	12.26	6.16	3.45	13.07	4.29	*segv*	n/a	n/a
372.smithwa	1.89	2.19	2.18	1.45	1.45	1.50	2.58	2.62	2.61

times for the different benchmarks, compilers and measurement approaches are displayed in Table 3. There are several interesting differences between compilers and measurement methods which we discuss below.

In the NAS suite of benchmarks, we observe that the LU-HP benchmark has very high measurement overhead for all methods due to the fact that it executes ~300,000 parallel region iterations of very small granularity. It is also interesting to note that the LU benchmark with Opari instrumentation has significantly higher overhead, due to the fact that ten times as many timer invocations $(34, 239, 023)$ were added to the application as compared to those added by the ORA/OMPT methods $(< 3, 456, 152)$.

Because they are task-based, the BOTS benchmarks provide some of the most striking differences between compiler / runtime execution times. For nearly all task based benchmarks, the GCC benchmarks lag far behind the other OpenMP runtimes. The floorplan GCC profile measured that nearly all of the execution time is spent creating tasks and waiting for their execution (97% of $234s$).

The Intel OMPT profile measured very little processing overhead in comparison (< 1% of 7.4s). The OpenUH profile measured a significant amount of time spent suspending tasks, rather than just executing them (51% of 21.464s). These profiles reflect the behaviors of the different task creation and scheduling implementations used in the runtimes. The GCC runtime has a queueing mechanism for processing tasks, but the TAU profiles show that there is considerable lock contention in the task creation and execution steps. Locked access to the queue perturbs the execution when thread counts increase, the work per task is small and the `taskwait` directive is used. With the FFT benchmark, we verified that

Table 4. Best execution times for BOTS benchmarks using baseline and modified GCC 4.8.2 runtime with lock-free queues

Benchmark	Baseline	Lock-free
alignment	70.59	0.73
fft	132.55	4.18
fib	23.91	0.80
floorplan	226.58	1.42
health	38.78	5.72
nqueens	120.18	0.73
sort	20.76	2.00
sparselu	4.11	4.05
strassen	0.02	11.85
uts	53.54	45.73

adding the `if(0)` clause to the last task directive before all `taskwait` directives executes those tasks immediately without queuing, reducing lock contention and improving performance. These measurements clearly suggest that reducing the lock contention within the GCC task scheduler would be helpful. To test this theory, we rewrote the GCC 4.8.2 task scheduler using lock-free bounded queues for both the main queue and the child queues for all parent tasks, along with other necessary changes. The measured times for our modified scheduler are in Table 4. While the execution times for most benchmarks are reduced, the strassen test performed worse. We will continue to study the runtime in the interest of contributing a faster task scheduler to the GCC runtime.

The BOTS benchmarks also demonstrate that instrumenting and measuring lightweight tasks can incur significant overheads. Returning to the floorplan example, consider the difference between the unperturbed Intel execution and those which use Opari instrumentation or process OMPT events. The execution in question generates millions of short-lived, lightweight tasks whose lifetimes are far shorter than the amount of time required to measure them. The Intel OMPT profile executes an average of $601,046$ tasks *per thread* in an execution that, unperturbed, executes in 0.70 seconds. In the profile observed with OMPT, the exclusive time per task ranges between 7.1 and 13 μs. Clearly, the work granularity is too small for instrumentation and is better measured with ORA or OMPT sampling state support. In a sampled TAU profile of the OpenUH version, the runtime shows no significant thread scheduling overhead. Comparing these OpenUH profiles suggests that the main cause of measurement overhead in this benchmark is in monitoring every `CREATE_TASK` and `SUSPEND_TASK` event.

The SPEC benchmarks had a few problems building and executing without errors. The 351.bwaves benchmark crashed at the first parallel region with both the Intel and OpenUH compilers when running the baseline build, and the OpenUH build of 371.applu331 also failed to execute. 357.bt331 and 363.swim failed to link with the POMP framework after instrumentation and compilation. The minimally instrumented 357.bt331 benchmark also failed to link with TAU and OpenUH. These build issues underscore the reasoning why users sometimes are reluctant to rely on instrumentation techniques in order to measure the performance of an application. Otherwise, the benchmarks executed as expected. Like the related NPB LU.B benchmark, the 371.applu331 benchmark showed significantly higher overhead with Opari.

The most interesting SPEC performance case is the 360.ilbdc benchmark. The execution times are much higher when compiled with GCC than with Intel or OpenUH. Using both the event tracking and sampling support in ORA to collect a TAU profile, we observe that a vast majority of the time is spent in the GOMP runtime. Examining the benchmark source code revealed that the parallel regions use the runtime scheduler, which in the case of GCC defaults to dynamic with a chunk size of 1 (Intel and OpenUH use static scheduling by default). Changing the scheduler to guided (or static) eliminated the runtime overhead and reduced the execution times for the baseline, Opari and ORA measurements to 39.25, 43.08 and 42.25 seconds, respectively. Having a cross-platform OpenMP measurement system allows performance differences between compilers to identify possible operational characteristics that might be adjusted, such as the scheduling option.

4.2 MPAS-Ocean

The Model for Prediction Across Scales (MPAS) [15] is a framework project jointly developed by the National Center for Atmospheric Research (NCAR) and Los Alamos National Lab (LANL) in the United States. The framework is designed to perform rapid prototyping of single-component climate system models. Several models have been developed using the MPAS framework. MPAS-Ocean [30] is designed to simulate the ocean system for a wide range of time scales and spatial scales from less than 1 km to global circulations.

MPAS-Ocean is developed in Fortran using MPI for large scale parallelism. MPAS-Ocean has been ported to several architectures and compilers, and in an effort to increase concurrency and efficiency on a wider range of large-scale distributed systems with multicore nodes OpenMP work-sharing regions have been introduced.

The MPAS-Ocean application had previously been instrumented with internal timing functions. TAU was integrated by replacing the timing infrastructure with TAU timers. The application instrumentation was mostly at a high level, encapsulating key phases in the simulation model. Linking in the TAU library also provides measurement of MPI communication through the PMPI interface, hardware counter data using PAPI, and OpenMP measurement through ORA (GCC) or OMPT (Intel).

A large scale parameter sweep was performed to examine the scaling behavior for a number of design decisions, including decomposition methods, solver implementations and OpenMP runtime scheduler. MPAS-Ocean was compiled with Intel 13 compilers and executed on Hopper [16], a Cray XE6 system at NERSC

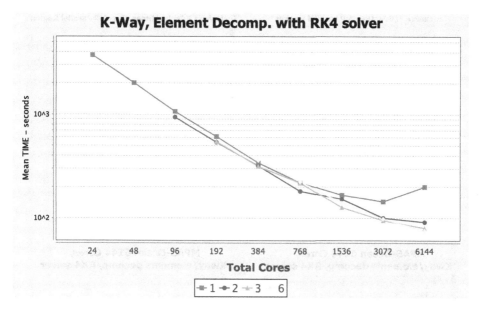

Fig. 2. Scaling performance of MPAS-ocean using K-way data partitioning, element decomposition, the RK4 solver and a guided OpenMP schedule. Each series represents the number of threads per process. Scaling performance tails off for single-threaded executions with greater than 768 processes.

with 2 twelve-core AMD 'MagnyCours' 2.1-GHz processors and 32 GB DDR3 1333-MHz memory per node. Figure 2 shows the scaling for one combination. The x-axis represents the number of total cores used, and each series represents the number of threads per process. The tail end of the figure shows that single-threaded executions using more than 768 processes do not continue to scale, with diminishing returns at 6144 total cores. The multi-threaded executions do not show this behavior as severely.

The diminishing scaling results when using just one thread is related to the domain decomposition. In a common run scenario, the problem domain is decomposed into N blocks, where N is equal to the number of processes. Because each process also has to process halo (ghost) cells from neighboring blocks, increasing the number of blocks in the partition has the effect of increasing the total calculations in the system as a whole. Increasing the thread count per process is a more efficient approach than increasing the number of processes when increasing the core count. However, increasing thread count beyond 2 threads per process doesn't appear to improve performance significantly. Figure 3 shows the reason why - as the thread count per process is increased, the FLOPs per thread decreases as expected but cache misses increase, effectively wiping out any potential performance benefit. Figure 4 shows that not all work-sharing regions are affected equally – the high_ord_hori_flux memory behavior appears unaffected. The conclusion is that false and/or real sharing of data structures

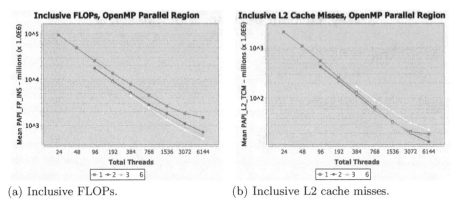

(a) Inclusive FLOPs.   (b) Inclusive L2 cache misses.

Fig. 3. Hardware counters for the OpenMP parallel region in MPAS-Ocean

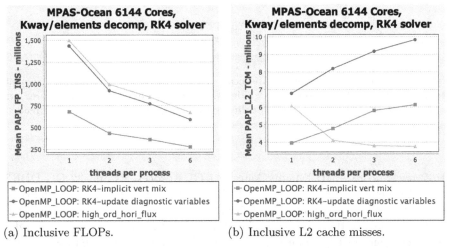

(a) Inclusive FLOPs.   (b) Inclusive L2 cache misses.

Fig. 4. Hardware counters for selected OpenMP work-sharing loops in MPAS-Ocean

in some OpenMP loops are the likely problems, and will be addressed as we continue to study the performance of this code.

5   Conclusion and Future Work

It is preferable that the portability of OpenMP as a parallel programming model extends to OpenMP performance measurement and analysis tools. However, until a tools API is adopted in the OpenMP standard, a common means for performance observation will not be available. This has been the case in the OpenMP community for several years, leading to the collection of techniques discussed in this paper. The main contribution of our research is the integration of these methods within a parallel measurement infrastructure with the objective to enable cross-platform performance analysis of OpenMP applications. We show that it is possible to relate the different approaches with respect to the type of performance insight they provide and to compare/contrast performance across different compilers and platforms through a common performance measurement system. The NPB, SPEC, and BOTS benchmarks allow us to evaluate the versatility of the methods and to assess the overheads associated with their implementation.

Our involvement with the OpenMP Tools Working group on the OMPT specification allowed a prototype OMPT implementation to be developed and included in our evaluation. Given its lineage from experience with the POMP API and the Collector API, the proposed OMPT gives a view of what can be expected in future OpenMP compiler environments. We intend to fully implement OMPT with TAU as a measurement backend, including blame shifting support. However, this does not mean that we will abandon the other work reported here. On the contrary, until OMPT is widely adopted, there will still be cause to provide support for multiple alternatives. OMPT will be another arrow in our OpenMP observation quiver, albeit a powerful one, making it possible to do cross-evaluation studies with systems that still offer only one of the other approaches. Presently, our integrated OpenMP support in TAU makes it the most portable and cross-platform of any OpenMP performance analysis tool.

Acknowledgements. This work is supported by NSF SI2-SSI grant 1148346 and DOE SciDAC grant DE-SC0006723. Doug Jacobsen was supported by the US DOE Office of Science, Biological and Environmental Research program. ACISS was supported by an NSF OCI Major Research Instrumentation grant 0960354. The authors would like to thank and acknowledge John Mellor-Crummey and the rest of the OpenMP Tools Working Group for both their contributions to the draft OMPT standard and the opportunity to work together on the initial implementation of OMPT in the Intel runtime.

References

1. Bui, V., et al.: Towards an implementation of the OpenMP collector API. Urbana 51, 61801 (2007)
2. Dagum, L., Menon, R.: OpenMP: An industry standard API for shared-memory programming. IEEE Computational Science Engineering 5(1), 46–55 (1998)
3. Eichenberger, A., et al.: OMPT and OMPD: OpenMP tools application programming interfaces for performance analysis and debugging (2014), (OpenMP 4.0 draft proposal)
4. Eichenberger, A.E., et al.: OMPT: An OpenMP tools application programming interface for performance analysis. In: Rendell, A.P., Chapman, B.M., Müller, M.S. (eds.) IWOMP 2013. LNCS, vol. 8122, pp. 171–185. Springer, Heidelberg (2013)
5. Fürlinger, K., Gerndt, M.: ompP: A profiling tool for OpenMP. In: Mueller, M.S., Chapman, B.M., de Supinski, B.R., Malony, A.D., Voss, M. (eds.) IWOMP 2005/2006. LNCS, vol. 4315, pp. 15–23. Springer, Heidelberg (2008)
6. Geimer, M., et al.: The Scalasca performance toolset architecture. Concurrency and Computation: Practice and Experience 22(6), 702–719 (2010)
7. GNU: GCC, the GNU Compiler Collection (2014), http://gcc.gnu.org
8. GNU: GNU Binutils (2014), http://www.gnu.org/software/binutils
9. GNU: GNU libgomp (2014), http://gcc.gnu.org/onlinedocs/libgomp/

10. Hernandez, O., et al.: Open source software support for the OpenMP runtime api for profiling. In: Proceedings of ICPPW 2009, pp. 130–137. IEEE (2009)
11. Intel: Intel open source OpenMP runtime (2014), http://www.openmprtl.org
12. Intel: Intel® Thread Profiler - Product Overview (2014), http://software.intel.com/en-us/articles/intel-thread-profiler-product-overview/
13. Itzkowitz, M., et al.: An OpenMP Runtime API for Profiling. OpenMP official ARB White Paper 314, 181–190 (2007)
14. Knüpfer, A., et al.: The Vampir performance analysis tool-set. In: Tools for High Performance Computing, pp. 139–155. Springer (2008)
15. LANL and NCAR: MPAS (2014), http://mpas-dev.github.io
16. LBL: Hopper, NERSC's Cray XE6 System (2014), http://www.nersc.gov/
17. Liao, C., et al.: OpenUH: An optimizing, portable OpenMP compiler. Concurrency and Computation: Practice and Experience 19(18), 2317–2332 (2007)
18. Liao, C., et al.: OpenUH: An optimizing, portable OpenMP compiler. Concurrency and Computation: Practice and Experience 19(18), 2317–2332 (2007)
19. Lin, Y., Mazurov, O.: Providing observability for OpenMP 3.0 applications. In: Müller, M.S., de Supinski, B.R., Chapman, B.M. (eds.) IWOMP 2009. LNCS, vol. 5568, pp. 104–117. Springer, Heidelberg (2009)
20. Liu, X., et al.: A new approach for performance analysis of OpenMP programs. In: ICS 2014, pp. 69–80. ACM, New York (2013)
21. Mohr, B., et al.: Towards a performance tool interface for OpenMP: An approach based on directive rewriting. Citeseer (2001)
22. Mohr, B., et al.: Design and Prototype of a Performance Tool Interface for OpenMP. Journal of Supercomputing 23(1), 105–128 (2002)
23. Mohr, B., Wolf, F.: KOJAK–a tool set for automatic performance analysis of parallel programs. In: Kosch, H., Böszörményi, L., Hellwagner, H. (eds.) Euro-Par 2003. LNCS, vol. 2790, pp. 1301–1304. Springer, Heidelberg (2003)
24. Mohsen, M.S., et al.: A survey on performance tools for OpenMP. World Academy of Science, Engineering and Technology 49 (2009)
25. OpenMP Architecture Review Board: The OpenMP® API specification for parallel programming (2014), http://openmp.org/wp/openmp-specifications/
26. Oracle: Oracle Solaris Studio (2014), http://www.oracle.com/technetwork/server-storage/solarisstudio/overview/
27. Qawasmeh, A., Malik, A., Chapman, B., Huck, K., Malony, A.: Open Source Task Profiling by Extending the OpenMP Runtime API. In: Rendell, A.P., Chapman, B.M., Müller, M.S. (eds.) IWOMP 2013. LNCS, vol. 8122, pp. 186–199. Springer, Heidelberg (2013)
28. Quinlan, D.: ROSE: Compiler support for object-oriented frameworks. Parallel Processing Letters 10(02n03), 215–226 (2000)
29. Quinlan, D.J., et al.: ROSE compiler project (2014), http://www.rosecompiler.org
30. Ringler, T., et al.: A multi-resolution approach to global ocean modeling. Ocean Modelling 69(0), 211–232 (2013)
31. Shende, S., Malony, A.D.: The TAU Parallel Performance System. International Journal of High Performance Computing Applications 20(2), 287–311 (2006)
32. Shende, S., et al.: Characterizing I/O Performance Using the TAU Performance System. In: Exascale Mini-symposium, ParCo 2011 (2011)
33. The Libunwind Project: The libunwind project (2014), http://www.nongnu.org/libunwind/
34. University of Oregon: ACISS (2014), http://aciss.uoregon.edu/

A Comparison between OPARI2 and the OpenMP Tools Interface in the Context of Score-P[*]

Daniel Lorenz[1], Robert Dietrich[2], Ronny Tschüter[2], and Felix Wolf[1,3]

[1] German Research School for Simulation Sciences, 52062 Aachen, Germany
[2] Technische Universität Dresden, Center for Information Services and High Performance Computing, 01062 Dresden, Germany
[3] RWTH Aachen University, Department of Computer Science, 52056 Aachen, Germany

Abstract. The upcoming OpenMP tools interface (OMPT) has been designed as a portable interface for performance analysis tools. It provides access to OpenMP-related information at program runtime and can thus extend the analysis capabilities of current performance tools. This paper compares the functionality and convenience of OMPT with OPARI2 for event-based performance analysis. For this purpose, we integrated OMPT into the measurement infrastructure Score-P, which previously accessed OpenMP-related information using only source-level instrumentation with OPARI2. For comparison, we performed Score-P measurements of the NAS Parallel Benchmark suite and the LULESH code with OPARI2 instrumentation and with OMPT. In each case, we determined the overhead and evaluated the output. We found that the measurement overhead is dominated by the measurement system, while the contribution of the event source remains negligible. Moreover, OMPT and OPARI2 provide complementary views of the performance behavior. Whereas OPARI2 maintains a strictly source-code-centric perspective that reflects OpenMP standard abstractions, OMPT mirrors the behavior of the OpenMP runtime and exposes compiler optimizations.

1 Introduction

OpenMP is a widely used parallel programming specification for shared-memory platforms. Many compilers support it to exploit thread-level parallelism on modern hardware architectures. In the past, several analysis tools [5,6,8,9,11,16] that are capable of recording and displaying OpenMP related performance data emerged, assisting users in the optimization of their parallel programs. However, the OpenMP specification does not define a performance monitoring interface that enables tool developers to write portable measurement libraries. The emerging OpenMP tools interface (OMPT) [3] is intended to address this need.

In this work, we discuss OMPT in the context of the performance measurement infrastructure Score-P [9]. So far, Score-P captures OpenMP-related performance data using the source-to-source instrumenter OPARI2 [14]. However, since OMPT provides

---

[*] This material is based upon work supported by the Department of Energy under Grant No. DE-FG02-13ER26158 / DE-SC0010668.

L. DeRose (Eds.): IWOMP 2014, LNCS 8766, pp. 161–172, 2014.

callbacks signaling the begin and the end of OpenMP constructs and other important events, it offers an attractive alternative to the current OPARI2-based instrumentation.

To evaluate the capabilities of OMPT for the event-based acquisition of OpenMP performance data, we integrated an OMPT adapter into Score-P and compared it in a set of different profiling and tracing scenarios with the default instrumentation via OPARI2. Our experiments are based on an OMPT implementation in the open-source version of the Intel OpenMP runtime [12]. To compare OMPT and OPARI2, we ran the NAS Parallel Benchmarks and the LULESH code, either with OMPT or with OPARI2 instrumentation. We determined the overhead for both cases, and evaluated the performance reports generated by Score-P.

The paper is organized as follows. Section 2 describes related work, in particular, further approaches to capture OpenMP-related performance data. Afterwards, in Section 3, we discuss the differences between the approaches taken by OPARI2 and OMPT in more detail. Section 4 outlines our prototypical OMPT adapter implementation in Score-P and the event model it adheres to. An evaluation of the experimental results is given in Section 5. Finally, in Section 6, we present our conclusions.

2 Related Work

Several tools [5,6,8,9,11,16] have emerged to provide insight into the parallel execution of OpenMP applications. Because there is no tools interface defined in the OpenMP specification yet, analysis tools rely on different methods to acquire their data. Performance tools based on sampling do not depend on an instrumenter like OPARI2. HPCToolkit [11], for example, collects the call path along with performance metrics at every sampling point. The routines are identified by their name and embedded in a calling-context. HPCToolkit recently implemented OMPT support to enable advanced analysis features like blame shifting for OpenMP applications. Another data acquisition strategy is instrumentation, which inserts hooks into the code to capture relevant events subject to further analysis. Advantages and drawbacks of the two approaches have been investigated in [13].

This work focuses on the measurement infrastructure Score-P [9], which uses instrumentation for data collection. Score-P is a joint performance measurement infrastructure for several analysis tools, including Vampir [8], Scalasca [6], TAU [16], and Periscope [1]. Currently, the performance-data collection of OpenMP events rests on the source-code instrumenter OPARI2 [14], which provides a portable way of instrumenting OpenMP pragmas by inserting calls to measurement functions around those pragmas into the program code. Score-P can produce both event traces and call-path profiles.

An alternative to OPARI2 is the ROSE compiler [15], which has been developed at Lawrence Livermore National Laboratory. It is an open-source compiler infrastructure to build source-to-source program translation and analysis tools for large-scale C/C++ and Fortran applications. ROSE can be used to identify and instrument all OpenMP 3.0 constructs in the source code [10]. Instead of transforming the source code, Paraver with Extrae as trace generator instruments OpenMP runtime routines based on a preloading mechanism (LD_PRELOAD) or DynInst [2]. The major drawback of this approach is the limited portability, as currently only Intel, GNU and IBM OpenMP runtimes are supported. Furthermore, only visible OpenMP runtime library routines can be instrumented, which limits the obtainable information.

3   Instrumentation Approaches

Among event-based performance analysis tools, the instrumenter OPARI2 is widely used. OMPT also aims to support event-based tools. This section gives an overview of OPARI2 and OMPT in the context of event-based performance analysis.

3.1   OPARI2

OPARI2 [14] is a source-to-source instrumentation tool for OpenMP applications. It annotates OpenMP directives and runtime library calls with calls to the POMP2 measurement interface. A performance measurement infrastructure can implement these calls to obtain information about the execution of OpenMP parallel applications. OPARI2 is independent of a specific OpenMP implementation. It parses the source code and modifies it directly. To instrument a program using OPARI2, the application must be recompiled. The POMP2 event model provides events marking the begin and the end of an OpenMP construct. If an OpenMP construct refers to a structured block, OPARI2 inserts extra enter and exit events around this block—with the exception of loop constructs. If an OpenMP construct implies an implicit barrier, OPARI2 replaces the implicit barrier with an explicit barrier and instruments the explicit barrier. As an example, Listing 1.2 shows how OPARI2 instruments the OpenMP construct from Listing 1.1.

3.2   OMPT

OMPT [3] is an extension proposal for the OpenMP specification. It defines a standardized interface to obtain information from the OpenMP runtime system. OMPT pursues different objectives. First, the OpenMP tools API provides state information on the OpenMP runtime to be queried by an analysis tool. This feature is mainly intended for sampling. OMPT distinguishes three classes of states: mandatory, optional, and flexible. In contrast to optional states, mandatory states have to be maintained by all standard-compliant OpenMP implementations. Finally, implementations have some freedom if and when they indicate the transition to a flexible state.

Second, OMPT allows event-based performance tools to register function callbacks for events of interest. For most constructs, OMPT provides begin and end events that are triggered when a thread encounters a construct and when it finishes its execution, respectively. Furthermore, events exist to notify a tool when threads or tasks are created, a thread switches between the execution of two tasks, or a thread starts waiting or ends waiting in synchronization constructs. The event callbacks are classified as mandatory and optional. Mandatory events have to be implemented by all standard-compliant OpenMP implementations. The set of mandatory events is small but sufficient for basic performance analysis of OpenMP programs. For example, mandatory events include the start and the end of threads, tasks, and parallel regions. Nevertheless, the majority

Listing 1.1. Example of a simple OpenMP parallel loop

```
#pragma omp parallel for
for (i=0; i < 100000; i++)
    c[i] = a[i] + b[i];
```

Listing 1.2. Code generated by OPARI2 for a simple OpenMP parallel loop

```
POMP2_Parallel_fork( ... );
#pragma omp parallel   ...
{
    POMP2_Parallel_begin( ... );
    {
        POMP2_For_enter( ... );
        #pragma omp for nowait
        for (i=0; i < 100000; i++)
            c[i] = a[i] + b[i];
        {
            POMP2_Implicit_barrier_enter( ... );
            #pragma omp barrier
            POMP2_Implicit_barrier_exit( ... );
        }
        POMP2_For_exit( ... );
    }
    POMP2_Parallel_end( ... );
}
POMP2_Parallel_join( ... );
```

of information needed by Score-P is available only as optional events. An OpenMP implementation can support an arbitrary set of optional events and analysis tools can not rely on the availability of any optional event.

3.3   Comparison

Functionality and portability: OPARI2 accesses only the source code of an application. Therefore, OPARI2 is independent of a specific OpenMP runtime. The source code is parsed and rewritten by OPARI2 before the code is compiled which may alter code optimization decisions of the compiler. Performance measurement tools that want to use OMPT need an OpenMP runtime that implements OMPT. Neither error-prone source code parsing nor recompilation are needed with OMPT, shifting development and maintenance costs from tool to OpenMP runtime developers. It is only necessary to implement measurement adapters. However, tools have to live with the possibility that certain optional events are absent.

Obtainable information: The callbacks provided by OMPT and the instrumentation inserted by OPARI2 follow a similar event model. For example, both methods indicate start and completion of a construct. On the other hand, the view the two methods provide of the application behavior is different in many regards. As a source-to-source instrumenter, OPARI2 has access to source-code information, but not to runtime information. Thus, it supplies many source-code details like the source-code location of constructs or additional clauses. Essentially, the instrumentation reflects the source-code structure and is agnostic of compiler optimizations. In contrast, OMPT is implemented in the OpenMP runtime library. Hence, it can access runtime information but lacks direct knowledge of the source code. It therefore does not know the original source-code structure but only the optimized binary code, which is why it can deliver insight into compiler optimizations. However, this implies that OMPT provides function pointer addresses for outlined functions of parallel regions and tasks as the only meta information on constructs. The function pointers can be used to obtain source code information if available. In principle, OMPT provides events for all constructs. However, most of the callbacks are optional in OMPT. Thus, the set of available events depends on the OpenMP implementation. With OPARI2, all events are always available, but a user can disable the instrumentation of any set of constructs. Additionally, OMPT allows direct measurement of waiting time in synchronization constructs. With OPARI2 a user can only assume waiting time if the execution time of a synchronization construct is large. Figure 1 shows the respective event trace of the OpenMP parallel loop construct from Listing 1.1 in the Vampir trace browser. The upper two charts (white background) depict the event trace recorded with OMPT callbacks. A timeline representation of the parallel loop execution with four threads is illustrated in the first chart and the corresponding call stack of the master thread is shown in the second chart. The lower two charts (purple background) present the data obtained from the OPARI2 instrumentation for the execution of the same OpenMP construct. OMPT reflects that the OpenMP runtime completes the execution of the parallel loop with an implicit barrier (blue region), whereas the OPARI2 instrumentation inserts an explicit barrier to the parallel loop construct.

4 Score-P Implementation

For the purpose of this study, we implemented a Score-P prototype supporting the OMPT interface. It was our goal to measure OpenMP applications even if the OpenMP runtime implements only mandatory events. If optional events are available, they should enrich the measurement with additional information. The Score-P architecture [9] consists of an adapter layer which captures events and a measurement layer which passes the data to the profiling or tracing backend. Event traces are written in the Open Trace Format 2 (OTF2) [4], which can be analyzed with Vampir or Scalasca. Call-path profiles are stored in the CUBE4 format.

First, we implemented a new support component for the internal thread management under OMPT, making no assumption about the availability of optional events. Unfortunately, the callbacks indicating the begin and end of an implicit task are optional events in OMPT. However, the information when a worker thread starts or ends its execution is essential in Score-P. Although we can estimate these times from the begin and end of a parallel region on the master thread, we still need to know which threads belong

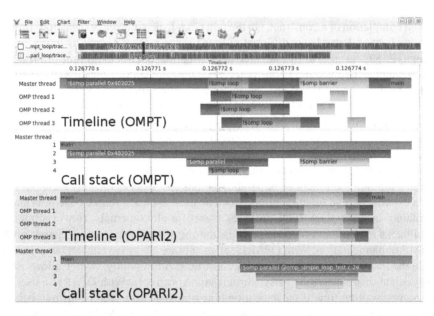

Fig. 1. OMPT (white background) and OPARI2 (purple background) perspective on an *OpenMP parallel for* region executed with four threads. The Vampir compare view shows the timeline and call stack view on the respective event traces.

to the parallel region. However, Score-P only learns that a thread is executing a parallel region if this thread triggers an event inside the region, which is not guaranteed. Thus, if no events appear inside a parallel region, Score-P can show that there is a parallel region but does not know about any worker threads running inside.

Second, we developed a new adapter that implements the OMPT callback functions and translates the call-backs to Score-P events. The OpenMP runtime version that we used for our experiments does not implement all optional events. However, for most OpenMP constructs that occurred in our experiments, OMPT call-backs exist.

5   Evaluation

In this section, we compare OPARI2 and OMPT on the basis of performance experiments with several benchmarks. We ran the NAS Parallel Benchmark (NBP) suite in profiling mode, while we ran LULESH in tracing mode. For each test case, we chose the minimum execution time of ten measurements.

5.1   Profiling Overhead

Our test platform was the the Linux cluster JUROPA at Forschungszentrum Jülich. JUROPA has 2208 compute nodes, each equipped with two Intel Xeon X5570 quad-core processors running with 2.93 GHz We used the Intel compiler version 11.1 to build the OpenMP runtime, Score-P and the NPB suite. The number of threads was always eight.

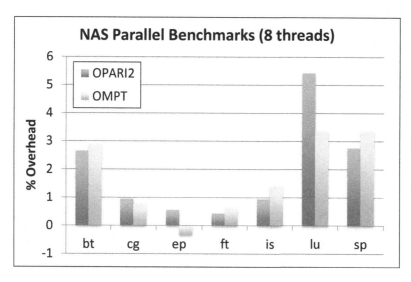

Fig. 2. Overhead of NPB measurements with OPARI2 instrumentation and with OMPT callbacks on JUROPA

We measured the runtime of (i) the uninstrumented codes, (ii) with OPARI2 instrumentation of OpenMP constructs, and (iii) with OMPT callbacks to record OpenMP related data. In addition to OPARI2 instrumentation and OMPT callbacks, we instrumented the main function manually. The measured overheads are shown in Figure 2.

The overhead is low in all cases. Only the OPARI2-instrumented lu benchmark shows an overhead of 5.4%. In all other cases the overhead is less than 3.4%. For cg, ep, and ft, the overhead is even less than the standard measurement deviation for these applications. With the exception of lu, the overheads of the OMPT and OPARI2 instrumentation are very similar. The difference in runtime is less than the standard deviation. The negative overhead measured for the OMPT instrumented ep is due to measurement deviation.

Only in the lu benchmark code, we observed a significant difference between the overheads of OMPT call backs and OPARI2 instrumentation. The reason is due to the more than 140,000,000 visits to OpenMP flush constructs in lu. They are instrumented by OPARI2, where they produce more than 95% of the events, but do not trigger any call backs in our OMPT implementation. This is because the Intel OpenMP runtime has no support for flush callbacks yet.

Except for the creation of a new system thread, the Score-P measurement system performs no communication or synchronization between threads during the measurement. Thus, we expect Score-P to be embarrassingly parallel. Measurements with the lu benchmark on JUROPA with up to 16 threads show that the speedup of the OPARI2 instrumented code, the OMPT based measurement and the uninstrumented code are identical.

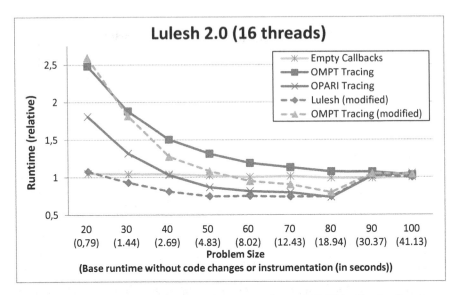

Fig. 3. Runtimes of LULESH with OPARI2 instrumentation and OMPT callbacks. Runtimes are relative to the runtime of the uninstrumented LULESH code. In the modified (and also uninstrumented) version, the implicit barrier was manually exchanged for an explicit barrier, similar to the transformation performed by OPARI2 (Listings 1.1 and 1.2).

5.2   Tracing Overhead

LULESH [7] is a shock hydrodynamics code developed at Lawrence Livermore National Laboratory. It is known to challenge machine performance. Furthermore, it stresses compiler vectorization, OpenMP overheads, and intra-node parallelism. For the latter, it employs for loops in simple non-nested parallel regions. We used LULESH version 2.0 and conducted our experiments on the Sandy Bridge partition of the HPC cluster Taurus at Technische Universität Dresden. We ran the job with 16 threads on a single node, which is equipped with two Intel Xeon CPU E5-2690 (8 cores) at 2.90GHz and hyperthreading disabled. LULESH, the open source version of the Intel OpenMP runtime, and the measurement system Score-P were compiled with the Intel compiler version 13.0.1. To record a similar set of events with both instrumentation approaches and enable the visualization of worker threads, we inserted calls to the implicit task begin and end callbacks into the the Intel OpenMP runtime.

We ran LULESH with different problem sizes for a fixed number of 200 iterations. Figure 3 shows the the runtimes relative to the original LULESH code without instrumentation. The runtime of the LULESH code without any instrumentation increases from $0.79sec$ for a problem size of 20 to $41.13sec$ for the problem size 100. The problem size defines the workload and increases the total computation time, whereas the number of OpenMP events stays constant. As the number of measurement events is independent of the problem size, large instrumentation overheads can be forced with small problem sizes and vice versa. For problem sizes smaller than 90, the OPARI2 instrumented version has between 9 and 73 percentage points less overhead than the

Table 1. Number of constructs distinguished by OPARI2 and OMPT for `bt` and `ft`. The OMPT implementation in our version of the Intel OpenMP runtime does not yet support atomic regions. For most OpenMP constructs, OMPT-based measurements merge constructs of the same type and aggregate their data.

Construct	bt		ft	
	OPARI2	OMPT	OPARI2	OMPT
atomic	2	–	0,	–
barrier	19	aggregated	9,	aggregated
loop	30	aggregated	8	aggregated
master	5	aggregated	1	aggregated
parallel	10	10	9	10

OMPT version. For problem sizes from 50 to 80, the OPARI2 instrumented code was even faster than the uninstrumented code. During instrumentation, OPARI2 substitutes explicit barriers for implicit barriers, as depicted in Section 3.1. If we apply this change manually to the LULESH source code, the uninstrumented code runs up to 26% faster than the unmodified version. As a consequence, the measurements with OMPT are much faster, too. The measurements with the modified code are shown in Figure 3 as dashed lines. We believe that this change alters the compile-time optimization decisions and constitutes the major reason why the OPARI2-based and the OMPT-based measurements are different.

5.3   Structural Differences in Performance Content

In the following, we highlight structural differences in the output of the two methods. As these differences are based on the instrumentation technique, our observations apply to both profiling and tracing equally.

The first observation is that OPARI2 provides source code information on every OpenMP construct, which allows the user to distinguish them during analysis. Except for parallel constructs and tasks, OMPT does not provide any information to distinguish constructs of the same type. Thus, for all remaining construct types, constructs of the same type appear merged and their performance data aggregated. This can be illustrated with profiling data from NPB. Since OPARI2 measurements can distinguish multiple OpenMP constructs of the same type appearing inside the same call path, the call tree of the OPARI2-instrumented code might look more differentiated. Table 1 shows the number of distinguishable constructs OPARI2 and OMPT recognize. To quantify the additional information the distinction among constructs of the same type provides, we counted the number of call paths (i.e., nodes) in the call tree (Table 2).

Table 2 shows that in most cases the OPARI2 profiles contain significantly more call paths than the OMPT profiles. For `bt`, `cg`, and `lu`, the OPARI2 profiles show more than twice as many call paths as the OMPT profiles. A remarkable exception is `ft`, where the OMPT instrumentation leads to more call paths than the OPARI2 instrumentation because it shows one additional outlined function for a parallel construct. Both profiles

Table 2. Number of visits and different call paths in the profile of NPB codes, measured with OPARI2 and OMPT

		bt	cg	ep	ft	is	lu	sp
OPARI2	Visits	47,994	147,990	154	2682	810	148,517,435	133,690
	Call paths	67	54	12	28	23	95	79
OMPT	Visits	34,197	127,571	54	172	626	1,712,033	90,265
	Call paths	32	26	11	31	18	34	44

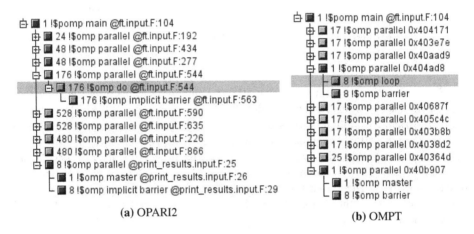

(a) OPARI2   (b) OMPT

Fig. 4. Comparison of the `ft` call trees generated with OPARI2 and with OMPT

are shown in Figure 4a and Figure 4b. The source code contains nine parallel constructs, as identified by OPARI2.

A second observation are the different visit counts produced by the two methods. This has several reasons. First, our OMPT implementation did not yet support all constructs that appeared. For example, in `lu` more than 95% of the visits in the OPARI2 instrumented measurement stem from flush constructs, for which the OMPT implementation does not produce events yet. Another reason is that the OPARI2 module of Score-P counts the start and the end of the implicit task inside the parallel region for every thread. Because the implicit task begin event is optional in OMPT, the OMPT module in Score-P must rely on the begin of the parallel region itself, which happens only on the master thread. However, this could be easily changed in a post-processing step, or by implementing the implicit task-begin event callback in the OpenMP runtime.

In some cases, compiler optimizations affect the visit count, which is the number of times a call path has been visited. For example, a loop in the main routine of `ft` iterates over subroutine calls to `evolve`, `fft`, and `checksum`, which contain parallel constructs. The OPARI2 measurement shows 20 or more visits per thread for these parallel constructs. However, the OMPT measurement shows only one visit for each of its 10 parallel constructs. Our explanation is that the compiler applied optimizations, e.g., moved the parallel region creation around the loop. Optimizations like unrolling are also a possible explanation why the number of parallel constructs in the OMPT result for ft differs from the number of parallel constructs in the source code. Furthermore, optimizations may result in outlined functions which cannot be easily mapped to the user code. We recompiled ft with optimization level zero to prove this assumption. The measurement result of the unoptimized ft with OMPT shows 9 outlined functions for parallel constructs. However, every parallel construct is still visited only once.

Obviously, OMPT measurements may provide insight into compiler optimizations. However, understanding this information may require knowledge of the compiler and may even then not be comprehensible at the first glance. In contrast, OPARI2 delivers information that strictly reflects the source code.

6 Conclusion

We compared OMPT callbacks and OPARI2 instrumentation with respect to their suitability for event-based performance measurements. OPARI2's source-to-source translation approach neither has access to object code nor to intermediate representations, but reflects the structure of the source code very well. An advantage is that a user can easily map the measurement results onto his mental image of the program. Since OPARI2 passes along all relevant source code information, the results can even be explored in a source-code browser. On the other hand, the instrumentation may interfere with compiler instrumentation and optimization.

For the development of OMPT, one of the initial design guidelines was to create an interface that can be implemented in the OpenMP runtime without having to change the compiler. Thus, it provides a view of the OpenMP runtime level, including compiler optimization artifacts. This may reflect the execution behavior of the application more accurately. On the other hand, differences to the source code representation may obscure measurement results sometimes. Overall, OPARI2 and OMPT provide complementary information, which makes it reasonable to combine both approaches. The information gathered with OMPT could be extended with source code correlation via OPARI2, whereas events that are not available with OPARI2 (e.g. thread begin/end, wait barrier begin/end) could be captured using OMPT. The measurement overhead is generally low for both, OMPT and OPARI2. In most cases, the measurement system itself dominates the overhead regardless of the instrumentation method. However, in cases where the source code instrumentation of OPARI2 interferes with compiler optimization, OPARI2 instrumentation may lead to different execution times.

The mandatory set of callback functions in OMPT allows call-path profiles to be constructed from the events produced by our instrumentation—provided that no tasks are used. However, if a worker thread does not trigger any events inside a parallel region, it may remain invisible in the measurement. To construct call-path profiles for tasks, the measurement system must be notified of task switches. Thus, to support event-based performance tools, we recommend to support at least the optional callbacks for the events `ompt_event_implicit_task_begin` and `ompt_event_task_switch` in OMPT implementations.

References

1. Benedict, S., Petkov, V., Gerndt, M.: PERISCOPE: An online-based distributed performance analysis tool. In: Tools for High Performance Computing 2009, pp. 1–16. Springer, Heidelberg (2010)
2. Buck, B., Hollingsworth, J.K.: An API for runtime code patching. The International Journal of High Performance Computing Applications 14(4), 317–329 (2000)
3. Eichenberger, A.E., et al.: OMPT: An OpenMP tools application programming interface for performance analysis. In: Rendell, A.P., Chapman, B.M., Müller, M.S. (eds.) IWOMP 2013. LNCS, vol. 8122, pp. 171–185. Springer, Heidelberg (2013)
4. Eschweiler, D., Wagner, M., Geimer, M., Knüpfer, A., Nagel, W.E., Wolf, F.: Open Trace Format 2 - The next generation of scalable trace formats and support libraries. In: Proc. of the Intl. Conference on Parallel Computing, ParCo 2011, Ghent, Belgium, August 30 – September 2. Advances in Parallel Computing, vol. 22, pp. 481–490. IOS Press (2012)
5. Fürlinger, K., Gerndt, M.: ompp: A profiling tool for openmp. In: Mueller, M.S., Chapman, B.M., de Supinski, B.R., Malony, A.D., Voss, M. (eds.) IWOMP 2005/2006. LNCS, vol. 4315, pp. 15–23. Springer, Heidelberg (2008)
6. Geimer, M., Wolf, F., Wylie, B.J.N., Becker, D., Abraham, E., Mohr, B.: The Scalasca performance toolset architecture. Concurrency and Computation: Practice and Experience 22(6), 702–719 (2010)
7. Karlin, I., Keasler, J., Neely, R.: LULESH 2.0 updates and changes. Technical Report LLNL-TR-641973, Lawrence Livermore National Laboratory (August 2013)
8. Knüpfer, A., Brunst, H., Doleschal, J., Jurenz, M., Lieber, M., Mickler, H., Müller, M.S., Nagel, W.E.: The Vampir performance analysis tool-set. In: Tools for High Performance Computing, Proceedings of the 2nd International Workshop on Parallel Tools for High Performance Computing, Stuttgart, Germany, pp. 139–155. Springer (July 2008)
9. Knüpfer, A., Rössel, C., an Mey, D., Biersdorff, S., Diethelm, K., Eschweiler, D., Geimer, M., Gerndt, M., Lorenz, D., Malony, A.D., Nagel, W.E., Oleynik, Y., Philippen, P., Saviankou, P., Schmidl, D., Shende, S.S., Tschüter, R., Wagner, M., Wesarg, B., Wolf, F.: Score-P – A joint performance measurement run-time infrastructure for Periscope, Scalasca, TAU, and Vampir. In: Proc. of 5th Parallel Tools Workshop, 2011, pp. 79–91. Springer, Heidelberg (2012)
10. Liao, C., Quinlan, D.J., Panas, T., de Supinski, B.R.: A ROSE-based OpenMP 3.0 research compiler supporting multiple runtime libraries. In: Sato, M., Hanawa, T., Müller, M.S., Chapman, B.M., de Supinski, B.R. (eds.) IWOMP 2010. LNCS, vol. 6132, pp. 15–28. Springer, Heidelberg (2010)
11. Liu, X., Mellor-Crummey, J., Fagan, M.: A new approach for performance analysis of OpenMP programs. In: Proceedings of the 27th International ACM Conference on Supercomputing, pp. 69–80. ACM (2013)
12. Mellor-Crummey, J., et al.: OMPT support branch of the open source Intel OpenMP runtime library (December 2013),
    http://intel-openmp-rtl.googlecode.com/svn/
    branches/ompt-support
13. Metz, E., Lencevicius, R., Gonzalez, T.F.: Performance data collection using a hybrid approach. SIGSOFT Software Engineering Notes 30(5), 126–135 (2005)
14. Mohr, B., Malony, A.D., Shende, S.S., Wolf, F.: Design and prototype of a performance tool interface for OpenMP. The Journal of Supercomputing 23(1), 105–128 (2002)
15. Quinlan, D.J., et al.: ROSE compiler project (April 2014),
    http://www.rosecompiler.org
16. Shende, S.S., Malony, A.D.: The TAU parallel performance system. The International Journal of High Performance Computing Applications 20(2), 287–311 (2006)

A User-Guided Locking API for the OpenMP* Application Program Interface

Hansang Bae[1], James Cownie[2], Michael Klemm[3], and Christian Terboven[4]

[1] Software and Services Group, Intel Corporation, Champaign, IL, USA
[2] Software and Services Group, Intel Corporation (UK) Ltd., Bristol, UK
[3] Software and Services Group, Intel GmbH, Feldkirchen, Germany
{hansang.bae,james.h.cownie,michael.klemm}@intel.com
[4] IT Center, RWTH Aachen University, Aachen, Germany
terboven@itc.rwth-aachen.de

Abstract. Although the OpenMP API specification defines a set of runtime routines for simple and nested locks, there is no standardized way to select different lock implementations. Programmers have to use vendor extensions to globally alter the lock implementation for the application; fine-grained control is not possible. Proper use of hardware-based speculative locks can achieve significant runtime improvements but, if used inappropriately, they can lead to severe performance penalties. Thus programmers need to be able to explicitly choose the right lock implementation on a per-lock basis. In this paper, we extend the OpenMP API for locks with functions to provide such hints to the implementation. We also extend the syntax and semantics of the `critical` construct with clauses to contain hints. Our performance results for micro-benchmarks show that the runtime selection of lock implementations does not add any noticeable overhead. We also show that using an appropriate runtime hint can improve application performance.

Keywords: OpenMP, locks, lock elision, speculative locks, Intel TSX.

1 Introduction

The OpenMP* API specification [12] defines lock routines for both simple and nested locks. However, there is no standard technique to allow programmers to pass information about the usage of a lock to the runtime. Vendor extensions such as the `KMP_LOCK_KIND` environment variable for the Intel OpenMP runtime change the implementation of all locks; fine-grained control of a lock implementation is not possible. Hence, it is impossible for programmers to choose a lock implementation that is optimized for the specific usage of a particular lock in an application. Even in the absence of hardware to support speculative locks, spin locks may be optimal for an uncontended lock, whereas more complicated queuing locks should be used for a heavily contended lock.

With hardware support for speculative lock elision in processors from vendors such as IBM [6] and Intel [8], this lack of per-lock control has become more important. Locks using hardware speculation can achieve significant performance

L. DeRose (Eds.): IWOMP 2014, LNCS 8766, pp. 173–186, 2014.

improvements, but can also cause tremendous penalties if used inappropriately. Using environment variables to change the implementation of all locks in a program is therefore no longer sensible; instead the programmer needs to select the best implementation for each significant lock based on the contention for the lock and the properties of the code inside the guarded critical section.

In this paper we propose to extend the OpenMP API for locks. We define new functions to pass contention information on a per-lock basis to the OpenMP runtime. Changes are only necessary where the new functionality is desired and are kept to a minimum to enable a smooth, incremental, transition. We demonstrate how the new API can be implemented efficiently while maintaining compatibility with code that has already been compiled and thus cannot be changed. We also extend the existing OpenMP `critical` construct with a clause to pass hints to the underlying lock. Our benchmarks prove that the performance impact of our implementation is minimal. Our measurements show that performance can be improved by using the new interface to exploit the Intel® Transactional Synchronization Extensions (Intel® TSX).

The remainder of the paper is organized as follows. Section 2 surveys related work. Section 3 provides a brief introduction to Intel TSX. In Section 4, we discuss possible design choices for API extensions to support per-lock hints. The specification of the extensions for the lock API and `critical` construct we propose are shown in detail in Section 5. Section 6 presents our implementation in the Intel OpenMP runtime and Section 7 evaluates its performance. Finally, Section 8 concludes the paper.

2   Related Work

Work from the 1990s such as that of Mellor-Crummey and Scott [10] discusses the differing properties of spin and queuing locks.

The POSIX thread library [4] contains support for different kinds of locks including speculative locks as part of glibc [9,11]. Although programmers can select the type of lock to use on a per-lock basis, the POSIX interface is not part of the OpenMP API definition and thus cannot be used from OpenMP without writing code that no longer conforms to OpenMP.

There are several papers on how to apply TSX-like technologies in HPC [13,15] and the performance improvements that can be obtained. Although hardware lock elision and transactional memory share similarities at the machine level, the programming models differ greatly. These papers augment the source code with target-specific constructs, whereas we propose a standard API to avoid the need for non-portable modifications.

IBM has implemented hardware specific pragmas in their C/C++ compiler for the Blue Gene/Q machine, such as `#pragma tm_atomic` [7]. There is a proposal for OpenMP [1,14], which defines OpenMP constructs to support transactional memory. However, this is fundamentally different from lock-based programming and complements our proposal from a different angle.

3 Intel TSX

Intel Transactional Synchronization Extensions are new capabilities introduced in the processors formerly known as Haswell which provide support for transactional execution while using cache-coherence protocols to detect memory access conflicts. On a transactional abort, the architectural state of the processor is restored to that at the start of the transaction (all transactional memory writes are discarded, and register state is restored). At transaction commit all transactional writes become atomically visible to other cores.

By using Intel TSX it is possible to execute multiple dynamic instances of a critical section simultaneously, with the required mutual exclusion enforced by the hardware when conflicting memory accesses occur. This allows code written with a single, coarse lock to behave as if it were implemented with fine-grain reader-writer locks.

Intel TSX provides two different interfaces to speculation: Hardware Lock Elision (HLE) and Restricted Transactional Memory (RTM). HLE is a backwards binary compatible interface that can be added to an existing lock. It requests that the processor speculate the critical section. If the speculation fails the processor takes the lock "for real" and executes the critical section non-speculatively. HLE preserves all of the semantics of the existing lock, so if the lock value is read inside the critical section it appears to be locked, as it would if there were no speculation.

Restricted Transactional Memory uses new instructions to place the processor into a speculative execution state and to commit the speculative state. With RTM the user has to provide the non-speculative backup path, since no lock is visible to the hardware.

Since some operations (inter alia any exception that would enter the kernel, or any system call) cannot be executed speculatively and cause an abort of speculation, converting all critical sections to use speculative locks may be counter-productive since much speculative work may have been performed before the abort, which then has to be replicated. Consider a lock used to serialize output, for instance, effort may be expended formatting data before the write system call is made. If this is done inside a speculative lock the formatting work will all be lost and have to be repeated.

We use both HLE and RTM in our speculative lock implementations.

4 Design Choices

The following section presents the design principles and decisions for the new locking API. We considered a number of ways in which the OpenMP lock interface could be extended.

The fundamental requirement of the new API is not to break any existing code to maintain a smooth transition from the old API to the new one. We also strive for an incremental refinement approach, in which a programmer can easily modify parts of the application code by adding lock hints. This should lead to improvements for the modified parts, while other, untouched, code is not negatively affected in terms of either correctness or performance.

Since not all OpenMP implementations can support multiple lock types and not all hardware supports speculative lock elision, we choose to make the new locking API a hint. If accepted into the OpenMP standard, an OpenMP runtime will have to support the proposed API, however it would be permitted to map the new API to the existing locking API and behavior without performance penalties. The additional information passed to the runtime is merely a hint that can be ignored.

If we consider the existing OpenMP API, there are only a few options available that maintain the programming style of current OpenMP and that do not break base-language compatibility:

- Use pragmas to prefix the existing lock routines with the desired hint.
- Introduce a full set of new locking routines and a new lock type.
- Add new lock initialization routines while keeping the existing lock API.

The pragma-based approach seems viable, but requires changes to both the compiler and the runtime to support the pragma. Since the OpenMP lock API is currently solely based on runtime functions, we would like to avoid splitting it across the compiler and runtime.

Adding a new lock type (e. g., `omp_lock_hint_t`) would require changes to every source code location where the given lock was operated upon, making the changes associated with lock tuning much harder than necessary. Programmers would need to touch the lock definition, lock initialization, function declarations (if locks are passed as arguments), and the lock operations themselves. It also prevents the use of the new lock type where a lock is declared in one part of the code but used in a separately compiled library for which the source may be not available or that cannot be changed for other reasons (e. g., compatibility with other library users).

The option of a new initialization function that leaves the rest of the lock API unchanged avoids these problems. To add the hint to the lock, a programmer only has to change the lock initialization routine to pass the desired hint to the runtime. The formal type of the lock and all lock operations stay the same. Programmers thus can incrementally alter application code on a per-lock basis and improve lock performance by modifying individual locks.

To make our approach more generic and to keep it open for additions, we provide a space for vendor-specific hints. While this may limit portability (e. g., missing declarations of additional hints in the `omp.h` header file), such errors will be detected at compile time. This allows programming and tuning for specific machines and OpenMP implementations, which is in the OpenMP spirit of providing support to enable the highest performance.

5   The API for User-Guided Locks

The guiding design principles of Section 4 lead to a straightforward definition of an OpenMP API that supports user-guided lock routines. Our proposal is based on an extension of the existing lock API (Section 5.1) and new clauses for the `critical` construct (Section 5.2). Without loss of generality, the following section only shows the proposal for C and C++ as the base languages. A translation to Fortran is straightforward but omitted for brevity.

5.1 User-Guided Lock Routines

An OpenMP lock is declared as a variable of the formal type `omp_lock_t` or `omp_nest_lock_t`. Before its first use, it must be initialized by calling the lock initialization functions `omp_init_lock` or `omp_init_nest_lock`, respectively. Once the lock has been initialized it can be set, unset, tested, and destroyed using the `omp_set_lock`, `omp_unset_lock`, `omp_test_lock`, and `omp_destroy_lock` functions (or their counterparts for `omp_nest_lock_t`). Each of these functions takes a pointer to the lock variable as an argument.

To provide additional information to the runtime system, we propose to add two additional lock initialization functions:

```
void omp_init_lock_hinted(omp_lock_t*, omp_lock_hint_t)
void omp_init_nest_lock_hinted(omp_nest_lock_t*, omp_lock_hint_t)
```

These functions may be used as a replacement of the existing `omp_init_lock` and `omp_init_nest_lock` functions to initialize a lock before it is used. The additional argument to `omp_init_lock_hinted` and `omp_init_nest_lock_hinted` is a "lock hint", which passes extra information about the expected usage of the lock to the runtime.

We propose a list of mnemonic lock hints through the enumeration type `omp_lock_hint_t` (of course, the specific numeric values implied here are not normative):

```
typedef enum omp_lock_hint_t {
  omp_lock_hint_none,
  omp_lock_hint_uncontended,      // Optimize for an uncontended lock
  omp_lock_hint_contended,        // Optimize for a contended lock
  omp_lock_hint_nonspeculative,   // Do not use hardware speculation
  omp_lock_hint_speculative,      // Do use hardware speculation
  omp_lock_hint_adaptive,         // Adaptively use HW speculation
  // Additional standard hints as desired

  // Vendors can add additional hints after this definition
  omp_lock_hint_vendor_first = ...
} omp_lock_hint_t;
```

To support vendor-specific or platform-dependent hints, vendors can add their own mnemonics at the end of enumeration with values higher than the pseudo-mnemonic `omp_lock_hint_vendor_first`.

5.2 User-Guided `critical` Sections

Most OpenMP implementations translate a `critical` section into a matching pair of `omp_set_lock` and `omp_unset_lock` invocations on a global lock. If the section is named, then a global lock with a matching mangled name is created for the lock routines. With our additions to the OpenMP lock API, it is desirable to augment the `critical` section with additional information about the preferred lock implementation to be used.

To provide the hint to the `critical` section, we define a new clause:

`#pragma omp critical` *[(name)]* ***[hint(hint-kind)]*** *new-line*
    structured-block

with *hint-kind* being one of: `none`, `uncontended`, `contended`, `nonspeculative`, `speculative`, and `adaptive`. Adding the `hint` clause to the `critical` section requests that the runtime use a suitably hinted lock. Again, the *hint-kind* is merely a hint to the runtime and may be ignored if the runtime does not support different locks or if the hardware does not support speculative locking. If no `hint` clause is present, the default hint `none` is used, which corresponds to the current semantics of OpenMP.

To ensure proper interaction between the traditional (named) `critical` and those with hints added, we require two restrictions. First, if a `hint` clause is specified, the `critical` construct must be a named construct. Second, all `critical` constructs with the same name must have the same `hint` clause. The restrictions ensure that all `critical` constructs with a hint use the same lock implementation. If two constructs had the same name but different hints, then the OpenMP runtime could no longer ensure correctness and mutual exclusion for these `critical` regions at runtime. The second restriction ensures that the runtime can choose the same lock implementation for all `critical` constructs with the same name.

6   Implementation

To implement user-guided locks with hints the OpenMP runtime needs to decide which internal lock implementation to use. Often this is achieved by having several different internal locking functions that can be called from the runtime functions to implement the lock semantics.

6.1   Implementation Strategies

The Intel OpenMP runtime provides a variety of different lock implementations (of which we show only an incomplete set here, since the additional ones add no new challenges). A specific implementation is enabled for all locks by setting the `KMP_LOCK_KIND` environment variable.

TAS: a "test and test-and-set" spin-lock that operates directly on the space allocated by the compiler, i. e., the lock structure itself.

Futex: a lock that uses the Linux futex [3] system call to operate directly on the space allocated by the compiler, i. e., the lock structure itself.

Queuing: a fair queuing lock that uses the space allocated by the compiler as a pointer to the actual lock structure if it is large enough, otherwise the lock stores an index into a table of lock structures.

Adaptive: a "test and test-and-set" lock that uses Intel TSX technology if speculation was previously successful. It requires more space than that allocated by the compiler, since it has to maintain statistics on speculation success.

These lock types are implemented in different internal functions that are (globally) bound to the OpenMP lock API according to the setting of the environment variable KMP_LOCK_KIND and thus can only be selected for the whole application.

We refer to lock implementations that maintain all of their state in the space allocated by the compiler as *direct* implementations, and those which use the compiler allocated space to hold a pointer or index as *indirect* implementations.

In the implementation without omp_init_lock_hinted only a single lock type can be in use in a given process, and which implementation that is can therefore be maintained in global state. The lock dispatch code does not need to inspect the lock itself to determine which type of lock it is. We describe this as *static* dispatch. However, once we have hinted locks there can be instances of many different lock types in the same process, and the runtime has to distinguish them dynamically, while also handling both direct and indirect locks. We describe the lock implementation that can handle different lock types for each lock as *dynamic* dispatch.

The obvious way to implement dynamic dispatch is to use virtual functions that are stored along with the lock structure. This is the technique normally used to implement virtual methods for C++ objects. However, it expands the lock structure to include a pointer to a virtual function table (commonly known as a *vtable*).

Unfortunately, such an implementation is not viable for our proposal. First, simple locks implemented with atomic operations or Linux futexes are direct locks, so there is no lock object that can store the vtable pointer. Second, in some implementations which we wish to support (e.g., OpenMP code compiled by GCC targeting a 64-bit processor) the lock's size is less than the size of a pointer, so the lock cannot contain a pointer to a vtable-like structure. Third, to maintain compatibility with existing compiled code, we cannot modify omp_lock_t to change its size. This would result in undefined data accesses and correctness issues.

6.2   Decoding the Dynamic Lock Type

Our solution deals with the above constraints and is based on the observation that an indirect lock is a pointer to an internal object that is at least four byte aligned. Therefore the least significant two bits of the value stored in an indirect lock will always be zero. Thus, we can distinguish direct locks from indirect locks if we ensure that at all times the bottom two bits of indirect locks are not both zero. (We actually rely only on the value of the bottom bit.) Since the runtime fully controls the lock implementations, it is easy to require that our implementations respect this constraint. Linux futex locks also allow us to store any value in the lock word, so they can still be used.

Fig. 1 shows the code to extract the lock type from the lock structure whatever the lock type is. The code fragment exploits the properties of two's complement

```
enum lock_info_e {
  lock_value_shift = 8,
  lock_type_mask   = (1<<lock_value_shift)-1,
};

static uint32_t extract_direct_type(uint32_t *l) {
  uint32_t value = *l;
  return value & lock_type_mask & -(value & 1);
}
```

Fig. 1. Code fragment to efficiently decode the lock type from the least significant byte of the lock word

```
void omp_set_lock(omp_lock_t *l) {
  (set_lock_functions[extractDirectType((uint32_t *)l)](l);
}
```

```
omp_set_lock:
# parameter 1: %rdi
    movb      (%rdi), %dl
    movb      %dl, %al
    andb      $1, %al
    negb      %al
    andb      %al, %dl
    movzbl    %dl, %ecx
    movq      direct_setOps(,%rcx,8), %rsi
    jmp       *%rsi
```

Fig. 2. Example of `omp_set_lock` with decoding (top) and the assembly code generated by the compiler (bottom)

arithmetic. The value of `-(value & 1)` is -1 (i.e., all bits set to one) if the bottom bit of `value` is one. Conversely, it is zero if the bottom bit is zero. Therefore when the bottom bit is zero (as it is when the value is a pointer, i.e., we have an indirect lock) `extract_direct_type` will return zero, whereas if the bottom bit is one it will return the bottom byte of the lock word. Using this sequence avoids any conditional branches, which could lead to branch mispredictions when several different lock types are active simultaneously.

Once the lock type has been decoded, we use it as an index into a table of function pointers. To avoid additional lookups for indirect locks, the table contains the decoder for indirect locks as the zeroth pointer, while the values for the various direct locks will be 1, 3, 5, etc., so we have their implementation functions at those positions in the function table. Although this creates holes in the function table and wastes a few bytes of memory, it improves function lookup by avoiding expensive conditional branch instructions. Fig. 2 shows the

Table 1. Lock overhead of static and dynamic dispatch of the lock implementation.

Lock Type	Min time (cycle)		Mean time (cycle)	
	Static	Dynamic	Static	Dynamic
Direct (TAS)	58.53	58.14	62.37	59.88
Indirect (Queuing)	107.54	90.43	109.46	91.34

implementation of the dispatch of `omp_set_lock` and the generated assembly code for it. Note that the compiler has avoided building a stack frame and is using a branch for the tail call to the appropriate lock implementation function.

7   Performance Evaluation

For performance evaluation we compare the performance of the lock API of the Intel OpenMP runtime that includes dynamic lock dispatch with the released version which does not. All measurements are made on one socket of a dual-socket Intel® Xeon® E5-2697v3 processor (former code name "Haswell") at 2.6 GHz (no turbo). The machine runs Red Hat Enterprise Linux Server release 7.0 with kernel version 3.10.0-123.el7.x86_64. We use the Intel® Composer XE for C/C++ 2013 SP1 2.144 with -O3 optimization. Because the OpenMP runtime links dynamically, the same executable is used for all measurements, only the runtime is changed.

7.1   Microbenchmarks and Lock Overhead Timing

We compare the performance of locks using the EPCC benchmark suite's [2] "Lock Overhead" measure. We also use our own microbenchmark for the overhead measurements which we run with a single OpenMP thread measuring the time to enter and leave the lock through `omp_set_lock` and `omp_unset_lock`. We are not interested in the contention behavior of the locks, but merely in the latency of getting into and out of the lock code since that is the changed code path. Note that the EPCC suite only measures the performance of fully contended locks, and has no data references inside the critical section, though in real OpenMP codes locks are frequently uncontended.

The time shown in Table 1 is the difference between the time spent executing the kernel with a lock and same kernel, but without the lock operations. We measure a loop repeating these kernels 10,000 times, and divide the resulting time by 10,000. We also repeat that experiment 1000 times, accumulating statistics of minimum, mean, maximum, and standard deviation over the runs. We show both the minimum and mean times.

As discussed in Section 6 we are concerned with two types of locks (*direct* locks which store the lock value in the space allocated by the compiler and *indirect* locks which store a pointer in that space) and two types of lock dispatch: *static*, where all locks are of the same type (as in the existing code) and *dynamic*, where each lock may have a different implementation (as is required to implement

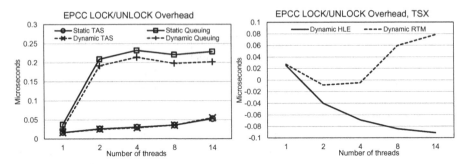

Fig. 3. EPCC LOCK/UNLOCK overhead - (a) static dispatch vs. dynamic dispatch, (b) dynamic TSX locks

our proposal). The interesting comparisons for lock overhead here are therefore between the static and dynamic dispatch columns.

The results of our microbenchmark (see Table 1) and the EPCC results in Fig. 3a show that on a modern processor our implementation of dynamic dispatch does not add any extra latency compared to the existing static lock dispatch code in the Intel OpenMP runtime. Therefore using dynamic lock dispatch (and allowing the user to choose lock types) will not slow down existing OpenMP codes that use locks.

The EPCC results in Fig. 3b demonstrate that the EPCC lock overhead measurement code cannot correctly measure the performance of speculative locks. It assumes that the locks serialize the code to ensure isolation, whereas speculative locking correctly enforces isolation without (always) serializing. As a result the speculative locks appear to have negative overhead.

7.2   Application Performance with User-Guided Locks

To evaluate the performance of lock hints in real code, we use the UA benchmark [5] from the NPB 3.3 benchmark suite. The original implementation of UA uses an array of fine-grain locks to protect the irregular update operation to a shared array A, as shown in Fig. 4a. The first experiment we conducted is to try different lock implementations by setting KMP_LOCK_KIND. This shows that using the TAS lock globally results in best performance; the first bar ("Static TAS") in Fig. 5 shows a speedup from 0.5 to 6.6 over the sequential version. Then, we enabled global use of the HLE lock in place of the TAS lock, but the performance degraded substantially as shown in the second bar ("Oblivious HLE") in Fig. 5. This result indicates that, as expected, just replacing existing fine-grain locks with TSX locks may not improve performance.

Next, we changed the code slightly to introduce coarser grained locking. We found that every statement guarded by a lock in the most time-consuming loop in UA is in the form of Fig. 4a (irregular reduction). An alternative way of computing this irregular reduction is to postpone the update to the shared data until each thread finishes computing local sums acopy as in Fig. 4b. Updates to

```
c$ omp do                                c$ omp do
do i = 1, N                              do i = 1, N
  ...                                      ...
  call omp_set_lock(L(f(i)))               acopy(f(i)) = acopy(f(i))+expr
  A(f(i)) = A(f(i))+expr                   ...
  call omp_unset_lock(L(f(i)))           enddo
  ...                                    c$ omp enddo
enddo                                    c$ omp critical
c$ omp enddo                               A(1:M) = A(1:M) + acopy(1:M)
                                         c$ omp end critical
           (a)                                      (b)
```

```
call omp_init_lock_hinted (LCK,hle)      k = (M/NUM_THREAD)*thread_num
c$ omp do                                do j = k+1, k+M
do i = 1, N                                call omp_set_lock(LCK)
  ...                                      if (j .gt. M) then
  acopy(f(i)) = acopy(f(i))+expr             A(j-M) = A(j-M) + acopy(j-M)
  ...                                      else
enddo                                        A(j) = A(j) + acopy(j)
c$ omp enddo                               endif
c continue...                              call omp_unset_lock(LCK)
                                         enddo
```

                                    (c)

Fig. 4. Code excerpt from UA – (a) original implementation, (b) postponed reduction optimization, (c) further optimization with hinted TSX locks. Shared variables were capitalized and the code was simplified for presentation.

the shared data are then executed within the critical section sequentially. This optimization results in better performance with one to 8 threads as shown in Fig. 5 ("Static Reduce").

Notice that in this implementation the update operation to the shared data is performed in a regular fashion, which means we can control when they are updated by different threads; i. e., data contention can be easily tuned. The implementation presented in Fig. 4c avoids data contention by making each thread update a different portion of the shared array at each iteration of the loop. This transformation exposes an optimization opportunity when lock speculation is available because the chance of data contention is much lower. This suggests that an HLE lock will work well for this version ("Hinted HLE Reduce"). The results of each of these experiments are shown in Fig. 5 and Fig. 6.

We used TAS locks as the default lock for Static TAS and Static Reduce as it delivers the best performance for each version; critical sections also use the TAS lock internally. Oblivious HLE enables HLE locks globally in the code, and Hinted HLE Reduce uses an HLE lock only for the code presented in Fig. 4c. In addition to the code in the figure, we also performed loop blocking in Hinted HLE Reduce to avoid excessive calls to the lock functions, and enabled shared sum update only when local sum is not zero. With these changes Static Reduce outperforms Static TAS with one to 8 threads, at the cost of increased memory

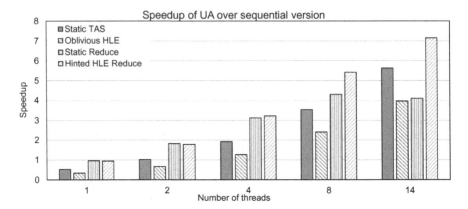

Fig. 5. Speedup UA with different implementation of shared data synchronization. **Static TAS** – original implementation with TAS lock, **Oblivious HLE** – original implementation with HLE lock, **Static Reduce** – reduction optimization with critical section, **Hinted HLE Reduce** – reduction optimization with coarse-grain HLE lock. Speedup is based on the runtime of the sequential version of UA without OpenMP.

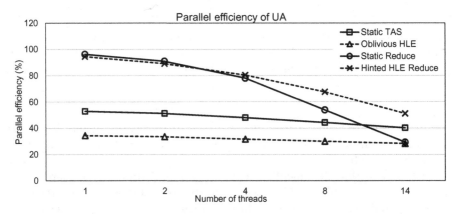

Fig. 6. Parallel efficiency of UA (all normalized to the sequential version) with different implementation of shared data synchronization

usage to hold private copies of the shared array. When the hinted HLE lock is used, the performance is close to, but not better than that of Static Reduce with one to two threads. As the thread count increases, Hinted HLE Reduce starts to outperform synchronization based on a `critical` section. Again, the poor performance of Oblivious HLE indicates one cannot simply use TSX locks everywhere without having information about the application. The optimization used in Static Reduce may not be a good solution in general, in that its scalability is limited by the sequentially executed code section, and Fig. 6 indicates this problem does exist. However, using TSX locks in the right place alleviated the problem and resulted in best performance in our experiments.

8   Conclusion

In this paper we have shown how the existing OpenMP API for locks can be extended with a user-guided locking API. Through the new API, programmers can provide hints to the OpenMP runtime to select appropriate lock implementations for each lock at application level. The proposed API extension of adding a new lock initialization function minimizes code changes and allows for incremental refinement of the application code. We have shown that our efficient decoder implementation does not add any measurable performance overhead to the OpenMP lock routines. Our benchmark demonstrates that a proper selection of lock implementations on a per-lock basis can lead to performance improvements.

Acknowledgments. We thank the anonymous reviewers for their constructive comments.

Intel and Xeon are trademarks or registered trademarks of Intel Corporation or its subsidiaries in the United States and other countries.

* Other brands and names are the property of their respective owners.

Software and workloads used in performance tests may have been optimized for performance only on Intel microprocessors. Performance tests, such as SYSmark and MobileMark, are measured using specific computer systems, components, software, operations and functions. Any change to any of those factors may cause the results to vary. You should consult other information and performance tests to assist you in fully evaluating your contemplated purchases, including the performance of that product when combined with other products. For more information go to `http://www.intel.com/performance`.

Intel's compilers may or may not optimize to the same degree for non-Intel microprocessors for optimizations that are not unique to Intel microprocessors. These optimizations include SSE2, SSE3, and SSSE3 instruction sets and other optimizations. Intel does not guarantee the availability, functionality, or effectiveness of any optimization on microprocessors not manufactured by Intel. Microprocessor-dependent optimizations in this product are intended for use with Intel microprocessors. Certain optimizations not specific to Intel microarchitecture are reserved for Intel microprocessors. Please refer to the applicable product User and Reference Guides for more information regarding the specific instruction sets covered by this notice.

References

1. Bihari, B.L., Wong, M., Wang, A., de Supinski, B.R., Chen, W.: A Case for Including Transactions in OpenMP II: Hardware Transactional Memory. In: Chapman, B.M., Massaioli, F., Müller, M.S., Rorro, M. (eds.) IWOMP 2012. LNCS, vol. 7312, pp. 44–58. Springer, Heidelberg (2012)
2. Bull, J.M.: Measuring Synchronisation and Scheduling Overheads in OpenMP. In: Proc. of the 1st European Workshop on OpenMP, Lund, Sweden, pp. 99–105 (1999)

3. Drepper, U.: Futexes are Tricky. Technical report, Redhat, Version 1.6 (2011)
   http://www.akkadia.org/drepper/futex.pdf
4. Drepper, U., Molnar, I.: The Native POSIX Thread Library for Linux. Technical
   report, Redhat (2003)
5. Feng, H., Van der Wijngaart, R.F., Biswas, R., Mavriplis, C.: Unstructured Adaptive (UA) NAS Parallel Benchmark, Version 1.0. Technical Report NAS-04-006,
   NASA (2004)
6. Haring, R.A., Ohmacht, M., Fox, T.W., Gschwind, M.K., Satterfield, D.L., Sug-
   avanam, K., Coteus, P.W., Heidelberger, P., Blumrich, M.A., Wisniewski, R.W.,
   Gara, A., Chiu, G.L.-T., Boyle, P.A., Christ, N.H., Kim, C.: The IBM Blue Gene/Q
   Compute Chip. IEEE Micro 32(2), 48–60 (2013)
7. IBM XL C/C++ for Blue Gene/Q, V12.1 (2012),
   http://pic.dhe.ibm.com/infocenter/compbg/v121v141/index.jsp?topic=
8. Intel Corporation. Intel® Architecture Instruction Set Extensions Programming
   Reference, Document number 319433-014 (2012)
9. Kleen, A.: Lock Elision in the GNU C Library. LWN.net 12(1) (2013),
   http://lwn.net/Articles/534758/
10. Mellor-Crummey, J.M., Scott, M.L.: Algorithms for Scalable Synchronization on
    Shared-memory Multiprocessors. ACM Trans. Comput. Syst. 9(1), 21–65 (1991)
11. Miller, D.: The GNU C Library version 2.18 is now available, Announcement on
    the info-gnu mailing list (2013),
    http://lists.gnu.org/archive/html/info-gnu/2013-08/msg00003.html
12. OpenMP Architecture Review Board. OpenMP Application Program Interface,
    Version 4.0 (2013), http://www.openmp.org/
13. Schindewolf, M., Bihari, B., Gyllenhaal, J., Schulz, M., Wang, A., Karl, W.: What
    Scientific Applications Can Benefit from Hardware Transactional Memory? In:
    Proc. of the Intl. Conf. on High Performance Computing, Networking, Storage
    and Analysis, SC 2012, Salt Lake City, pp. 90:1–90:11 (2012)
14. Wong, M., Bihari, B.L., de Supinski, B.R., Wu, P., Michael, M., Liu, Y., Chen, W.:
    A Case for Including Transactions in OpenMP. In: Sato, M., Hanawa, T., Müller,
    M.S., Chapman, B.M., de Supinski, B.R. (eds.) IWOMP 2010. LNCS, vol. 6132,
    pp. 149–160. Springer, Heidelberg (2010)
15. Yoo, R.M., Hughes, C.J., Lai, K., Rajwar, R.: Performance Evaluation of Intel®
    Transactional Synchronization Extensions for High-performance Computing. In:
    Proc. of the Intl. Conf. on High Performance Computing, Networking, Storage and
    Analysis, Denver, CO, pp. 19:1–19:11 (2013)

Library Support for Resource Constrained Accelerators

Laust Brock-Nannestad and Sven Karlsson

Technical University of Denmark, Lyngby, Denmark
{laub,svea}@dtu.dk

Abstract. Accelerators, and other resource constrained systems, are increasingly being used in computer systems. Accelerators provide power efficient performance and often provide a shared memory model. However, it is a challenge to map feature rich APIs, such as OpenMP, to resource constrained systems. In this paper, we present a lightweight system where an accelerator can remotely execute library functions on a host processor. The implementation takes up 750 bytes but can replace arbitrary library calls leading to significant savings in memory foot print. We evaluate with a set of SPLASH-2 applications and show that the impact on execution time is negligible when compared to GCCs OpenMP implementation.

1 Introduction

Accelerators, small custom compute units, have recently gained in popularity. They can be found in a wide range of systems from supercomputing systems to small embedded systems. Accelerators can be designed for a specific purpose or application. Alternatively, they can also be programmable. In this paper, we only consider the latter programmable type. Accelerators are connected to a *host* machine and act as co-processors to the host machine.

Programmable accelerators are very power efficient which has made them popular in embedded systems. However to make accelerators power efficient, they are very resource constrained. This means for example that the available amount of efficiently accessed memory is low. More concretely, this means that caches or scratchpad memories are small. At the same time, many accelerators embrace a shared memory model, for example the Epiphany accelerators [2]. The current version of the Epiphany core has 32 kilobytes of local memory. Accesses outside this memory space are permitted but incur a high memory latency. Hence, efficient software must have a small memory foot print.

The shared memory model employed by Epiphany and other accelerators makes OpenMP an attractive programming model. However, it is a challenge to manage the low amount of memory available.

In this paper, we present a lightweight system where an accelerator can remotely execute library functions on the host. This is a departure from the traditional model where accelerators are co-processors to the host. However, it also

L. DeRose (Eds.): IWOMP 2014, LNCS 8766, pp. 187–201, 2014.

means that the accelerator memory foot print can be reduced as rarely executed library functions do not take up space in the accelerator's memory.

We demonstrate our approach by developing a lightweight system for executing OpenMP applications. The applications can call arbitrary library functions located on the host. Our approach can be used on any accelerator system which embraces a shared memory model and so can support the data sharing model of OpenMP. We use OpenMP versions of SPLASH-2 benchmarks to evaluate our approach and compare to a homogeneous SMP system.

Our implementation only takes up 750 bytes and the results show that the impact on the execution time, when compared to GCCs OpenMP implementation, is negligible.

In short, we make the following contributions:

- We describe a lightweight system which allow accelerators to execute arbitrary library functions on the host.
- We evaluate the system using SPLASH-2 benchmarks. We measure execution time and memory foot print and compare to a traditional homogeneous system.

The rest of this paper is organized as follows: In section 2 we discuss the architecture of our approach. Section 3 provides some details on our implementation. Then, in section 4 we evaluate our system with a set of SPLASH-2 benchmarks. In section 5 we give an overview of related work and finally, in section 6, we conclude.

2   Architecture

We assume that the system consists of a host processor connected to a multi-core accelerator. We will refer to the main thread of execution on the accelerator as the *master* thread [7]. This thread is responsible for coordinating the execution and controlling one or more *worker* threads which participate in the execution of parallel code. The threads are statically mapped to accelerator cores.

The system may be heterogeneous. We do not propose that the master thread executes on the host. Instead, execution is driven by the accelerator and the host assists.

In this paper, we focus on the *runtime* system. Typically, the compiler uses techniques such as function outlining of parallel regions, so that they can easily be executed by threads, and replaces OpenMP `pragmas` with function calls to the runtime, e.g. for barriers. We also rely on the compiler performing these tasks.

An application has any number of C libraries at its disposal and may call ANSI C library functions. This will typically occur during initialization but is also possible from within parallel computation regions. These calls include calls for memory management, string to value conversions, and I/O. These calls are relatively infrequent and we argue they should be off-loaded to the host, thus freeing up resources on the accelerator.

We assume that a shared memory interface exists between the host and the accelerator. Each worker uses a *mailbox* data structure in the shared memory as the interface to the host. The mailbox is readable and writable from both the host and the accelerator.

To invoke a call, the mailbox is filled with data corresponding to the function call: i) a identifier describing the function to call and ii) the function call arguments required by the call.

The host checks each mailbox. If a mailbox contains a new request, the host parses it, executes the call, and updates the mailbox with the return value. The actual interface between the host and the accelerator and the contents of the mailbox is device specific but can be hidden by the runtime system. On the accelerator side, a remote function call is nothing more than a function call.

The caller places parameters in registers or on the stack. The caller then calls a stub. The stub interfaces with the host. Depending on the architecture, this can either require that the stub sends a notification to the host and that it passes along the function call arguments. In a shared memory design, where the caller's stack is visible to the host, all arguments is passed on the stack allowing the host to retrieve them directly.

Lets look at a concrete example using malloc. A worker puts a {malloc,size} message in its mailbox. The host reads the message, performs the allocation, keeping track of all memory allocations on the accelerator to ensure there are no conflicts, and returns the pointer to the allocated memory region. While the host is executing, the worker can poll for the response or use more effective mechanisms if offered by the hardware.

3   Experimental Setup

We implement our approach as a runtime on a homogeneous multicore platform. While our approach works on heterogeneous platforms the aim of our implementation is to validate our design and provide initial results. To simulate the host and the accelerator on the same system, we use a multi-threaded application. One thread acts as the host and is executed using the Linux system's normal C runtime. Another set of threads acts as the accelerator but do not access to the C runtime, only the lightweight runtime.

The lightweight runtime contains a small amount of bootstrapping code, the host interface, as well as threading and synchronization primitives. The accelerator runtime has only one dependency on the underlying Linux operating system, which is to create worker threads during initialization, performed directly using the syscall trap instruction. This keeps the design as close as possible to bare metal.

To simulate the host–accelerator interface we use the memory which is implicitly shared between threads.

3.1   Accelerator Side

The implementation relies on specific C features to enable remote function calls without modifications to the application source code. We depend on variadic functions, preprocessor macros with named arguments, and the union type.

A variadic function is a function that takes a variable number of arguments. It can be decided at execution time how many arguments each call takes. Declaring a variadic function causes GCC to pass all arguments on the stack. We utilize this to let the host to read them directly.

All calls to library functions are redirected to a single local function on the accelerator. This variadic function takes an identifier followed by a varying number of arguments. The identifier encodes the identity of the function call. The other arguments are the same as for the library function.

To transparently add the additional identifier, we define a macro for each standard library function. The macro takes the same number of arguments. The macro expands to a call to the stub with the identifier *and* the original arguments. The macro is named as the function it replaces. For C functions that are already variadic, such as `printf`, we do the same, but use a variadic macro, as introduced in C99. Examples of macros can be found in figure 1.

```
#define getopt(a, b, c) __accstub(1, a, b, c).i
#define atoi(a) __accstub(2, a).i
#define printf(...) __accstub(5, __VA_ARGS__).i
```

Fig. 1. Macros to redirect library calls to the accelerator stub

We assign one mailbox per thread. We assume each thread has a unique identifier and there is a one to one mapping from the identifier to a mailbox. The stub uses this mapping to locate the correct mailbox.

Library functions have different return types. To handle this, we use the union type, as shown in figure 2. The macro ensures that the correct type is extracted from the return value.

Synchronization between host and accelerator is highly dependent on the memory models of the two architectures. The accelerator must ensure that the call arguments on the stack are readable from the host side before the host is notified of an incoming call. A memory barrier or fence will ensure this. A sequence number is added to each remote call to allow the host to identify when a new call has been issued. The stub increases the sequence number once the call is setup. Pseudocode for the stub is presented in figure 3.

3.2   Host Side

The host contains only a small amount of code. It monitors the mailboxes for activity. The implementation polls them in round robin fashion. Pseudocode for

```
/* Number of threads */
const int num_threads = MAX_NBR_OF_THREADS;

/* Union large enough to hold argument types */
typedef union {
    uintptr_t i;
    double d;
    /* ... */
} ARGTYPE;

/* Written by accelerator, read by host */
volatile typedef struct {
    int func_id     /* Defines the function */
    int seq;        /* Sequence number */
    va_list args;   /* Defines call arguments */
} mailbox;

/* One mailbox per thread */
mailbox mbox[num_threads];

/* Written by host, read by accelerator */
volatile typedef struct {
  int seqnr;
  ARGTYPE retval;
} replybox;

/* One replybox per thread */
replybox rbox[num_threads];
```

Fig. 2. Data types used by the accelerator and host

```
/* Interacts with the host */
ARGTYPE __accstub (int func_id , ...) {
  /* Locate caller's unique id */
  /* Could be encoded as part of the func_id */
  int t_id = locate_tid ();
  va_list ap;
  va_start (ap, id );

  /* Prepare the call arguments */
  va_copy (mbox[ t_id ]. args , ap);
  mbox[ t_id ]. func_id = func_id ;

  /* Ensure that arguments are visible to host */
  /* This is architecture specific */
  memory_fence ();

  /* Increase sequence number */
  mbox[ t_id ]. seq++;

  memory_fence ();

  /* Wait for host to indicate completion */
  while (rbox[ t_id ]. seq != mbox[ t_id ]. seq) {
    /* sleep and then memory fence */
    memory_fence ();
  }

  va_end (ap);

  return rbox[ t_id ]. retval;
}
```

Fig. 3. Pseudo code for the accelerator stub

this is shown in figure 4. If an active mailbox is found, the host performs the following steps:

1. Determine function call based on `func_id`.
2. Fetch arguments from shared memory.
3. Call real function with arguments.
4. Place return value in mailbox, using the union type.
5. Set acknowledgment flag in mailbox.

In our current implementation, the host is polling each mailbox. Many accelerators allow for efficient event queues or interrupts between the accelerator and host and such mechanisms should be used to avoid the overhead of busy wait.

Similarly, we use busy wait on the accelerator side. Many architectures support efficient hardware mechanisms for waking up accelerator cores and these should be used to avoid the busy wait approach.

4   Evaluation

We use benchmarks from the SPLASH-2 [12] suite to evaluate performance. We use the *Modified SPLASH-2* benchmarks [10]. This is a minor update to the original benchmarks which improves compatibility on 64 bit platforms. The parameters we use for SPLASH-2 are shown in table 1. The SPLASH-2 benchmarks utilize the following C library functions: `malloc`, `printf`, `getopt`, `atof`, `drand48`, as well as several functions from the math library.

Table 1. SPLASH-2 benchmarks used and their parameters

Benchmark	Data set size
FFT	2^{26} data points
LU contiguous	8192×8192 matrix
LU non-contiguous	8192×8192 matrix

We modify the original benchmarks in two ways: First, we construct a baseline. The baseline uses OpenMP `parallel` regions, barriers and locks. These OpenMP directives are compiled by GCC to generate parallel code for the GNU OpenMP library.

For our lightweight runtime, we replace all C library calls with calls to the stub and then manually insert parallelization and synchronization calls. We match the locations where GCC's inserts calls to the GNU OpenMP runtime library.

We execute the SPLASH-2 benchmarks with the normal libgomp OpenMP library and use this as a baseline for performance. We then compare it to the performance of our lightweight runtime.

To measure the size of our runtime we compile each benchmark as a static *freestanding* binary without C library dependencies. This also allow us to verify

```
/* Performs the actual call on the host side */
ARGTYPE perform_call(int func_id, va_list args, ...) {
  ARGTYPE a; /* Used to hold first argument */
  /* Return value */
  ARGTYPE retval.i = 0;

  /* Determine call */
  switch (func_id) {
    case 1: /* drand48 */
      /* No arguments */
      retval.d = drand48();
      break;
    case 2: /* srand48 */
      /* Extract argument */
      a.i = va_arg(args, long);
      /* No return value */
      srand48(a.i);
      break;
    /* The rest of the supported library calls here. */
  }
  return retval;
}

while (1) {
  /* Ensure that data is transferred from the accelerator */
  /* This is architecture specific */
  memory_fence();

  for (n=0; n<num_threads; n++) {
    /* Determine if there is activity */
    if (mbox[n].seq == rbox[n].seq+1) {
      /* Perform call*/
      rbox[n].retval =
          perform_call(mbox[n].func_id, mbox[n].args);

      /* Ensure that data is transferred to the accelerator */
      /* This is architecture specific */
      memory_fence();

      /* Increase sequence number to indicate completion */
      rbox[n].seq = mbox[n].seq + 1;
      memory_fence();
    }
  }
  /* Repeat */
}
```

Fig. 4. Pseudocode for the host side of the interface

that no calls to the C library remain as that would cause linking to fail. We then analyze the size of the object code using the `readelf` tool.

Experiments were executed on an Intel production server, with the specifications outlined in table 2. All timing experiments were executed 30 times and we present the averages with standard deviations shown using error bars. Timing is carried out using the processor's time stamp counter and then converted to seconds. The processor's time stamp counter always runs at the same rate and can be used for timing measurements.

Table 2. Experimental machine

Processor	Dual socket Intel Xeon X5570
Memory	48 GB
Disk	Samsung SSD 840
OS	64 bit Debian GNU/Linux 3.2.57
Compiler	GCC 4.8.1.
glibc	2.17

4.1 Execution Time Analysis

We have instrumented the system so that we can split the execution time into two parts, the initialization time and the computation time. For completeness we also present the total execution time.

Figure 5 shows the initialization time for each benchmark, for the baseline and our lightweight runtime and for different number of threads. In SPLASH benchmarks, initialization is mainly serial code so there is no speed up as the number of threads increase. Initialization contains the most library calls. FFT's initialization phase is noticeably longer than for the OpenMP implementation. FFT initializes each data point with a random value. This value is obtained by calling `drand48`. This results in 2^{26} calls to the host during initialization.

Figure 6 and table 3 shows the parallel computation part of each benchmark as we vary the number of threads from 1 to 4. We see the expected speed up when the benchmark is parallelized. The performance when using our runtime matches the baseline.

For completeness, figure 7 shows the total wall clock time for each benchmark. When not dominated by initialization time we are competitive when compared to the baseline.

4.2 Memory Foot Print Analysis

We have also examined the size of object code in the lightweight runtime and the benchmarks. Based on which C functions are executed remotely, we also estimate the savings in object code. We assume a shared memory model where shared variables are shared between host and accelerator. We therefore do not include

Table 3. Computation time in seconds

Benchmark	Threads	Lightweight runtime	Baseline
FFT	1	11.33	11.18
FFT	2	5.81	6.06
FFT	4	3.29	3.16
LU contiguous	1	18.36	20.10
LU contiguous	2	9.67	10.91
LU contiguous	4	5.39	6.07
LU non-contiguous	1	44.37	45.39
LU non-contiguous	2	26.04	26.59
LU non-contiguous	4	14.67	14.74

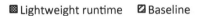

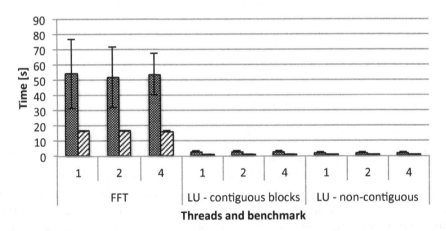

Fig. 5. *Initialization* time for each benchmark. The number of threads is varied from 1 to 4.

shared variables in our discussion. We acknowledge, however, that efficient data caching mechanisms are needed to support the shared memory model.

Table 4 shows the size of all the functions that comprise the runtime system. Sizes are in bytes. These functions are available and executed on the accelerator. We place the functions in two categories, those that are only called during initialization and those that are called during runtime. The runtime functions handle thread synchronization and host communication.

Table 5 shows the size of the application object code for FFT and LU contiguous. The benchmarks rely on the C library functions shown in table 6. We examine the size of these functions in the GNU C library. As the C library has many implementations optimized for different situations, we choose a likely candidate. The following results are therefore only an estimate.

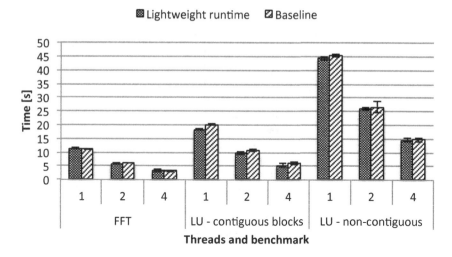

Fig. 6. *Computation* time for each benchmark. The number of threads is varied from 1 to 4.

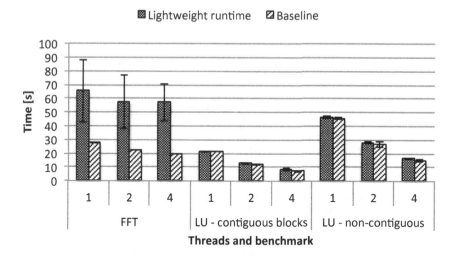

Fig. 7. The total execution time for each benchmark. The number of threads is varied from 1 to 4.

In total, the library functions used by FFT occupy more than 34 kilobytes. For LU contiguous it is more than 21 kilobytes. Using these values we can estimate the total object code size for FFT as 45029 bytes with the GNU C library and 10734 bytes with our runtime. This is a saving of at least 75%. For LU contiguous the GNU C library version is 32121 bytes, but 10755 bytes with our runtime. Here we see a saving of 66%.

Table 4. Object code sizes for the lightweight runtime

Group	Function name	Object code size (bytes)
Runtime	__accstub	209
	__barrier_wait	87
	__strtod_wrapper	51
	__barrier_init	46
	__memset_wrapper	42
	__thread_wrapper	30
	__spinlock_lock	18
	__cmpxchg	7
	__spimlock_init	4
	__spinlock_unlock	4
	Sub-total	498
Initialization	__fakestart	183
	__create_thread	49
	__sys_clone	11
	__real_start	6
	__exit	2
	Sub-total	251
Total		749

Table 5. Object code sizes for FFT and LU contiguous

FFT		LU contiguous	
Function name	Size (bytes)	Function name	Size (bytes)
main	4812	main	4779
FFT1D	1165	lu	1649
Transpose	1072	CheckResult	924
SlaveStart	666	InitA	628
PrintArray	354	OneSolve	506
FFT1DOnce	330	PrintA	337
InitU	303	TouchA	319
InitU2	262	bmod	180
TouchArra	219	bmodd	169
InitX	188	bdiv	162
TwiddleOneCol	132	lu0	156
Reverse	126	SlaveStart	111
CheckSum	106	doxpy	46
Scale	63	printerr	46
log_2	50	BlockOwnerRow	41
CopyColumn	49	BlockOwner	17
printerr	46	BlockOwnerColumn	16
BitReverse	42		
FFT Total	9985	LU Total	10006

Table 6. Object code sizes for GNU C library functions and their use by FFT and LU contiguous

Function	Size (bytes)	FFT	LU
__printf_fp	9345	X	X
__sin_sse2	8569	X	
__cos_sse2	5159	X	
_getopt_internal_r	4391	X	X
_int_malloc	4776	X	X
_int_free	2796		
____memset_sse2	2705		X
malloc	333	X	X
fflush	249		X
free	136		X
__drand_iterate	96	X	
_getopt_internal	92	X	X
sqrt	38		X
drand48	33	X	
getopt	29	X	X
atoi	21	X	X
Total		35044	22115

5   Related Work

There are many similarities between our remote execution and *remote procedure calls*. Unlike an RPC interface, we do not have the uncertainty of invoking a function across an unreliable network, but can assume that the call does not fail. In many ways this is more similar to using hardware queues for events.

The OpenMP 4.0 standard [7] already addresses accelerators through the target directives, but these offload only selected parts of the program to the accelerator. Our aim is to run OpenMP programs, including the master thread, directly on the accelerator and let it be assisted by the host.

Prior work on executing OpenMP on bare metal hardware [3,5] solve similar issues regarding thread management and synchronization, but implement OpenMP on stand alone systems and do not consider host and accelerator combinations.

There have been many previous efforts to use OpenMP on accelerators. Most notable is perhaps IBM's Cell Broadband Engine Architecture, which combined a general purpose *PowerPC Processing Element* (PPE) with a set of *Synergistic Processor Elements* (SPEs), small accelerator cores optimized for vector operations. The Cell has been the target of much research. Wei and Yu [11] presented a source to source compiler which splits an application annotated with OpenMP directives into two parts. One part would be compiled for and executed on the PPE and the other for the SPEs. Unlike in our approach, the master thread executes on the host PPE processor.

As the Cell processor lacks shared memory and caches, much effort has been focused on efficiently utilizing its memory hierarchy. O'Brien et al. [6] present an OpenMP runtime for the Cell processor which in tight coupling with the PPE can execute threads on the SPEs. They implement the required thread synchronization and work distribution. Much of their work centers on buffering and overlapping DMA requests and implementing software caches to improve performance. As with the work by Wei and Yu, the master thread always executes on the host processor.

Stotzer et al. recently developed an OpenMP runtime for the Texas Instruments C66X series of DSPs [9]. The runtime sits very close to the hardware, but on top of a small real-time operating system, *Open Event Machine*, also developed by TI. The C66X is a powerful processor and not a resource constrained accelerator.

Pakin et al. [8] implemented a subset of MPI on the Cell processor. This allows each SPE to be part of the message passing network. They offload arbitrary C code to the PowerPC host, which is also responsible for communication between SPEs on different nodes.

Outside the area of OpenMP and especially in the area of high performance computing, there is a trend towards thin minimal software stacks. This can be seen in operating systems optimized for HPC systems, such as Sandia Labs' Kitten [4] and ZeptoOS from Argonne National Lab [1], both of which are minimalistic operating system that are optimized for the target hardware. In many ways, our host and accelerator setup also mirrors the design of modern day HPC clusters, where machines are divided into computation and I/O nodes, each with their dedicated tasks. In our mindset this would be the accelerator and the host, respectively.

6   Conclusion

In this paper, we have described a lightweight system where an accelerator can remotely execute functions on the host. This allow even resource constrained accelerators to utilize feature rich libraries. We show that an implementation of our system can be made as small as 750 bytes allowing for a significant reduction in object code size. We have evaluated our system with a set of SPLASH-2 applications and show that the impact on execution time is negligible when compared to GCCs OpenMP implementation.

References

1. The ZeptoOS project, http://www.zeptoos.org, (accessed: July 15, 2014)
2. Adapteva: Epiphany architecture reference, revision 14.03.11 (2014)
3. Jeun, W.C., Ha, S.: Effective openmp implementation and translation for multi-processor system-on-chip without using os. In: Proceedings of the 2007 Asia and South Pacific Design Automation Conference, pp. 44–49. IEEE Computer Society (2007)

4. Lange, J., Pedretti, K., Hudson, T., Dinda, P., Cui, Z., Xia, L., Bridges, P., Gocke, A., Jaconette, S., Levenhagen, M., et al.: Palacios and kitten: New high performance operating systems for scalable virtualized and native supercomputing. In: 2010 IEEE International Symposium on Parallel & Distributed Processing (IPDPS), pp. 1–12. IEEE (2010)
5. Liu, F., Chaudhary, V.: A practical openmp compiler for system on chips. In: Voss, M.J. (ed.) WOMPAT 2003. LNCS, vol. 2716, pp. 54–68. Springer, Heidelberg (2003)
6. O'Brien, K., O'Brien, K., Sura, Z., Chen, T., Zhang, T.: Supporting openmp on cell. International Journal of Parallel Programming 36(3), 289–311 (2008)
7. OpenMP Architecture Review Board: Openmp application program interface, version 4.0 (2013)
8. Pakin, S., Lang, M., Kerbyson, D.: The reverse-acceleration model for programming petascale hybrid systems. IBM Journal of Research and Development 53(5), 1–8 (2009)
9. Stotzer, E., Jayaraj, A., Ali, M., Friedmann, A., Mitra, G., Rendell, A.P., Lintault, I.: Openmp on the low-power ti keystone ii arm/dsp system-on-chip. In: Rendell, A.P., Chapman, B.M., Müller, M.S. (eds.) IWOMP 2013. LNCS, vol. 8122, pp. 114–127. Springer, Heidelberg (2013)
10. University of Delaware, CAPSL: The modified splash-2 home page (2007), http://www.capsl.udel.edu/splash/, (accessed: July 15, 2014)
11. Wei, H., Yu, J.: Loading openmp to cell: An effective compiler framework for heterogeneous multi-core chip. In: Chapman, B., Zheng, W., Gao, G.R., Sato, M., Ayguadé, E., Wang, D. (eds.) IWOMP 2007. LNCS, vol. 4935, pp. 129–133. Springer, Heidelberg (2008)
12. Woo, S.C., Ohara, M., Torrie, E., Singh, J.P., Gupta, A.: The splash-2 programs: Characterization and methodological considerations. In: ACM SIGARCH Computer Architecture News, vol. 23, pp. 24–36. ACM (1995)

Implementation and Optimization of the OpenMP Accelerator Model for the TI Keystone II Architecture

Gaurav Mitra[1,2], Eric Stotzer[1], Ajay Jayaraj[1], and Alistair P. Rendell[2]

[1] Texas Instruments, Dallas TX, USA
estotzer@ti.com, ajayj@ti.com
[2] Australian National University, Canberra ACT, Australia
{gaurav.mitra, alistair.rendell}@anu.edu.au

Abstract. The TI Keystone II architecture provides a unique combination of ARM Cortex-A15 processors with high performance TI C66x floating-point DSPs on a single low-power System-on-chip (SoC). Commercially available systems such as the *HP Proliant m800* and nCore *BrownDwarf* are based on this ARM-DSP SoC. The Keystone II architecture promises to deliver high GFLOPS/Watt and is of increasing interest as it provides an alternate building block for future exascale systems. However, the success of this architecture is intimately related to the ease of migrating existing HPC applications for maximum performance. Effective use of all ARM and DSP cores and DMA co-processors is crucial for maximizing performance/watt. This paper explores issues and challenges encountered while migrating the matrix multiplication (GEMM) kernel, originally written only for the C6678 DSP to the ARM-DSP SoC using an early prototype of the OpenMP 4.0 accelerator model. Single precision (SGEMM) matrix multiplication performance of 110.11 GFLOPS and and double precision (DGEMM) performance of 29.15 GFLOPS was achieved on the TI Keystone II Evaluation Module Revision 3.0 (EVM). Trade-offs and factors affecting performance are discussed.

1 Introduction

Embedded accelerators such as the TI C6678 DSP have been proven to provide high GFLOPS/Watt for HPC applications [1,2]. As a result there has been considerable interest in utilizing low-power SoCs containing these accelerators to build supercomputers capable of higher energy efficiency compared to current systems. The HP Proliant m800 Server Cartridge, part of HP's *Moonshot* [3] project, and nCore HPC's *BrownDwarf* [4] systems both use the TI Keystone II SoC [5]. In the context of these two systems, it remains to be proven whether existing HPC applications can use the OpenMP 4.0 accelerator model [6] to achieve maximum performance. Section 3 discusses the accelerator specific additions made to the OpenMP 4.0 specification after providing a brief overview of the Keystone-II architecture in section 2.

L. DeRose (Eds.): IWOMP 2014, LNCS 8766, pp. 202–214, 2014.

In previous work [5] we demonstrated the use of hardware queues to create a bare metal OpenMP runtime for the TI Keystone-I C6678 DSP. In section 4, we demonstrate our current implementation of the OpenMP accelerator model for the Keystone-II 66AK2H ARM-DSP SoC which is used to offload OpenMP parallel regions from ARM host cores to the target DSP cores. Matrix multiplication written for the C6678 DSP is ported to 66AK2H, and its performance is reported in section 5. The importance of leveraging performance optimizations such as using buffers in local SRAM, transferring data using DMA co-processors, allocating buffers in memory shared between the ARM and DSP cores is also highlighted in sections 4 and 5. Finally, we list related work in section 6 and conclude with future directions in section 7.

2   TI Keystone II

The 66AK2H SoC shown in figure 1 is composed of a quad-core ARM Cortex-A15 (up to 1.4 Ghz) cluster and an octa-core C66x DSP (up to 1.228 Ghz) cluster [7]. The Cortex-A15 quad cores are fully cache coherent, while the DSP cores do not maintain cache coherency. The DSP cores do not have any virtual memory support as they do not have an MMU and do not share the ARM MMU. The DSP cores have 32KB of L1D and L1P and 1MB L2 cache each. Each of these caches are configurable and can be partitioned into scratchpad RAM (SRAM)

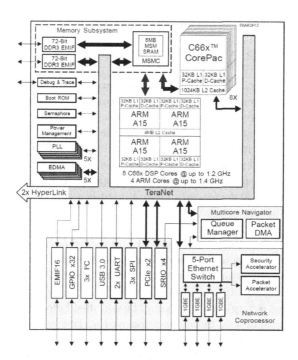

Fig. 1. 66AK2H SoC

as needed. The ARM cores also have 32 KB of L1D and L1P cache per core, but share a single 4 MB L2 cache. The Multicore Shared Memory Controller (MSMC) also provides 6 MB of SRAM which is shared by all ARM and DSP cores.

The DSP cores are 8-way VLIW with two 64-bit loads/stores and four single-precision FLOPS per cycle. 66AK2H provides five user-programmable Enhanced DMA 3 (EDMA3) channel controllers capable of three-dimensional data transfers to and from DDR,MSMC,L2 memory segments. Each EDMA controller has 64 DMA channels which support transfers triggered both by the user and interrupts/events in the case of chained transfers. It also provides a two Tb/s TeraNet interconnect and two 72-bit DDR3 interfaces (up to 1600 Mhz).

The 66AK2H SoC consumes an average of 9-14 Watts of thermal design power (TDP) at 55 degrees C case temperature [7]. The DSP cores have a theoretical peak performance of 19.648 GFLOPS per core and 157.184 GFLOPS aggregate single-precision GFLOPS (at 1.228 Ghz). The double-precision performance of the DSP cores is approximately one fourth single-precision, 39.296 GFLOPS. The ARM cores are capable of one double-precision FLOP per cycle and therefore have a peak performance of 2.4 GFLOPS per core [8] and 9.6 GFLOPS aggregate double-precision GFLOPS (at 1.2 Ghz). Using the NEON extensions [9], the peak single-precision performance would approximately be four times the double-precision performance, 38.4 GFLOPS. Taking the SoC TDP into consideration, the maximum energy efficiency achievable for the DSP cores would be between 2.86 to 4.37 double precision GFLOPS/Watt. Counting the ARM cores, we could expect between 3.49 to 5.43 double precision GFLOPS/Watt.

3   The OpenMP Accelerator Model

The OpenMP 4.0 specification added an accelerator model that enables a programmer to direct execution to heterogeneous cores. Using this model, programmers have the capability to identify the code segments that they want to run on a compute accelerator. The OpenMP accelerator model is portable across a variety of different instruction set architectures (ISAs) including GPGPUs, DSPs and FPGAs. The model is host-centric with a *host device* and multiple *target devices* of the same type. A *device* is a logical execution engine with some type of local memory. A *device data environment* is a collection of variables that are available to a *device*. Variables are *mapped* from a host device data environment to a target device data environment. The model supports both shared and distributed memory systems between host and target devices.

Program execution begins on the initial host device. The `target` construct indicates that the subsequent structured block is executed by a target device. Variables appearing in map clauses are mapped to the device data environment. The map clause has a *map-type* which may be specified before the list of variables. The *map-type* is one of `to`, `from`, `tofrom` and `alloc` and is used to optimize the mapping of variables. Array section syntax is supported on pointer and array variables that appear in map clauses to indicate the size of the storage that is mapped.

In figure 2 the `target` construct indicates that the subsequent structured block may execute on a target device. The array sections specified for the variables A and B and the variables N and sum are mapped to the target device data environment. Because of its `from` map-type the corresponding variable sum on the target device is not initialized with the value of original variable sum on the host. Once on the device, the iterations of the loop after the `parallel for` construct are executed in parallel by the team of threads executing on the target device. When the `target` region is complete the value of the original variable sum on the host is assigned the value of the corresponding variable sum on the target device and it and the other variables previously mapped are un-mapped. The thread on the host device that encountered the `target` construct then continues execution after the `target` region.

```
 1 │ double f(double * restrict A, double * restrict B, int N)
   │ {
 3 │     double sum;
   │     #pragma omp target map(to: A[0:N], B[0:N], N) map(from:sum)
 5 │     {
   │         sum = 0.0;
 7 │         #pragma omp parallel for reduction(+:sum)
   │         for (int i=0; i<N; i++)
 9 │             sum += A[i] * B[i];
   │     }
11 │     return sum;
   │ }
```

Fig. 2. Target construct

Depending on the hardware memory system, a mapped variable might require copies between host and target device memories, or no copies if the host and target device share memory. Even if memory is shared, a pointer translation or memory coherence operation might still be required when mapping a variable. The OpenMP accelerator model supports all of these hardware configurations. When an original variable in a host data environment is mapped to a corresponding variable in a device data environment, the model asserts that the original and corresponding variable may share storage. Writes to the corresponding variable may alter the value of the original variable. Therefore, a program cannot assume that a mapped variable resulted in a copy of that variable.

Other device constructs include the `target data` and `target update` constructs which are used to manage the placement and consistency of variables mapped to device data environments. The `teams` and `distribute` constructs were also added to facilitate a new type of work-sharing pattern that exploits accelerator style loop-level parallelism. For the purposes of this paper, the `target` construct is sufficient.

4   Accelerator Model Implementation

The implementation is split across a front-end source-to-source lowering tool (S2S) and a host library (libompaccel). The S2S tool takes as input a source file with target constructs and: (a) replaces the target region with API calls to make the data available on the target device, trigger execution on the target and make any data computed by the target region available to the host device; and (b) takes the target region and compiles it for the target device

OpenCL^{TM} [10] is an industry standard approach to programming heterogeneous SoCs. TI's OpenCL 1.1 compliant runtime implements an extension which supports dispatching OpenCL kernels with calls to functions containing OpenMP parallel regions. This feature enabled us to leverage the OpenCL runtime to perform the mechanics of making data available on the target device and triggering execution. Libompaccel is implemented as a thin layer that implements the target API calls and maps them to corresponding OpenCL APIs and performs book keeping required by the accelerator model. The target region is dispatched as an OpenCL kernel.

4.1   Optimizing Data Synchronization

Data synchronization between the host and target device can be a significant source of overhead. This overhead has implications for the amount of computation that needs to be performed by a target region to outweigh the data synchronization overhead. On the 66AK2H SoC, the host and target device share internal and external memory. However as noted earlier: (a) the target device does not have a memory management unit (MMU); and (b) there is no hardware cache coherency between the target and host device.

As a result, the host accesses shared memory using virtual addresses and the target accesses the shared memory using physical addresses. Moreover, host device variables can span multiple non-contiguous pages in Linux virtual memory whereas the target device operates on contiguous physical memory. When mapping variables from the Linux process space, the variables must be copied into contiguous memory for target operation. This copy is inefficient, especially for large variables. To eliminate this copy, the implementation provides a special purpose dynamic memory allocation API, __malloc_ddr() and __malloc_msmc() shown in figure 3. The physical memory associated with this heap is contiguous and is mapped to a contiguous chunk of virtual memory on the host. If any host variables allocated via this API are mapped into target regions, the map clauses translate to cache management operations on the host, significantly reducing the overhead.

```
  float* buf_in_ddr  = (float*) __malloc_ddr(size_bytes);
2 float* buf_in_msmc = (float*) __malloc_msmc(size_bytes);
```

Fig. 3. __malloc_ddr and __malloc_msmc API

In figure 4 we report the advantage of mapping buffers allocated using this API compared to those allocated using standard malloc() on the host. The overhead times of offloading buffers with sizes varying between 4 KB to 163840 KB (160 MB) created using both the __malloc_ddr() API and standard malloc() were measured. The speed-up obtained by using __malloc_ddr() is shown. A buffer was first read and written to in order to populate the host caches. Following this the host timer was started and the buffer was offloaded to a target region using map(tofrom:buffer[0:size]). Within the target region, all eight

DSP cores wrote to the buffer using an OpenMP parallel region. Upon returning from the target region, timing was stopped and recorded on the host. The elapsed DSP time measured within the target region was then subtracted from the host time to obtain the overhead times. All measurements were taken on the TI 66AK2H EVM using compilers and tools listed in section 5. Execution times were measured in microseconds averaged over 100 iterations with a standard deviation of 0.5 microseconds.

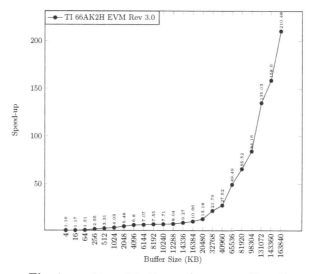

Fig. 4. __malloc_ddr() speed-up vs. malloc()

Using our shared memory allocation API results in a maximum overhead of 3.75 ms for a 12288 KB (12 MB) buffer whereas using malloc results in overheads increasing proportional to buffer size. Speed-up factors shown in figure 4 suggest that for small buffer sizes up to 64 KB malloc'd buffers have almost equivalent performance compared to __malloc_ddr'd ones. However, larger buffers, especially ones above 1 MB should be allocated using __malloc_ddr as it results in a considerable performance advantage.

4.2   Utilizing Target Scratchpad Memory

On the 66AK2H, each DSP core's 1MB L2 memory can be configured such that a portion of it is fast scratchpad memory and the rest is L2 cache. The OpenMP 4.0 map clause specification does not allow taking advantage of the scratchpad memory. Our implementation added a new local map-type, which maps a variable to the L2 scratchpad memory. In terms of data synchronization, such variables are treated as map-type alloc. They have an undefined initial value on entry to the target region and any updates to the variable in the target region cannot be reflected back to the host. Mapping host variables to target scratchpad memory provides significant performance improvements.

5 Porting Matrix Multiplication for Keystone II

Fundamental to a majority of HPC applications are Basic Linear Algebra Subprograms (BLAS). For an emerging HPC platform, achieving good scalable performance for fundamental BLAS routines is a key factor. General Matrix multiplication (GEMM) is a level 3 BLAS routine that has been used extensively to benchmark and test the performance of HPC platforms.

```
double MatmulOptTarget(real* A, real* B, real* C,
                       int m, int k, int n,
                       real* MSMC_buf, int msmc_size, int num_threads)
{
    int size_A = m*k; int size_B = k*n; int size_C = m*n;
    /* Local L2 SRAM scratch total: 768 Kbytes = 786432 bytes */
    /* Do not need to allocate here, passing a null pointer as local is adequate */
    real *pL2 = NULL;
    uint64_t elapsed_cycles;
    #pragma omp target map(to: A[0:size_A], B[0:size_B], m, k, n, num_threads) \
                       map(alloc: MSMC_buf[0:msmc_size]) \
                       map(local: pL2[0:L2_SRAM_NUM_REALS]) \
                       map(tofrom: C[0:size_C]) \
                       map(from: elapsed_cycles)
    {
        omp_set_num_threads(num_threads);
        /* Set start address of a core's L1D SRAM that is about to be created */
        real* pL1 = (real*) L1D_SRAM_START;
        int lda = m, ldb = k, ldc = CORE_PROCESS_ROWS*((m+(CORE_PROCESS_ROWS-1))/CORE_PROCESS_ROWS);
        int tid, mLocal;
        uint64_t start = __clock64();
        #pragma omp parallel default(none) \
                            private(tid, mLocal) \
                            firstprivate(pL1, pL2, m, n, k, lda, ldb, ldc) \
                            shared(A, B, C, MSMC_buf)
        {
            /* Configure L1D on each core to have 16KB SRAM and 16 KB Cache */
            __cache_l1d_16k();
            int nthreads = omp_get_num_threads();
            int mRemaining = 0;
            tid = omp_get_thread_num();
            mLocal = (nthreads > m ? 1 : m/nthreads);
            if (tid == nthreads-1)
                if (m % nthreads != 0) mRemaining = m % mLocal;
            gemm(mLocal + mRemaining, n, k, A + mLocal*tid, lda, B, ldb, C + mLocal*tid, ldc,
                 pL1, pL2, MSMC_buf, tid);
            /* Restore L1D Cache config on each core to entire 32KB Cache */
            __cache_l1d_all();
        }
        uint64_t end = __clock64();
        elapsed_cycles = end - start;
    }
    /* Assuming the clock speed of the DSP is 1.228Ghz Calculate the elapsed seconds */
    double elapsed_time_sec = ((double)elapsed_cycles)/1.228e9;
    return elapsed_time_sec;
}
```

Fig. 5. Target region for GEMM

It provides a good basis for comparing the cost of data movement vs. raw FLOPS across different systems. Several approaches have been used to perform blocking/panelling of matrices to maximize utilization of caches and scratchpad RAM. In [1,2], GEMM was written for the C6678 DSP and the performance measured across 8 DSP cores was 79.4 GFLOPS for SGEMM and 21 GFLOPS for DGEMM with the DSPs running at 1Ghz. To port GEMM for 66AK2H, the same algorithm, inner kernel and matrix panelling scheme was used. In order to maximize the use of a larger L2 and MSMC SRAM, the number of inner panels was increased to use all 768 KB of L2 and 4.5 MB of MSMC SRAM. The runtime reserves 128 KB of L2 and 1.5 MB MSMC SRAM. The remaining 128 KB of L2 is configured as cache.

The GEMM implementation for the C6678 DSP used the EDMA3 co-processor for data transfer and intrinsics such as _cmpysp() to perform four single precision floating-point multiplies and _daddsp() to perform four single precision additions in one cycle. The accelerator model requires that each function used within a target region must have an equivalent implementation for the host. The if() clause specification mandates this. However, it is important to note that every accelerator specific function or API might not be implementable for the host side. We accounted for this situation by allowing C66x specific code to be compiled separately and linked into the final executable. In this case we compiled the GEMM API function with instrumentation code and the inner kernel using the DSP compiler cl6x and called the GEMM function from within the target region as shown in figure 5. Timing within the target region was done using the built-in __clock64() function that provides a cycle count by reading a DSP performance counter register.

In figure 5 we note several key optimizations to effectively use the Keystone II memory system. The *local* map-type is used to allocate a 768 KB buffer on each DSP core's L2 SRAM. Upon entering the target region, the L1D cache size is halved to create 16 KB L1D SRAM and 16 KB L1D Cache per DSP core. This optimization is critical to the performance of the particular panelling scheme used. It ensures that a 16KB panel is retained in L1D SRAM as long as possible while the other 16KB cache usage is maximized using the __touch(void* array, int size) built-in function that allows fast reading of a memory segment into cache. The arrays A, B and C were allocated in shared memory using __malloc_ddr(). The MSMC_buf array used 4MB of usable 4.5 MB in MSMC SRAM and was allocated using __malloc_msmc(). Within the instrumentation code, the EDMA Manager API was used to start parallel DMA transfers on separate channels. Figure 6 shows the API function for a 2D block transfer which allows transferring a number of lines of contiguous chunks of memory with different source and destination start offsets (pitch).

```
int32_t EdmaMgr_copy2D2DSep( EdmaMgr_Handle h,void *restrict src, void *restrict dst,
                             int32_t    num_bytes, int32_t   num_lines,
                             int32_t    src_pitch, int32_t   dst_pitch);
```

Fig. 6. EDMA Manager 2D transfer API

5.1 Performance

The TI 66AK2H EVM (Rev 3.0) was used to measure performance. The ARM Cortex-A15 cores were clocked at 1.2 Ghz and the C66x DSP cores ran at 1.228 Ghz. In order to assess GEMM performance on the ARM cores, ATLAS CBLAS (using Pthreads) v3.10.1 library auto-tuned for ARM Cortex-A15 was used. The auto-tuning was performed on the 66AK2H EVM is using gcc 4.7.2. The following TI software packages were used: TI MCSDK Linux v3.00.04.18, TI OpenCL v0.10.0, OpenMP accelerator model v1.0.0 and TI C6000 Code Generation Tools v8.0.0.

Two sets of times were collected. The first set was measured from within the target region using __clock64() to time the OpenMP parallel region and DSP execution time. GFLOPS calculated using this time are denoted as SGEMM-DSP and DGEMM-DSP in figure 7. The second set was measured from the host using the clock_gettime() function call and the CLOCK_MONOTONIC_RAW clock with microsecond accuracy. This time measurement included the overhead of calling the accelerator model runtime library and the data transfer time to and from the target region along with execution time. SGEMM-DSP(+Overheads) and DGEMM-DSP(+Overheads) denote GFLOPS calculated using time measured from the host. clock_gettime() was also used to measure time for ATLAS Pthread CBLAS SGEMM and DGEMM on ARM. SGEMM-ARM and DGEMM-ARM denote GFLOPS for these measurements. Each time measurement was averaged over a 100 iterations with a standard deviation of 0.5 microseconds. GFLOPS values calculated using these time measurements are reported in figure 7.

The figures 7(a)-7(f) report strong scaling performance for a fixed total problem size each by varying the number of DSP threads used. Each DSP core runs a single thread. Near linear performance scaling is observed in all cases varying from 1-8 threads. The single DSP core performance peaks at 14.1 GFLOPS for SGEMM for the square 4096×4096 case and 3.66 GFLOPS for DGEMM for the square 2048×2048 case. The 4096×2048 rectangular matrix case provides the peak performance of 110.11 GFLOPS (with overheads) for SGEMM across all eight DSP cores while the square 2048×2048 case provides the peak DGEMM performance of 29.15 GFLOPS. For the smallest 512×512 matrices, the overheads recorded are significant in comparison to the rest of the cases. This is because an extra five buffers are mapped to the target region every time and the DSP execution times for smaller cases do not outweigh the cost of creating these buffers. The peak performance of ATLAS across four ARM cores is 8.45 GFLOPS for SGEMM in the largest case and 5.45 GFLOPS for DGEMM in the 2048×2048 case. In comparison a single DSP core is always faster than four ARM cores and eight DSP cores are at least $12\times$ faster in all cases. With respect to the peak performance of the DSP cluster, using the accelerator model on 66AK2H achieves 70.05% for SGEMM and 74.18% efficiency for DGEMM including all overheads. The original implementation for C6678 achieved 62% for SGEMM and 65% for DGEMM [1]. The increase in efficiency can be attributed to larger L2 and MSMC SRAM available in 66AK2H.

5.2   Power Efficiency

The exact power consumed by the DSP cores during computation of GEMM kernels is unavailable at this time and therefore energy or power efficiency using the TDP rating of the 66AK2H SoC, which is between 9-14 Watts, is reported. The GEMM execution on the ARM cores is not counted. The efficiency is reported as a range with the lower bracket calculated using 9 Watt TDP and the higher with 14 Watt TDP. Taking the peak performance numbers with offload overheads, power efficiency between 7.865 to 12.23 single precision GFLOPS/Watt and 2.08 to 3.23 double precision GFLOPS/Watt was achieved.

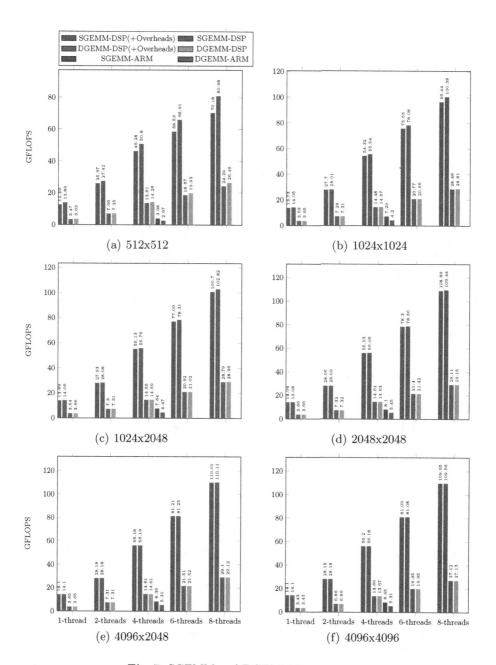

Fig. 7. SGEMM and DGEMM Performance

6   Related Work

OpenACC [11] provides an alternate specification for programming accelerators using compiler directives. The PGI accelerator model [12] and hiCUDA [13] have also been use to similar effect. Embedded TI C66x DSPs have also previously been shown to be effective building blocks for HPC platforms in [14,15]. Similar to our _malloc_ddr() method of allocating buffers in shared memory space NVIDIA CUDA 6[16] provides the concept of *unified memory* which allows creation of buffers in a shared memory space using cudaMallocManaged(). For the new NVIDIA Tegra K1[17] SoC which provides four ARM Cortex-A15 cores and a Tegra GPU on-chip, unified memory translates to physically shared memory similar to TI Keystone II. But for other discrete host CPU and PCiE connected NVIDIA GPUs unified memory goes across separate physical memory spaces. HOMP [18], an early implementation of the accelerator model for NVIDIA GPUs generated CUDA kernels similar to how we generate OpenCL kernels. The Intel Xeon Phi co-processor is another emerging HPC platform for which OpenMP was one of the first programming models to be ported [19,20,21,22]. Implementation of compiler directive based accelerator programming for it was also recently demonstrated by [23]. [24] measured the isolated power efficiency of running DGEMM provided in the SHOC benchmark on the Intel Xeon Phi co-processor. A maximum efficiency of 2.2 GFLOPS/Watt was reported.

7   Conclusion and Future Work

We demonstrated the effective use of the OpenMP accelerator model to offload SGEMM and DGEMM kernels from host ARM cores to the eight DSP cores on the TI 66AK2H Keystone II SoC. The acceleration of the GEMM kernels running on the eight DSPs vs. the four ARM cores was at least 12×. Further, we achieved slightly better performance (up to 74.18% efficiency) than the GEMM kernels that run on the TI C6678 Keystone I SoC with only 8 C66x DSP cores (up to 65% efficiency), demonstrating that performance can be maintained when offloading from the ARM Cores to the DSP cores. The slight performance improvement was due to extra L2 and MSMC scratch memory on Keystone II.

In the OpenMP accelerator model variables are *mapped* from a host device to a target device. The model supports systems that require copying the variables and those where a copy is not required. In our implementation of the accelerator model, we had to support both types of mapping. A copy is required for variables that have been allocated in the Linux processes' non-contiguous virtual memory, and a copy is not required when a variable is allocated from a special shared contiguous physical memory range. The runtime makes the decision to copy based on the address of the mapped variable. We extended the model to provide new API functions _malloc_ddr() and _malloc_msmc() to dynamically allocate memory from the host such that it is in contiguous physical memory, therefore avoiding any copies when mapping the memory to the target device.

The L1 and L2 memories on the TI C66x DSP core can be configured as both scratch, cache or both. We added a new `local` map-type to allocate a variable to L2 scratch memory. Optimal performance can be achieved when using the L1 and L2 as scratch memories, however, DMA co-processors are used to move data in and out of the scratch memories. Today programmers are required to use TI specific API functions to program the DMA co-processors. Our future work is to explore how to implement the DMA operations in portable OpenMP style pragmas.

In summary, with its combination of ARM Cortex-A15 and TI C66x DSP cores integrated on a single SoC with shared memory among all the cores, the TI Keystone II architecture is a good fit for the OpenMP accelerator model. The few extensions we have added for performance are general enough to be considered for future versions of the OpenMP accelerator model.

Acknowledgment. GM and APR acknowledge the support of Australian Research Council Discovery Project DP0987773.

References

1. Ali, M., Stotzer, E., Igual, F.D., van de Geijn, R.A.: Level-3 BLAS on the TI C6678 multi-core DSP. In: IEEE 24th International Symposium on Computer Architecture and High Performance Computing (SBAC-PAD), pp. 179–186. IEEE (2012)
2. Igual, F.D., Ali, M., Friedmann, A., Stotzer, E., Wentz, T., van de Geijn, R.A.: Unleashing the high-performance and low-power of multi-core DSPs for general-purpose HPC. In: Proceedings of the International Conference on High Performance Computing, Networking, Storage and Analysis, p. 26. IEEE Computer Society Press (2012)
3. HP: HP moonshot system (2014), http://h17007.www1.hp.com/us/en/enterprise/servers/products/moonshot/index.aspx
4. nCore HPC: ncore browndwarf y-class supercomputer (2014), http://ncorehpc.com/browndwarf/
5. Stotzer, E., Jayaraj, A., Ali, M., Friedmann, A., Mitra, G., Rendell, A.P., Lintault, I.: OpenMP on the Low-Power TI Keystone II ARM/DSP System-on-Chip. In: Rendell, A.P., Chapman, B.M., Müller, M.S. (eds.) IWOMP 2013. LNCS, vol. 8122, pp. 114–127. Springer, Heidelberg (2013)
6. OpenMP ARB: OpenMP Application Program Interface, v.4.0 (2013), http://www.openmp.org/mp-documents/OpenMP4.0.0.pdf
7. Texas Instruments Literature: SPRS866: 66AK2H12/06 Multicore DSP+ARM Keystone II System-on-Chip (SoC)
8. Rajovic, N., Rico, A., Puzovic, N., Adeniyi-Jones, C., Ramirez, A.: Tibidabo: making the case for an ARM-based HPC system (2013)
9. Mitra, G., Johnston, B., Rendell, A.P., McCreath, E., Zhou, J.: Use of SIMD vector operations to accelerate application code performance on low-powered ARM and Intel platforms. In: Parallel and Distributed Processing Symposium Workshops & PhD Forum (IPDPSW). IEEE (2013)

10. Khronos: OpenCL: The open standard for parallel programming of heterogeneous systems (2011), http://www.khronos.org/opencl

11. Reyes, R., Lopez, I., Fumero, J.J., de Sande, F.: Directive-based programming for gpus: A comparative study. In: IEEE 14th International Conference on High Performance Computing and Communication & 2012 IEEE 9th International Conference on Embedded Software and Systems (HPCC-ICESS), pp. 410–417. IEEE (2012)

12. Wolfe, M.: Implementing the PGI accelerator model. In: Proceedings of the 3rd Workshop on General-Purpose Computation on Graphics Processing Units, pp. 43–50. ACM (2010)

13. Han, T.D., Abdelrahman, T.S.: hi CUDA: A high-level directive-based language for GPU programming. In: Proceedings of 2nd Workshop on General Purpose Processing on Graphics Processing Units, pp. 52–61. ACM (2009)

14. Ahmad, A., Ali, M., South, F., Monroy, G.L., Adie, S.G., Shemonski, N., Carney, P.S., Boppart, S.A.: Interferometric synthetic aperture microscopy implementation on a floating point multi-core digital signal processer. In: SPIE BiOS, International Society for Optics and Photonics, pp. 857134–857134 (2013)

15. Note, F.W., Van Zee, F.G., Smith, T., Igual, F.D., Smelyanskiy, M., Zhang, X., Kistler, M., Austel, V., Gunnels, J., Low, T.M., et al.: Implementing level-3 blas with blis: Early experience (2013)

16. NVIDIA: Unified Memory in CUDA 6 (2014), http://devblogs.nvidia.com/parallelforall/unified-memory-in-cuda-6/

17. NVIDIA: NVIDIA Tegra K1 Processor (2014), http://www.nvidia.com/object/tegra-k1-processor.html

18. Liao, C., Yan, Y., de Supinski, B.R., Quinlan, D.J., Chapman, B.: Early Experiences With The OpenMP Accelerator Model. In: Rendell, A.P., Chapman, B.M., Müller, M.S. (eds.) IWOMP 2013. LNCS, vol. 8122, pp. 84–98. Springer, Heidelberg (2013)

19. Schmidl, D., Cramer, T., Wienke, S., Terboven, C., Müller, M.S.: Assessing the performance of OpenMP programs on the Intel Xeon Phi. In: Wolf, F., Mohr, B., an Mey, D. (eds.) Euro-Par 2013. LNCS, vol. 8097, pp. 547–558. Springer, Heidelberg (2013)

20. Barker, J., Bowden, J.: Manycore Parallelism through OpenMP. In: Rendell, A.P., Chapman, B.M., Müller, M.S. (eds.) IWOMP 2013. LNCS, vol. 8122, pp. 45–57. Springer, Heidelberg (2013)

21. Cramer, T., Schmidl, D., Klemm, M., an Mey, D.: OpenMP Programming on Intel Xeon Phi Coprocessors: An Early Performance Comparison, pp. 38–44 (2012)

22. Leang, S.S., Rendell, A.P., Gordon, M.S.: Quantum chemical calculations using accelerators: Migrating matrix operations to the nvidia kepler gpu and the intel xeon phi. Journal of Chemical Theory and Computation 10(3), 908–912 (2014)

23. Newburn, C., Dmitriev, S., Narayanaswamy, R., Wiegert, J., Murty, R., Chinchilla, F., Deodhar, R., McGuire, R.: Offload Compiler Runtime for the Intel Xeon Phi Coprocessor. In: 2013 IEEE 27th International on Parallel and Distributed Processing Symposium Workshops PhD Forum (IPDPSW), pp. 1213–1225 (May 2013)

24. Li, B., Chang, H.C., Leon Song, S., Su, C.Y., Meyer, T., Mooring, J., Cameron, K.W.: The Power-Performance Tradeoffs of the Intel Xeon Phi on HPC Applications. In: Parallel and Distributed Processing Symposium Workshops & PhD Forum (IPDPSW). IEEE (2014)

On the Roles of the Programmer, the Compiler and the Runtime System When Programming Accelerators in OpenMP

Guray Ozen, Eduard Ayguadé, and Jesús Labarta

Barcelona Supercomputing Center (BSC-CNS), Barcelona, Spain
Universitat Politècnica de Catalunya (UPC–BarcelonaTECH)

Abstract. *OpenMP* includes in its latest 4.0 specification the accelerator model. In this paper we present a partial implementation of this specification in the OmpSs programming model developed at the Barcelona Supercomputing Center with the aim of identifying which should be the roles of the programmer, the compiler and the runtime system in order to facilitate the asynchronous execution of tasks in architectures with multiple accelerator devices and processors. The design of OmpSs is highly biassed to delegate most of the decisions to the runtime system, which based on the task graph built at runtime (*depend* clauses) is able to schedule tasks in a data flow way to the available processors and accelerator devices and orchestrate data transfers and reuse among multiple address spaces. For this reason our implementation is partial, just considering from 4.0 those directives that enable the compiler the generation of the so called "kernels" to be executed on the target device. Several extensions to the current specification are also presented, such as the specification of tasks in "native" CUDA and OpenCL or how to specify the device and data privatization in the *target* construct. Finally, the paper also discusses some challenges found in code generation and a preliminary performance evaluation with some kernel applications.

Keywords: OpenMP accelerator model, OmpSs, OpenCL, CUDA.

1 Introduction

The use of accelerators has been gaining popularity in the last years due to their higher peak performance and performance per Watt ratio when compared to homogeneous architectures based on multicores. However, the heterogeneity they introduce (in terms of computing devices and address spaces) makes programming a difficult task even for expert programmers.

Some alternatives have been proposed to address the programmability of these accelerator–based systems. CUDA [1] and OpenCL [2] provide low-level API's that allow computation to be offloaded to accelerators. the management of their memory hierarchy and the data transfers between address spaces. Other alternatives, such as OpenACC [3], have appeared with the aim of providing a higher–level directive–based approach to program accelerator devices. OpenMP

L. DeRose (Eds.): IWOMP 2014, LNCS 8766, pp. 215–229, 2014.

[4] also includes in its latest 4.0 specification the accelerator model with the same objective. These solutions based on directives still rely on the programmer for the specification of data regions, transfers between address spaces and for the specification of the computation to be offloaded in the devices; these solutions also put a lot of pressure on the compiler–side that has the responsibility of generating efficient code based on the information provided by the programmer.

The OmpSs [5] proposal has been evolving during the last decade to lower the programmability wall raised by multi–/many–cores, demonstrating a task–based data flow approach in which offloading tasks to different number and kinds of devices, as well as managing the coherence of data in multiple address spaces, is delegated to the runtime system. Multiple implementations were investigated for the IBM Cell (CellSs [6]), NVIDIA GPU (GPUSs [7]) and homogeneous multicores (SMPSs [8]) before arriving to the current unified OmpSs specification and implementation. Initially OmpSs relied on the use of CUDA and OpenCL to specify the computational kernels. This paper presents the latest implementation of OmpSs which includes partial support for the accelerator model in OpenMP 4.0 specification. We just adopted those functionalities that are necessary to specify computational kernels in a more productive way. The paper analyzes the roles of the programmer, the compiler and the runtime from this new OmpSs perspective.

2   "Pure" Accelerator-Specific Programming

"Pure" accelerator-specific programming initially put all responsibility in the programmer, who should take case of transforming computational intensive pieces of code into kernels to be executed on the accelerator devices and write the host code to orchestrate data allocations, data transfers and kernel invocations with the appropriate allocation of GPU resources. Nvidia CUDA [1] and OpenCL [2] are the two APIs commonly used today.

In favor of programmability, the latest releases of the Nvidia CUDA architecture improved programming productivity by moving some of the burden to the CUDA runtime, including Unified Virtual Addressing (CUDA 4) to provide a single virtual memory address space for all memory in the system (enabling pointers to be accessed from GPU) no matter where in the system they reside) and Unified Memory (CUDA 6) to automatically migrate data at the level of individual pages between host and devices, freeing programmers from the need of allocating and copying device memory. Although these additions may be seen as a need for beginners, they make it possible to share complex data structures and eliminate the need to handle "deep copies" in the presence of pointed data inside structured data. Carefully tuned CUDA codes may still use streams and asynchronous transfers to efficiently overlap computation with data movement when the CUDA runtime is unable to do it appropriately due to lack of lookahead.

3   Directive-Based Approaches in OpenMP and OpenACC

With the aim of providing a smooth and portable path to program accelerator-based architectures, OpenACC [3] and OpenMP 4.0 [4] provide a directive-centric programming interface. Directives allow the programmer to specify code regions to be offloaded to accelerators, how to map loops inside those regions onto the resources available in the device architecture, the data mapping in their memory and data copying between address spaces. This directive–based approach imposes a high responsibility on the compiler that needs to be able to generate optimized device–specific kernels (considering architectural aspects such as the memory hierarchy or the amount of resources available) as well as taking care of accelerator startup and shutdown, code offloading and implementing data allocations/transfers between the host and accelerator[1].

The directive–based approach frees the programmer from the need to write accelerator-specific code for the target device (e.g. CUDA or OpenCL kernels). We think this is important in terms of programming productivity, but we also believe that the directive–based approach should allow a migration path for existing CUDA applications by reusing device–specific OpenCL or CUDA kernels already optimized by experienced programmers.

In the following subsections we briefly summarize OpenMP 4.0 and OpenACC constructs with the aim of splitting responsibilities between the compiler and the runtime system, with the overall objective of lowering the programmability wall.

3.1   Offloading, Kernel Configuration and Loop Execution

OpenMP 4.0 offers the *target* directive to start parallel execution on the accelerator device. Similarly, OpenACC offers the *parallel* directive with the same purpose. In OpenACC these regions can be declared asynchronous removing the implicit barrier at the end of the accelerator parallel region, allowing the host to continue with the code following the region.

Inside these accelerator regions in the OpenMP 4.0, the programmer can specify *teams*, representing a hierarchy of resources in the accelerator: a league of *num_teams* teams, each with *thread_limit* threads. The execution in the *teams* region initially starts in the master thread of each team. Later, the *distribute* and *parallel for* directives can be used to specify the mapping of iterations in different loops to the resources available on the accelerator. On the other hand, OpenACC offers *kernels*, i.e. regions that the compiler should translate into a sequence of kernels for execution on the accelerator device. Typically, each loop nest will be a distinct kernel. OpenACC also includes the *loop* directive to describe what type of parallelism to use to execute a loop and declare loop-private variables and arrays and reduction operations. Inside kernels and loops resources are organized in gangs, workers and vectors (indicated with the *num_gangs*, *num_workers* and

---

[1] If the accelerator can access the host memory directly, the implementation may avoid this data allocation/movement and simply use the host memory.

vector_length clauses, respectively), similar to the teams, threads and SIMD in OpenMP 4.0.

Figure 1 shows the use of the above mentioned directives and clauses in OpenMP 4.0. Lines 7 and 11 in the code on the left specify the mapping of iterations of the *i* and *j* loops among 16 teams and 512 threads inside each team, respectively as declared in lines 5–6. Similarly, line 6 in the code on the right informs the compiler to map iterations of the *i* loop to both teams and threads inside each team; lines 8 and 13 also map iterations of the *j* loop to threads, probably using the multidimensional organization available in current accelerator devices.

```
1 #define n 128
2 #define m 10240
3
4 #pragma omp target device(0)
5 #pragma omp teams
6          num_teams(16) thread_limit(512)
7 #pragma omp distribute
8 for (i = 0; i < n; i++)
9 {
10
11      #pragma omp parallel for
12      for (j = 0; j < m ; j++)
13          // loop body
14
15 }
```

```
1 #define nX 4
2 #define nelem 12000
3
4 #pragma omp target device(0)
5 #pragma omp teams thread_limit(64)
6 #pragma omp distribute parallel for
7 for (i=0; i < nelem; i++) {
8      #pragma omp parallel for private(k)
9      for (j=0; j < nX*nX; j++)
10         for (k=0; k < nX; k++)
11             // loop body
12     #pragma omp parallel for
13     for (j=0; j < nX*nX; j++)
14         // loop body
15 }
```

Fig. 1. Two simple examples using OpenMP 4.0 directives for offloading

Figure 2 shows another OpenMP 4.0 code where the programmer defines the thread hierarchy (line 9) and maps to it the execution of the loop in line 10. The *target* region is inside a *task*, so in this case the execution in the device is asynchronous to the execution of the master thread in the processor.

```
1 for (begin=0 ; begin < n; begin+=stride)
2 {
3   int end = begin + stride - 1;
4   int dev_id = (begin / stride) % omp_get_num_devices();
5
6   #pragma omp task
7   #pragma omp target device(dev_id) \
8              map(to: y[begin:end], x[begin:end]) map(from: z[begin:end])
9   #pragma omp teams num_teams(16) thread_limit(32)
10  #pragma omp distribute parallel for
11  for (i = 0; i < stride; ++i)
12      z[i] = a * x[i] + y[i];
13 }
```

Fig. 2. Code in OpenMP 4.0 asynchronously offloading to multiple accelerator devices

The *target* directive in OpenMP 4.0 includes the *device* clause, which offloads the execution of the region kernel to a given physical device (indicated by the integer value in the clause). This direct mapping makes it difficult to write applications that dynamically offload work to accelerators in order to achieve load balancing or adapt to device variability, since it forces the programmer to embed in the application logic code to manage resources.

For example the code in Figure 2 shows how the programmer could statically map consecutive *target* regions to the accelerators available in the target architecture (line 4 to compute the device identifier and *device* clause in line 7), allowing in this case to use two devices. Observe that the iteration range for the *for* loop at Line 11 goes from 0 to *stride*, so the program is not "sequentially equivalent" since it should iterate from *begin* to *end*. This is how OpenMP 4.0 forces the specification of the work to be offloaded; we assume that this has to be done in this way in order to ease code generation by the compiler although at the expenses of reducing code portability and reusability, in addition to potential programming errors.

3.2 Data Motion

Data copying clauses may appear on the *target* construct in OpenMP 4.0 and *parallel* and *kernels* constructs in OpenACC. With these clauses the programmer specifies the data motion needed to bring in and out the data for the execution of the region in the accelerator.

For the data items (including array regions) that appear in an OpenMP 4.0 *map* clause, corresponding new data items are created in the device data environment associated with the construct. Each data item has an associated map type which specifies the data copying on entry and exit (*to*, *from* or *tofrom*) or just allocation (*alloc*). OpenACC offers similar clauses (*copyin*, *copyout*, *copy* and *create*). With all this information, the compiler schedules the associated data allocations and transfers accordingly.

The example in Figure 2 shows the use of the *map* clause in Line 8. It is important to notice that *map(to: ...)* forces the movement of data when the *target* region is found; similarly for *map(from: ...)* which copies from device to host when the *target* region finishes.

Both OpenMP 4.0 and OpenACC offer the possibility of defining data environments in the accelerator for the extent of the region: *target data* and *data*, respectively. Inside these regions, multiple kernel offloading actions may occur without data copying between them, unless explicitly specified. An executable directive (*target update* in OpenMP 4.0 and *update* in OpenACC) is offered to the programmer to update, inside the scope of a *data* region, the data from the host to the device or vice-versa. The use of multiple accelerators within a *target data* region is not clear since at most one *device* clause can appear in the *target data* directive. The Jacobi code in Figure 6 shows the use of *data* regions and *update* in an OpenACC example.

3.3 Memory Hierarchy in the Accelerator Device

Private, firstprivate and *reduction* clauses in *distribute* and *parallel for* directives give the compiler hints about the use of the memory hierarchy inside the accelerator. Again, OpenMP 4.0 and OpenACC rely on the programmer and the compiler for the management of the memory hierarchy, having a direct impact in the quality of the kernel codes to be executed on the accelerator device.

4   Accelerator Support in OmpSs

The accelerator support in the OmpSs programming model [5] leverages the tasking model with data directionality annotations already available in the model (that influenced the new *depend* clause in OpenMP 4.0). These annotations are used by the OmpSs runtime system to dynamically compute task dependences and build a dependence task graph. This graph is used to dynamically schedule tasks in a data–flow way conscious of the resources available at any time.

The OmpSs programming model offers *target* directive with the following syntax:

```
#pragma omp target [clauses]
    task construct | function definition | function header
```

where clauses specify:

- copy_in, copy_out and copy_inout - shared data that needs to be available in the device before the construct can be executed or available after the construct is executed.
- copydeps - copy semantics for the directionality clauses in the associated *task* construct.
- device - kind of devices that can execute the construct (smp, cuda, opencl or acc).
- implements - an alternative implementation of the function whose name specified in the clause for a specific kind of device.

In order to make hybrid with native CUDA and/or OpenCL kernels, the directive includes two additional clauses:

- ndrange - specification of the dimensionality, iteration space and blocking size to replicate the execution of the CUDA or OpenCL kernel.
- shmem - arguments (and their size) to be mapped into team shared–memory.

The *copy_in*, *copy_out* and *copy_inout* clauses, together with the lookahead provided by the availability of the task graph, are used by the runtime system to schedule data copying actions between address spaces (movements between host and accelerator or between two accelerator devices if needed). *Copydeps* is a simple shorthand to reuse the directionality annotations in the *task* directive.

Figure 3 shows a simple example based on SAXPY. In this example, the task computing *saxpy* is written as a CUDA kernel and offloaded to a device with CUDA architecture; task *check_results* is defined to be executed in the host. Observe that the output of CUDA task instances are inputs of the host task instances. The dependences computed at runtime will honor these dependences and the runtime system will take care of doing the data copying operations based on the information contained in the task graph (dynamically generated at runtime). The *ndrange* clause is used to replicate the execution of the CUDA kernel in the device block/thread hierarchy (one dimension with $na*na$ iterations in total to distribute among teams of na iterations in this example).

```
1 #pragma omp target device(cuda) ndrange(1, na*na , na) copy_deps
2 #pragma omp task in(a[0:stride] , b[0:stride]) out(c[0:stride])
3 __global__ void saxpy (double * a, double * b, double * c, int stride) {
4       // CUDA kernel code
5 }
6 #pragma omp target device(smp) copy_deps implements(saxpy)
7 #pragma omp task in(a[0:stride] , b[0:stride]) out(c[0:stride])
8 void saxpy_smp (double * a, double * b, double * c, int stride) {
9       // CPU code with OpenMP directives
10 }
11 #pragma omp target device(smp) copy_deps
12 #pragma omp task in(static_correct_result[0:stride], c[0:stride])
13 void check_results ( double * precalc_result, double * c, int stride) {
14       // CPU codes with OpenMP directives
15 }
16 int main (int argc, char ** argv) {
17       double a[SIZE], b[SIZE], c[SIZE];
18
19       for (begin=0 ; begin < nX ; begin+=stride)
20           saxpy(&a[begin], &b[begin], &c[begin], stride);
21
22       for (begin=0 ; begin < nX ; begin+=stride)
23           check_results(&precalc_result[begin], &c[begin], SIZE);
24 }
```

Fig. 3. Heterogeneous task example with OmpSs

With the *device* clause the programmer informs the compiler and runtime system about the kind of device that can execute the task, not an integer number that explicitly maps the offloading to a certain device as done in OpenMP 4.0. This is a big difference that improves programming productivity when targeting systems with different number and type of accelerators and regular cores. The code in Figure 3 could be executed on any number of devices without changes.

The *acc* device type is used to specify that the task will make use of OpenMP 4.0 directives to specify what to execute on the accelerator device, relying on the compiler to generate the kernel code to be executed on the device. We will describe in more detail the current compiler implementation in Section 5.

Multiple implementations tailored to different accelerators/cores can be specified for the same task (currently only available for tasks that are specified at the function declaration/definition). In this case, the programmer is delegating to the runtime system the responsibility of dynamically selecting the most appropriate device/core to execute each task instance, for example based on the availability of resources or the availability of the data needed to execute the task in the device (locality–aware scheduling). With the *implements* clause the programmer can indicate alternative implementations for a task function tailored to different devices (accelerator or host). Figure 3 shows the use of the *implements* clause: the *saxpy_smp* function in Line 6 is defined as an alternative implementation to the CUDA implementation of *saxpy* at Line 3. Observe that the programmer simply invokes *saxpy* in Line 20, delegating in the runtime the selection of the most appropriate implementation for each task instance.

5   MACC Compiler

A new compilation phase (MACC[2]) has been included in the Mercurium [9] compiler supporting the OpenMP 4.0 accelerator model with the OmpSs runtime. MACC takes care of kernel configuration, loop scheduling and appropriate use

---

[2] MACC is abbreviation for "Mercurium Accelerator Compiler".

of the memory hierarchy for those tasks whose *device* is set to *acc* in the *target* clause. Some of the OpenMP 4.0 directives for accelerators (*target data target update* directives and *map* clause) are simply ignored because we delegate their functionality to the runtime system. Others have been extended to better map with the OmpSs model or to provide additional functionalities.

OpenMP 4.0	MACC	OpenMP 4.0	MACC
target	extended (*implements*, *ndrange* for CUDA and OpenCL kernels)	device(*int*)	extended
map(*to/from/tofrom*)	implemented but different names (copy_in/out/inout)	distribute	new clauses *dist_private*
map(*alloc*)	ignored	teams	implemented
target data	currently ignored	parallel for	implemented
target update	ignored	distribute parallel for	implemented

Fig. 4. MACC vs OpenMP 4.0

5.1   Kernel Configuration, Loop Scheduling and Thread Mapping

When generating kernel code MACC needs to decide: 1) the dimensionality of the resources hierarchy (one-, two- or three-dimension teams and threads) and 2) the size in each dimension (number of teams and threads). In order to support the organization of the threads in multiple dimensions MACC allows the nesting of *parallel for* directives inside a *target* region (dimensionality equals the nesting degree). Other proposals considered the use of *collapse* which includes an integer to specify the number of nested loops with the same purpose [17].

MACC takes into account the restrictions of the device (for example maximum number of blocks and threads warp size in the CUDA computing capability) and the information provided by the programmer in the *num_teams* or *max_threads* clauses; if not specified, MACC simply assigns one iteration per block and one iteration per thread. MACC currently generates one dimensional teams (the current implementation does not support nesting of *distribute* directives). Thread dimensions are initially assigned in loop nesting order. As we will see in the experimental section[3], this ordering (for example outer loop for second thread dimension and inner loop for first thread dimension) may have a noticeable impact in performance; for now this is the responsibility of the compiler with no hints from the programmer in the current OpenMP 4.0 specification.

5.2   Coalesced Accesses and Use of Shared Memory

MACC code generation makes use of coalesced accesses to access global memory in warps. To that end MACC performs a cyclic mapping of loop iterations

---

[3] **opt3** in the experimental evaluation of DG-kernel in Section 6.

and tries to eliminate redundant "one–iteration" loops and simplifies increment expressions for induction variables in order to improve kernel execution time[4].

MACC also makes use of shared memory for threads in a team based on the specification of *private* and *firstprivate* data structures in the *distribute* directive, so that each team allocates a private copy in its own shared memory. MACC analyzes the size of the data structure to be privatized and generates code for its allocation and copying from global memory to shared memory in each team. However, for very large private arrays this is not possible to apply. For these cases we have implemented 3 new clauses (*dist_private*, *dist_firstprivate* and *dist_lastprivate*); with these clauses and the chunk size provided in the *dist_schedule(static,chunk_size)* clause in the *distribute* directive or near by array variable the compiler just allocates a portion of the arrays to each team and performs the necessary copies according to the *firstprivate* and *lastprivate* semantics[5].

- *dist_private(list)* : shared memory is only allocated up to indicated *chunk_size*.
- *dist_firstprivate(list)* : shared memory is allocated up to indicated *chunk_size* and it is filled with own part of array at global memory.
- *dist_lastprivate(list)* : shared memory is allocated up to indicated *chunk_size*. End of the *distribute* scope, allocated area from shared memory is recopied to own location at the global memory.
- *dist_first_lastprivate(list)* : it is a short-cut for specifying *dist_firstprivate(list)* and *dist_lastprivate(list)* at the same time.

Figure 5 shows the use of shared variables with *distribute* and *team* directives for the DG_kernel application (which is used later in the evaluation section). In this example, *delta*, *der* and *grad* are small arrays which are privatized with *private* and *firstprivate* at line 13. However, *flx* and `fly` are specified as *dist_first_lastprivate* with a chunk size of CHUNK at line 14.

6   Preliminary Performance Evaluation

The objective of the performance evaluation in this section is to show how the OmpSs proposal to program accelerators behaves, which just integrates those directives from OpenMP 4.0 accelerator model that are used to specify the kernel computations. For the evaluation we use three codes: Jacobi, DG-kernel [11] from NCAR and CG from NAS Parallel Benchmark [12].

For the experimental evaluation we have used a node with 2 Intel Xeon E5649 sockets (6 cores each) running at 2.53 GHz and with 24 GB of main memory, and two Nvidia Tesla M2090 GPU devices (512 CUDA cores each, compute capability 2.0) running at 1.3GHZ and with 6GB of memory per device. For the compilation of OpenACC codes we have used the HMPP (version 3.2.3) compiler from CAPS [13]. For the compilation of OmpSs codes we have used the

---

[4] **opt2** in the experimental evaluation of DG-kernel in Section 6.
[5] **opt1** in the experimental evaluation of DG-kernel in Section 6.

```
1#define nX 4
2#define NELEM 90000
3#define SIZE (NELEM*nX*nX)
4#define CHUNK 256
5#define NUM_TEAMS 5625
6
7double delta[nX*nX], der[nX*nX], grad[nX*nX], flx[SIZE], fly[SIZE];
8
9 for (it=0; it<nit; it++)
10 {
11    #pragma omp target device(acc) copy_deps
12    #pragma omp task inout(flx[0:SIZE], fly[0:SIZE])
13    #pragma omp teams num_teams(NUM_TEAMS) private(grad) firstprivate(delta,der)
14    #pragma omp distribute parallel for dist_first_lastprivate(flx[CHUNK],fly[CHUNK])
15    for (ie=0; ie < NELEM; ie++)
16    {
17       #pragma omp parallel for private(j,i)
18       for (ii=0; ii < nX*nX; ii++) {
19
20          // <..computation..>
21
22          for (j=0; j < nX; j++)
23          {
24             // <..computation..>
25
26             for (int i=0; i < nX; i++)
27                // <..computation..>
28
29             // <..computation..>
30          }
31
32          // <..computation..>
33       }
34
35       #pragma omp parallel for
36       for (j=0; j < nX*nX; j++)
37          // <..computation..>
38    }
39 }
```

Fig. 5. Example to explain MACC implementation of shared memory - DG Kernel

Mercurium/Nanos environment [9],[10]. GCC 4.6.1 has been used as back-end compiler for CPU code generation and the CUDA 5.0 toolkit for device code generation. Performance is reported in terms of execution time for the kernels generated and speed–up, with respect to sequential execution on a single core, for the complete application.

6.1 Jacobi

Jacobi is a simple iterative program to get an approximate solution of a linear system A*x=b. In each iteration of an outer *while* loop two nested loops are executed, the second one performing the main computation and including a reduction operation on a scalar variable used to control convergence in the *while* loop. The structure of the code is shown in Figure 6, with three different annotations that correspond to three different versions[6]:

- "OpenACC baseline" – each loop is a *kernels* region with the individual specification of data copying.
- "OpenACC optimized" – a *data* region is defined, which includes the two *kernels* regions mentioned in the previous version.
- "MACC/OmpSs" – equivalent to "OpenACC baseline" in terms of *target* regions but written in OpenMP 4.0. In this version the programmer relies

---

[6] The OpenACC versions could have equivalent versions in OpenMP 4.0.

on the runtime system to do all data allocations and copying when necessary. Observe that all *target* regions are *tasks*. This is because the current OmpSs implementation just supports asynchronous *target* regions (not yet in OpenMP 4.0 specification); in this code this does not have any influence due to the serialization caused by data dependences.

The left plot in Figure 7 shows the total execution time of the kernels generated by HMPP and MACC compilers for a data size of 2048 elements. For this code there are no significant differences in the quality of the CUDA kernels generated. The right plot in the same figure shows the speed–up that is obtained for the three versions mentioned above for three different problem sizes: 512, 1024 and 2048. First of all, observe that in OpenACC (and in OpenMP 4.0) the programmer needs to define an external *data* region to minimize data copying between consecutive *kernels* regions, while taking care of updating the scalar *error* variable in the device and host. This achieves a relative speed–up of 25 between the OpenACC optimized and baseline versions. And second, the performance plot also shows that the runtime system in OmpSs is able to achieve a slightly better performance even with the overheads incurred by keeping track of memory allocations, data copying and orchestration of kernel execution.

OpenACC baseline

```
1 while (( k <= mits) && (error > tol )) {
2    error = 0.0;
3
4    #pragma acc kernels copyin(u)
5                        copyout(uold)
6    #pragma acc loop
7    for (i = 0; i < n; i++)
8       // <..computation..>
9
10   #pragma acc kernels copyin(uold)
11              copyin(u) copy(error)
12   #pragma acc loop reduction(+:error)
13   for (i = 1; i < (n - 1); i++)
14      // <..computation..>
15
16   error = sqrt(error) / (n * m);
17   k++;
18 }
```

OpenACC optimized

```
1 #pragma acc data copy(u) copyout(error)
2                  create(uold, error)
3 while (( k <= mits) && (error > tol )) {
4    error = 0.0;
5
6    #pragma acc kernels loop
7    for (i = 0; i < n; i++)
8       // <..computation..>
9
10   #pragma acc update device(error)
11   #pragma acc kernels loop reduction(+:error)
12   for (i = 1; i < (n - 1); i++)
13      // <..computation..>
14
15   #pragma acc update host(error)
16   error = sqrt(error) / (n * m);
17   k++;
18 }
```

MACC/OmpSs

```
1 while (( k <= mits) && (error > tol )) {
2    error = 0.0;
3
4    #pragma omp target device(acc) copy_deps
5    #pragma omp task in(u) out(uold)
6    #pragma omp teams distribute parallel for
7    for (i = 0; i < n; i++)
8       // <..computation..>
9
10   #pragma omp target device(acc) copy_deps
11   #pragma omp task in(uold) out(u) inout(error)
12   #pragma omp teams distribute parallel for reduction(+:error)
13   for (i = 1; i < (n - 1); i++)
14      // <..computation..>
15
16   #pragma omp taskwait
17   error = sqrt(error) / (n * m);
18   k++;
19 }
```

Fig. 6. Annotated codes for Jacobi application

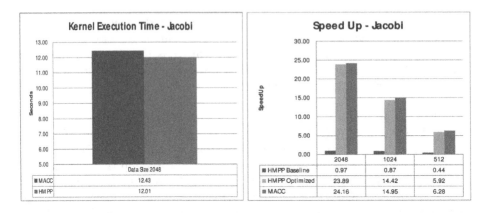

Fig. 7. Performance evaluation of Jacobi application

6.2 DG Kernel

DG is a kernel version of a climate benchmark developed by National Center for Atmospheric Research [11]. The structure of the code has been omitted in this submission version but will be included if the paper is accepted for publication. The code consists of a single *target* region that is executed inside an iterative time step loop that is repeated for a fixed number of iterations. Inside the *target* region the iterations of two nested loops are mapped to the teams/thread hierarchy as specified by the programmer.

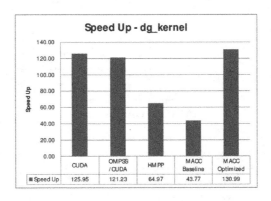

Fig. 8. Performance evaluation of for DG kernel

Figure 8 plots the performance that is achieved by different versions of the code, described in the following bullet points:

- CUDA: hand–optimized CUDA version of the application (with host and kernel code written in CUDA) available from NCAR.
- OmpSs/CUDA: OmpSs version of the application leveraging (only) the computational kernels written in CUDA.

- HMPP: OpenACC version available from NCAR.
- MACC: different versions of our OpenMP 4.0 implementation in the MACC compiler, including additional clauses to influence kernel code generation by the compiler.

Comparing bars labelled CUDA and OmpSs/CUDA in Figure 8 one can extract a first conclusion: OmpSs is able to leverage existing CUDA kernels with similar performance as full host/device CUDA codes. In this case we observe a small performance degradation probably due to overheads of the runtime in generating tasks in each iteration of the time step loop.

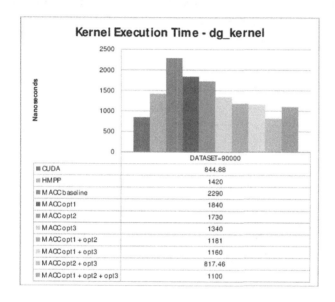

Fig. 9. Performance evaluation of CUDA Kernel for DG kernel

The second conclusion from this evaluation is the important role of the compiler in generating efficient kernel codes for the target device. The first 3 bars at Figure 9 show the execution time for the original CUDA kernel, the kernel generated by the HMPP compiler and the initial kernel generated by the MACC compiler. As one can observe, the manually programmed CUDA kernel clearly outperforms the kernels generated by the two compilers, which directly translate into significant performance degradation in terms of speed–up for the whole application (first, third and fourth bar, in Figure 8).

Thanks to the previous observation and to the study of the kernels available and generated by the compilers, we have been investigating alternative code generation schemes and proposed a new clause for the *distribute* directive (*dist_private*, as explained in Section 5). The impact of these optimizations is shown in the performance plot at Figure 9. Observe that there is plenty of room for improvement by using and combining these optimizations which result in a clear impact in the overall speed–up of the application (last bar in the left plot).

6.3   CG from NAS Parallel Benchmarks

The last code we have selected for the experimental evaluation in this paper is
NAS CG [12]. The main computational part of the application contains several
loops that can be made tasks and offloaded to a device or executed on the host.
The loop that contributes the most to the execution time performs a sparse
matrix vector operation. To execute this loop we want to use the two GPUs
available in the node.

The performance plot in Figure 10 shows the speed–up of the GPU accelerated
version of NAS CG (bars HMPP, MACC and MACC/2 GPU) and the speed–
up using 8 processors in the host, for three different classes of NAS CG. The
speed–up with 2 GPU is significant although we only refined one of the loops.
Note that data transfers between GPUs will take place, automatically handled
by the runtime.

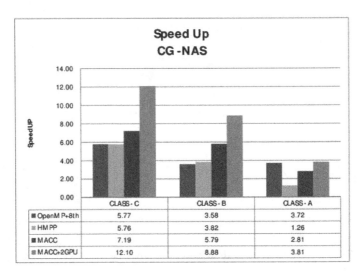

Fig. 10. Performance evaluation for NAS CG

7   Conclusions

In this paper we presented the main design considerations that are embedded in
our current implementation of the OpenMP 4.0 [4] accelerator model in OmpSs,
making emphasizing on the roles of the programmer, compiler and runtime system in the whole picture. The compiler plays a key role and for this reason previous efforts have been devoted to the automatic generation of device–specific
programs from high-level programs annotations such as OpenMP and OpenACC
[3], including both research efforts at academia [15–17] as well as commercial implementations [13, 14]. Our compiler implementation in Mercurium [9] has been
useful to experiment with different code generation strategies, trying to fore-
see the need for new clauses in current OpenMP 4.0 specification. OmpSs [5] is
strongly rooted on the assumption that the runtime system should play a key

role, making appropriate use of the information that can be gathered at execution time. In this paper we tried to emphasize this aspect supported by an experimental evaluation on three application kernels.

Acknowledgments. This work is partially supported by the Spanish TIN2012-34557 project and the IBM/BSC Technology Center for Supercomputing collaboration agreement. Thanks to John Dennis from NCAR for providing the OpenACC and CUDA versions of the DG kernel as part of the G8 ECS project.

References

1. Nvidia CUDA parallel computing and programming,
   http://www.nvidia.com/cuda
2. OpenCL Open Computing Language, http://www.khronos.org/opencl/
3. OpenACC: Directives for Accelerators, http://www.openacc-standard.org
4. The OpenMP API Specification for Parallel programming,
   http://www.openmp.org
5. Barcelona Supercomputing Center. The OmpSs programming model,
   http://pm.bsc.es/ompss
6. Bellens, P., Perez, J.M., Badia, R.M., Labarta, J.: CellSs: A programming model for the Cell/B.E. architecture. In: ACM/IEEE Supercomputing (November 2006)
7. Bueno, J., Planas, J., Duran, A., Badia, R.M., Martorell, X., Ayguade, E., Labarta, J.: Productive programming of GPU clusters with OmpSs. In: IEEE 26th International on Parallel Distributed Processing Symposium (IPDPS) (May 2012)
8. Perez, J.M., Badia, R.M., Labarta, J.: A dependency-aware task-based programming environment for multi-core architectures. In: IEEE International Conference on Cluster Computing (September 2008)
9. Barcelona Supercomputing Center. Mercurium source-to-source compiler,
   http://pm.bsc.es/mcxx
10. Barcelona Supercomputing Center. Nanos++ runtime library,
    http://pm.bsc.es/nanos
11. Vadlamani, S., Kim, Y., Dennis, J.: DG-kernel: A climate benchmark on accelerated and conventional architectures. In: Extreme Scaling Workshop (XSW) (August 2013)
12. NAS Division. NAS parallel benchmarks,
    http://www.nas.nasa.gov/resources/software/npb.html
13. CAPS Entreprise, CAPS Compiler, http://www.caps-entreprise.com
14. PGI Accelerator Compilers, http://www.pgroup.com/resources/accel.htm
15. Han, T.D., Abdelrahman, T.S.: Hicuda: A high-level directive-based language for gpu programming. In: 2nd Workshop on General Purpose Processing on Graphics Processing Units (GPGPU) (March 2009)
16. Lee, S., Min, S.-J., Eigenmann, R.: OpenMp to GPGPU: A compiler framework for automatic translation and optimization. In: 14th ACM SIGPLAN Symposium on Principles and Practice of Parallel Programming (PPoPP) (February 2009)
17. Liao, C., Yan, Y., de Supinski, B.R., Quinlan, D.J., Chapman, B.: Early experiences with the openMP accelerator model. In: Rendell, A.P., Chapman, B.M., Müller, M.S. (eds.) IWOMP 2013. LNCS, vol. 8122, pp. 84–98. Springer, Heidelberg (2013)

Author Index